Adorno, Aesthetics, Dissonance

Adorno, Aesthetics, Dissonance

On Dialectics in Modernity

William S. Allen

BLOOMSBURY ACADEMIC
NEW YORK • LONDON • OXFORD • NEW DELHI • SYDNEY

BLOOMSBURY ACADEMIC
Bloomsbury Publishing Inc
1385 Broadway, New York, NY 10018, USA
50 Bedford Square, London, WC1B 3DP, UK
29 Earlsfort Terrace, Dublin 2, Ireland

BLOOMSBURY, BLOOMSBURY ACADEMIC and the Diana logo are trademarks of
Bloomsbury Publishing Plc

First published in the United States of America 2023
Paperback edition published 2024

Copyright © William S. Allen, 2023

For legal purposes the Acknowledgments on p. ix constitute an
extension of this copyright page.

Cover design by Eleanor Rose
Cover image: Erwartung (Expectation), Scene 2, by Arnold Schoenberg. Watercolor and white bodycolor, pen and Chinese ink on paper. 10,2 × 17,2 cm. ca. 1911. Catalogue raisonné 16. Used by permission of Belmont Music Publishers, Los Angeles

All rights reserved. No part of this publication may be reproduced or transmitted in any form or by any means, electronic or mechanical, including photocopying, recording, or any information storage or retrieval system, without prior permission in writing from the publishers.

Bloomsbury Publishing Inc does not have any control over, or responsibility for, any third-party websites referred to or in this book. All internet addresses given in this book were correct at the time of going to press. The author and publisher regret any inconvenience caused if addresses have changed or sites have ceased to exist, but can accept no responsibility for any such changes.

Library of Congress Cataloging-in-Publication Data
Names: Allen, William S., 1971-author.
Title: Adorno, aesthetics, dissonance : on dialectics in modernity / William S. Allen.
Description: New York : Bloomsbury Academic, 2022. | Includes bibliographical references and index. | Summary: "An analysis of the development and range of Adorno's aesthetics, incorporating the influence of other thinkers and musicians"– Provided by publisher.
Identifiers: LCCN 2022015181 (print) | LCCN 2022015182 (ebook) | ISBN 9781501393860 (hardback) | ISBN 9781501393853 (paperback) | ISBN 9781501393877 (epub) | ISBN 9781501393884 (pdf) | ISBN 9781501393891
Subjects: LCSH: Adorno, Theodor W., 1903-1969. | Aesthetics.
Classification: LCC B3199.A34 A6485 2022 (print) | LCC B3199.A34 (ebook) | DDC 193–dc23/eng/20220808
LC record available at https://lccn.loc.gov/2022015181
LC ebook record available at https://lccn.loc.gov/2022015182

ISBN: HB: 978-1-5013-9386-0
PB: 978-1-5013-9385-3
ePDF: 978-1-5013-9388-4
eBook: 978-1-5013-9387-7

Typeset by RefineCatch Limited, Bungay, Suffolk

To find out more about our authors and books visit www.bloomsbury.com
and sign up for our newsletters.

Next to the pianino with the Mozart medallion hung a guitar in the [Hotel] Post's guest room. It was missing a string or two, and the rest were very out of tune. I couldn't play the guitar, but I tore at the strings all at once and let them vibrate, intoxicated by the dark dissonance, probably the first such polytonality that I came across, years before I knew a note by Schoenberg. I felt the wish: one should compose the way this guitar sounds.

Adorno, 1966

Contents

Acknowledgements	ix
Abbreviations	xi
Introduction: Dialectic of Aesthetics	1
Part One: The Development of Dialectics	
1 Kracauer and the Dialectic of Natural-History	23
2 Dialectics of the Avant-Garde in Music	79
Part Two: Refractions of Aesthetics	
3 Horkheimer, Sade, and Erotic Reason	131
4 Klossowski, Perversity, Criminality	149
5 Beside Herself with Desire: Musil	165
6 Modernity and Utopia	183
Notes	207
Index	247

Acknowledgements

Another version of Chapter Three has appeared in *Understanding Sade, Understanding Modernism*, ed. James Martell (New York: Bloomsbury, 2023). My thanks to Bloomsbury Academic for permission to reuse this material here. I must also express my warmest appreciation to the Arnold Schönberg Center (Wien), and Belmont Music Publishers (Los Angeles), for their kind permission to use an image of Schoenberg's *Erwartung*, Scene 2, on the cover of this book. My deepest thanks go to Haaris Naqvi, and Rachel Moore, at Bloomsbury for their continued support and enthusiasm for my work.

Abbreviations

Where double page references have been used, they refer to the German or French text and then the English versions, as translations have generally been modified.

AK Theodor W. Adorno and Ernst Křenek, *Briefwechsel*, ed. Wolfgang Rogge (Frankfurt am Main: Suhrkamp, 1974).

AN Siegfried Kracauer, *Die Angestellten*, in *Werke 1*, ed. Inka Mülder-Bach (Frankfurt am Main: Suhrkamp, 2006); tr. Quintin Hoare as *The Salaried Masses* (London: Verso, 1998).

AP Adorno, 'Die Aktualität der Philosophie', in *Philosophische Frühschriften*, ed. Rolf Tiedemann (Frankfurt am Main: Suhrkamp, 1973); tr. Benjamin Snow (Susan Buck-Morss) as 'The Actuality of Philosophy', in *The Adorno Reader*, ed. Brian O'Connor (Oxford: Blackwell, 2000).

AS Adorno, *Ästhetik (1958/59)*, ed. Eberhard Ortland (Frankfurt am Main: Suhrkamp, 2009); tr. Wieland Hoban as *Aesthetics 1958/59* (Cambridge: Polity, 2018).

AT Adorno, *Ästhetische Theorie*, ed. Gretel Adorno and Rolf Tiedemann (Frankfurt am Main: Suhrkamp, 1971); tr. Robert Hullot-Kentor as *Aesthetic Theory* (Minneapolis: University of Minnesota Press, 1997).

B Adorno, *Beethoven. Philosophie der Musik*, ed. Rolf Tiedemann (Frankfurt am Main: Suhrkamp, 1993); tr. Edmund Jephcott as *Beethoven: The Philosophy of Music* (Cambridge: Polity, 1998).

BW Adorno and Kracauer, *Briefwechsel 1923-1966*, ed. Wolfgang Schopf (Frankfurt am Main: Suhrkamp, 2008); tr. Susan Reynolds and Michael Winkler as *Correspondence 1923-1966* (Cambridge: Polity, 2020).

DA Max Horkheimer and Adorno, *Dialektik der Aufklärung. Philosophische Fragmente*, in *Gesammelte Schriften* 5, ed. Gunzelin Schmid Noerr (Frankfurt am Main: S. Fischer, 1987); tr. Edmund Jephcott as *Dialectic of Enlightenment: Philosophical Fragments* (Stanford: Stanford University Press, 2002).

DR	Kracauer, *Der Detektiv-Roman*, in *Werke 1*, ed. Inka Mülder-Bach (Frankfurt am Main: Suhrkamp, 2006).
DS	Adorno, *Drei Studien zu Hegel*, in *Gesammelte Schriften* 5, ed. Rolf Tiedemann (Frankfurt am Main: Suhrkamp, 1971); tr. Shierry Weber Nicholsen as *Hegel: Three Studies* (Cambridge: MIT Press, 1993).
EFB	Horkheimer, 'Egoismus und Freiheitsbewegung. Zur Anthropologie des bürgerlichen Zeitalters', in *Gesammelte Schriften* 4, ed. Alfred Schmidt (Frankfurt am Main: S. Fischer, 1988); tr. Frederick Hunter as 'Egoism and Freedom Movements: On the Anthropology of the Bourgeois Era', in *Between Philosophy and Social Science: Selected Early Writings* (Cambridge: MIT Press, 1993).
ING	Adorno, 'Die Idee der Naturgeschichte', in *Philosophische Frühschriften*, ed. Rolf Tiedemann (Frankfurt am Main: Suhrkamp, 1973); tr. Robert Hullot-Kentor as 'The Idea of Natural-History', *Telos* 60 (1984): 111-24.
K	Adorno, *Kierkegaard. Konstruktion des Ästhetischen*, ed. Rolf Tiedemann (Frankfurt am Main: Suhrkamp, 1979); tr. Robert Hullot-Kentor as *Kierkegaard: Construction of the Aesthetic* (Minneapolis: University of Minnesota Press, 1989).
LGF	Adorno, *Zur Lehre von der Geschichte und von der Freiheit (1964/65)*, ed. Rolf Tiedemann (Frankfurt am Main: Suhrkamp, 2001); tr. Rodney Livingstone as *History and Freedom: Lectures 1964-1965* (Cambridge: Polity, 2006).
MM	Adorno, *Minima Moralia. Reflexionen aus dem beschädigten Leben*, ed. Rolf Tiedemann (Frankfurt am Main: Suhrkamp, 1979); tr. E. F. N. Jephcott as *Minima Moralia: Reflections from Damaged Life* (London: New Left Books, 1974).
MMU	Adorno, *Moments musicaux*, in *Musikalische Schriften IV*, ed. Rolf Tiedemann (Frankfurt am Main: Suhrkamp, 1982); tr. Wieland Hoban in *Night Music* (London: Seagull Books, 2009).
MS4/5	Adorno, *Musikalische Schriften IV/V*, ed. Rolf Tiedemann and Klaus Schultz (Frankfurt am Main: Suhrkamp, 1982-84); *Essays on Music*, ed. Richard Leppert (Berkeley: University of California Press, 2002).
ND	Adorno, *Negative Dialektik*, ed. Rolf Tiedemann (Frankfurt am Main: Suhrkamp, 1972); tr. E. B. Ashton (Ernst Basch) as *Negative Dialectics* (New York: Seabury Press, 1973).

NL1/2 Adorno, *Noten zur Literatur*, ed. Rolf Tiedemann (Frankfurt am Main: Suhrkamp, 1974); tr. Shierry Weber Nicholsen as *Notes to Literature*, 2 vols (New York: Columbia University Press, 1991-92).

NP G.W.F. Hegel, *Die Naturphilosophie*, in *Enzyklopädie der philosophischen Wissenschaften im Grundrisse 1830, Bd. II*, ed. Eva Moldenhauer and Karl Markus Michel (Frankfurt am Main: Suhrkamp, 1970); *Philosophy of Nature*, tr. A. V. Miller (Oxford: Oxford University Press, 1970).

OM Kracauer, 'Das Ornament der Masse', in *Werke 5.2*, ed. Inka Mülder-Bach (Frankfurt am Main: Suhrkamp, 2006); tr. Thomas Y. Levin as 'The Mass Ornament', in *The Mass Ornament: Weimar Essays*, ed. Thomas Y. Levin (Cambridge: Harvard University Press, 1995).

PG Hegel, *Phänomenologie des Geistes*, ed. Wolfgang Bonsiepen and Reinhard Heede (Hamburg: Felix Meiner, 1980); tr. A. V. Miller as *Phenomenology of Spirit* (Oxford: Oxford University Press, 1977).

PNM Adorno, *Philosophie der neuen Musik*, ed. Rolf Tiedemann (Frankfurt am Main: Suhrkamp, 1975); tr. Robert Hullot-Kentor as *Philosophy of New Music* (Minneapolis: University of Minnesota Press, 2006).

QF Adorno, *Quasi una fantasia*, in *Musikalische Schriften I-III*, ed. Rolf Tiedemann (Frankfurt am Main: Suhrkamp, 1978); tr. Rodney Livingstone as *Quasi una fantasia: Essays on Modern Music* (London: Verso, 1992).

SER Georg Lukács, *Studies in European Realism*, tr. Edith Bone (London: Hillway Publishing, 1950).

SMP Pierre Klossowski, *Sade mon prochain* (Paris: Seuil, 1967); tr. Alphonso Lingis as *Sade My Neighbour* (London: Quartet, 1992).

UDT Walter Benjamin, *Ursprung des deutschen Trauerspiels*, in *Gesammelte Schriften I*, ed. Rolf Tiedemann and Hermann Schweppenhäuser (Frankfurt am Main: Suhrkamp, 1974); tr. Howard Eiland as *Origin of the German Trauerspiel* (Cambridge: Harvard University Press, 2019).

VA Hegel, *Vorlesungen über die Ästhetik III*, ed. Eva Moldenhauer and Karl Markus Michel (Frankfurt am Main: Suhrkamp, 1970); *Aesthetics: Lectures on Fine Art*, tr. T. M. Knox (Oxford: Clarendon, 1975).

VL Robert Musil, 'Die Vollendung der Liebe', in *Gesammelte Werke II. Prosa und Stücke*, ed. Adolf Frisé (Hamburg: Rowohlt, 1978); tr. Genese Grill as 'The Completion of Love', in *Unions: Two Stories* (New York: Contra Mundum Press, 2019).

VND Adorno, *Vorlesung über Negative Dialektik*, ed. Rolf Tiedemann (Frankfurt am Main: Suhrkamp, 2003); tr. Rodney Livingstone as *Lectures on Negative Dialectics* (Cambridge: Polity, 2008).

VW Adorno, *Versuch über Wagner*, in *Die musikalische Monographien*, ed. Rolf Tiedemann (Frankfurt am Main: Suhrkamp, 1971); tr. Rodney Livingstone as *In Search of Wagner* (London: New Left Books, 1981).

Introduction: Dialectic of Aesthetics

The aim of this book is to examine the development of Adorno's thinking on dialectics. The significance of this body of thought comes from its uniqueness, which derives from the wide range of sources that Adorno draws upon. It is partly because of this diversity that Adorno's thinking of dialectics has proved difficult to assess in relation to Hegel's thinking, and so the current project will attempt to draw out its constitutive dimensions in order to show how Adorno rethinks Hegel's ideas in modernity. Principal to this rethinking is the way that Adorno pursues a notion of dialectics that is not just material but aesthetic, which is not to translate the materialist critique into a discussion of artworks but to realize that materialism is deepened when it is considered in terms of the full range of aesthetics, as referring to experience that is sensual as well as artistic. Such a perspective responds to the materialist need to broaden its critique by taking account of bodily and sensual needs, and to realize a thinking of the sensual as material and historical, and with a range that is not limited to suffering but also takes account of pleasure. Nevertheless, the strength and singularity of Adorno's perspective is such that both the material and the sensual are rethought, and this transformation will affect the scope and possibility of his thinking. Initially, Adorno's thinking of dialectics develops through his understanding of natural-history, which is refracted through his extensive studies of music particularly in terms of musical interpretation and reproduction. In these ways his aesthetics is not only concerned with the analysis and demonstration of material dialectics but also with its transformation, and with the form of critique it uncovers. Intrinsic to this discovery is the fact that aesthetics bears its own logic and reason, its own form of thought, which will entail a rethinking of the notion of dialectics itself.

The significance of sensuality not only refers to the discourses of affect and corporeality, but also to its status in society, and the concomitant importance of perversion as a parallel model in which the inter-relation of thought and materiality is exposed. In this regard, the discussion of Adorno will lead into further studies of Sade, Pierre Klossowski, and Robert Musil, as writers who have examined how the (perverse) nature of desire is made concrete. The problem that arises here is of key importance for a materialist critique, since any notion of utopia would have to include sexual freedom, but complete sexual freedom does not seem compatible with the notion of a society free of oppression because of the nature of perversion. Hence sexuality is of pivotal importance for the actual stance of critical theory, as Adorno remarked in 1956, in reference to the need to bridge the gap between theory and praxis: 'One must find the point where it hurts. Offending against sexual taboos'.[1] There is nothing idle about this suggestion, but nor can it be removed from its consequences, and in doing so it takes up the arguments of Marx and Freud about how society operates to alienate individuals from the possibilities of their own freedom. Approaching critical theory from this perspective brings out the way that the dialectic of natural-history – the dynamic inter-relation of 'nature' and 'history' – is inflected in very different terms by sensuality. The position of critical theory on questions about the role and status of sexuality was never fully worked out, although it was always a central part of its programme. After Erich Fromm left the group in the late 1930s these issues were taken up by Herbert Marcuse, who took them in less dialectical directions by espousing an idealist vision of emancipated sexuality after the thinking of Friedrich Schiller and Charles Fourier. Adorno's interest in these concerns was always apparent but never fully developed (as was also the case for Max Horkheimer), and so it is not my intention simply to excavate his thoughts in this regard but to examine their possibilities by exploring how the aesthetic and material nature of the dialectic becomes transformed by the permutations of sensuality. Such a reading will thus show how Adorno's aesthetics and materialism are not limited to discussions of artworks and society but are extended, deepened, and problematized by the movements of sensuality. As a result, I will not be examining the general relation of critical theory to psychoanalysis, but more pointedly looking at why Adorno's thinking of dialectics necessitated an analysis of sensuality, and how such an analysis constitutes a critical theory that takes dialectics and aesthetics beyond themselves.[2]

The term that will help give shape to this discussion is dissonance, which emerges in Adorno's studies of music and becomes a form of non-dialectical dialectic that indicates the effects of aesthetics on thinking, both critical and otherwise. Through such a notion the form of utopia becomes rethought in its materiality and temporality, while nevertheless avoiding positive descriptions of such an alternative. For Musil this alternative was simply to be called the other state, and it is significant that he regarded both sexuality and aesthetics as possible ways of bringing it about. Of equal importance is the fact that the other state is no less reflective than it is sensual, and that its uniqueness comes from the way that its reflexivity seems to arise from and through its sensuality, rendering its thought radically different from what would be called instrumental reason. Adorno's thinking does not follow Musil (who would develop this notion into a quasi-mystical form), but he nevertheless finds that the dialectic of natural-history leads to a reformulation of thinking, and of the social and artistic forms that such a renewed thinking can unfold when it is pursued to its material extremes. It is the latter point, which develops through his studies of music, that becomes the basis for the tension between this reformulated thinking and the notion of utopia, which is in turn realized in the form of dissonance.

The discussion will proceed by examining the development of Adorno's notion of natural-history, and the dialectic this gives rise to, by exploring his relation to Siegfried Kracauer, who is the most important interlocutor of his early years. Alongside the sociological and philosophical work he was pursuing, there was an equally significant and intense engagement with music, arising from his appreciation of Arnold Schoenberg, his tuition with Alban Berg, and his discussions with Ernst Křenek. These discoveries were not just of aesthetic value but directly affected his thinking of the relation between nature and history, understood in terms of the dialectic between musical material and temporality. While this thought would not reach maturity until his 1941 essay on Schoenberg, later collected in *Philosophie der neuen Musik*, the first stages of its development can be found in the late 1920s. Together, these two aspects of Adorno's thinking, the sociological and musical, come to manifest themselves in a series of writings that culminate in the major works he wrote before 1933, which I will delineate to show how these ideas come about and how they are gradually transformed as some points are put aside in favour of others. It is clear that he begins to move closer to Horkheimer through the 1930s and as a result leaves behind some of the ideas picked up from Kracauer and Walter Benjamin. In doing so, Adorno's notion of the dialectic will become sharper and more materialist, taking on the form that will be known in his later works as negative. The analysis of music is a critical part of this change, as critical as his works in sociology or philosophy, and learning how this is the case also has an effect on the way that we approach his thinking as a project or work. Music is not simply adopted as an example as it has its own way of pursuing the dialectic of natural-history, which inevitably affects the form and status of the dialectic as such.

With this challenge in mind the rest of the book will examine the different possibilities of navigating this transformation in the relation of nature and history, with particular reference to the broader understanding of aesthetics that it has made apparent. Horkheimer's interest in Sade becomes crucial for understanding this change in Adorno's thinking, as he himself made clear, for it renders any thinking of an alternative to the present state of things dependent on a confrontation with the nature of sexual freedom and its ineradicable perversity. Once raised, this thought will need to be pursued through other avenues, as neither Adorno nor Horkheimer fully examined its implications. Fortunately, such a thinking can be found in the works of Klossowski, which not only examine the forms of perversity but also show how it affects thinking, as Sade had indicated.[3] A particularly resonant demonstration of the way that such a thinking would develop and what it would entail is brought out in the work of Musil, whose early writing provides an alternative notion of an aesthetic dialectic that enables Adorno's thinking to be put in contrast by showing the finitude inherent in Musil's thinking of desire. The dialectic of aesthetics thereby takes up a parallel situation to the dialectic of enlightenment by drawing out the tensions inherent in the notion of relation as such, which is what aesthetic and sexual experiences expose. For example, in opposition to the unity of will that subordinates the subject's impulses to reason, as is found in Kantian thinking and is consolidated in the unity of language, Adorno finds in aesthetics and sexuality an impulse towards the dissolute in its literal sense:

> The will is thus always a deflection from the immediate goal of the drives, it is sublimation. If we talk in general about the will of a person, if we say of a man that he has a strong will, then what is meant is his character, the harmonious unity of his actions according to a central principle that dominates him, which is in fact not at all foreign from Kant's localised principle on this point. The antithesis of the will and the character would then be the dissolved [*das Aufgelöste*] – just as, indeed, to tell you something you all know, the subtitle of Mozart's *Don Giovanni*, *il dissoluto punito*, that is, "The Punished Libertine", is one in which libertine [*Wüstling*] translates *dissoluto*: one who drifts apart in all directions without being organised by a consistent, harmonious principle of reason. So that – and this leads us, if you want, very deeply into the moral taboos on polygamy and libertinism – erotic infidelity

actually always stands as an example of how the unifying discipline of the ego-concept has failed in people.

LGF: 355/255; cf. ND: 237/238

Although it is only mentioned here briefly, the status of this dissolution of relation will be felt in the artwork and in sensuality and will have an impact on the nature of their dialectics as its reformulation of mediation and transformation is experienced as a form of dissonance. The significance of dissonance is not just in relation to music, language, or thought, but also due to the way that it reconfigures the relation of natural-history by making possible a material temporality and vice versa, which is precisely how its effects will be felt.

Thus, alongside the dialectic of enlightenment is a dialectic of aesthetics, which is its material complement in terms of both its tangibility and its refraction, so that it is neither the fulfilment of the former dialectic nor its mere ancillary. Such a thinking has implications for both conceptualization and socialization because of the way that the dialectic of natural-history is reconstrued in aesthetics on the basis of suffering and pleasure, which alter its grounds and scope. Suffering and pleasure implicate the material complex of thinking, which is not just the material complex of the individual in their contingency but also that of their social and historical background, which thereby affects the notion of relation as the basis of dialectical logic. Just as with the artwork, in suffering and pleasure we become implicated in something whose consequences are unknown, which reconstitutes both subject and object. The meaning or purpose of the interaction becomes dense and disruptive, a dissonance rather than a relation, which surpasses the logic known as mimetic on the basis of the fact that it bears its own thought.

The point is made quite concisely in the following statements: 'the liberation of happiness is a condition of right life; the intelligible sphere opens up from sensual fulfilment, not from denial' [NL2: 377/48]. But, in thereby opening up, intelligibility derives from the sensuous not only in its abstraction but also in its concreteness, which is to say that the sensuous is thought through itself. Adorno is making a connection between ethics and epistemology in view of the arguments made by Karl Kraus, whose works he is discussing, for whom an enlightened perspective leads to a better life. Adorno does not ascribe completely to the modesty of this claim, as he calls it, and so the two statements are not directly correlated. However, even in their paratactic coupling the strength of his own perspective becomes apparent: the sensuous is a condition of both a right life and of intelligibility as such, a claim that goes beyond Marx and Freud, and even Benjamin and Horkheimer, in its regard for the constitutive inter-relation of bodily and cognitive experience.

To begin this discussion, I will focus on Adorno's 1958-59 course on aesthetics, which is of key significance for the development of his ideas. While this course presents a concise overview of his aesthetics, which will situate my subsequent account by showing how and why the issue of dissonance will come to be important, it also takes place at a crucial point in his own thinking (as I will go on to show) as he is brought to respond to challenges that have arisen from those who have begun to think through the implications of his earlier works. That is, the emergence of what became known as new music in Germany in the 1950s took up some of Adorno's own ideas from his studies of Schoenberg and, in developing them practically, provided a response that he initially struggled to grasp. By examining this moment of transition, it is possible to gain a clearer idea of the scope of his thinking on aesthetics in general, which will then enable a return to his earlier works to explicate the various themes that have given rise to his thinking in the 1950s. I will come back to this lecture course in the final chapter to take account of the critical issues that mark this thinking, in terms of its status and actuality, and thereby reveal its current implications.

I Aesthetics and Nature

After some preliminary points Adorno starts his 1958-59 course on aesthetics with a discussion of Kant. In itself this is unremarkable, even considering that he proceeds by way of Kant's understanding of natural beauty, since it is central to any analysis of aesthetics that it takes the measure of the distance and difference between natural and artistic beauty. What is remarkable is the way that Adorno historicizes this argument, and in doing so reconfigures what is meant by both nature and beauty and, concomitantly, what is meant by art. This course is the fourth one on aesthetics that Adorno gave after returning to Germany in 1949 and it is contemporary with the beginning of his work on the manuscript that would later be published as *Ästhetische Theorie*. As such, it offers an initial view of Adorno's perspectives that is often more lucid than the later written work. The fact that he begins with the distinction between natural and artistic beauty not only refers us to the historicity of this distinction but also to the historical dialectic between art and reason. Hence aesthetics, and the dialectic it unfolds, becomes an aspect of the dialectic of enlightenment that marks the history of European thinking. This relation is not merely contingent to a particular phase in the development of Adorno's thinking but indicates how aesthetics plays a critical role in the history of reason, which is not fully grasped if we continue to think of it as merely ancillary, or even, as I have just noted, as an aspect of the dialectic of enlightenment. The relation between the two dialectics is never explicitly raised by Adorno but it is a central part of his argument, and it is very helpful to approach his thinking by way of it for what it exposes about the role and status of aesthetics in his and any post-Hegelian thinking.[4]

The importance of Hegel arises not just because of his predominant role in Adorno's thinking but also because he countered many of the points of Kant's aesthetics and in doing so established the major distinctions that mark the continuing history of aesthetics. Thus, it is necessary to approach Kant with Hegel's concerns in mind in order to grasp the broader context of arguments in the history of aesthetics and also because, in the transition from Kant to Hegel, there is in effect a transition to modernity that is still ongoing. As Adorno explains, although Kant spends much of his time in the third *Kritik* discussing natural phenomena, he still considers artistic beauty and natural beauty to have the same dignity [AS: 36/19]. It is only with Hegel that this relation is rethought, with artistic beauty becoming more significant, and of equal importance is the effect this change has on the division between the beautiful and the sublime in Kant's thought, which is to some degree sublated in Hegel's aesthetics. There are a number of reasons why this change came about, but it is largely due to the secularization of enlightenment thought (and its concomitant emphasis on self-determination) that spiritual feelings migrated into artworks, while traditional estimations of the beauty of nature became less significant. However, this change necessarily implies that the relation between natural and artistic beauty is constitutive (in that the notion of the latter derives from the former) and thus unsurpassable, with the consequence that it is still part of aesthetics – just as the dialectic of natural-history remains part of the dialectic of enlightenment. As a result, aesthetics becomes a major field for the renegotiation of the relation between nature and history because it is an intrinsic part of that relation, to the degree that this relation is perhaps only visible through aesthetics because it exposes the interchange of its aspects. What will need to be considered is how the dialectic of nature and history is related to aesthetics, and how far its dialectics is put in question by aesthetics.

Hegel's denigration of natural beauty in favour of artworks sets up the contrast that Adorno will pursue, as it unravels the subsequent history of aesthetics as a contrast between form and content, subjectivity and objectivity, materiality and ideality, and so on. As a result, it is necessary to understand this contrast for what it exposes about the nascent determination of art and the tensions that will subtend this determination. For what is uncovered is that neither Kant nor Hegel fully address the problem of natural beauty as it is not simply a sphere of formal beauty, whether this is seen as its strength or not, but also an encounter with that which resists assimilation to both myth and reason.[5] So, while the attempt to retrieve a sense of the formal beauty of nature is insufficient to our understanding of nature, it cannot be put aside; instead, it must be reformulated in a way that allows for the understanding of how it relates and does not relate to the emergence of rationality, and the basis for approaching natural beauty in this way comes about through the sublime. Kant emphasizes that beauty and the sublime are to be distinguished since beauty relates to the idea of formal harmony, while the sublime is the feeling that arises in the face of an experience that cannot be fully grasped and so exceeds any sense of harmonic unity. Adorno is aware of this distinction but passes over it by considering the way that Romanticism found beauty in the sublime, that is, it was the lack of formal harmony that began to be seen as the object of a universal, disinterested, and non-conceptual satisfaction, as Kant would define the beautiful. But as part of the reorganization of aesthetics that occurred with Romanticism, subjectivity became that in which expression took place, so that the object would give rise to a feeling in such a way that the subject could not remain unaffected. Adorno carefully explains this change in relation to the sublime insofar as it involves a sensation of being overwhelmed and a resistance to this overwhelming, which is not reducible to the mere sanctuary of contemplative reason.

First, it is necessary to understand how nature could only be grasped in the sense of natural beauty through a historical change that put it at a distance and thereby defined it. Nature was no longer threatening on the one hand, and not simply a resource to be plundered on the other hand, it could be contemplated and, almost as a kind of compensation, in Adorno's words, seen as beautiful [AS: 50/28]. Thus, the sense of nature as nature emerges historically and within a delimited framework, which is then reflected in the sense of formal beauty and the ornamental usage to which it is put (to the extent that cultivated 'wildernesses' appeared in formal gardens from the sixteenth century onwards). Such seeming natural order and purposiveness then becomes unsettled as natural phenomena that seemed to exceed such schemas were encountered and, conversely, as natural order itself became displaced by a sense of subjective freedom and empowerment (as is recorded by travellers who could now safely experience these 'dramatic' phenomena). The subject then found its reflection in those phenomena that seemed to exceed natural order, for in these experiences was a sense of being overwhelmed and also a kernel of resistance to this force. In this way there is not simply a dominance over nature but rather a dialectical interplay between domination and resistance, through which freedom is expressed, both subjectively and objectively. It can be seen how closely this model adheres to a kind of Hegelian thought, but Hegel's aesthetics is actually closer to Kant's than it is to Romanticism, in that Hegel cannot subscribe to the mere valorization of this feeling of freedom nor to the adoption of an aesthetics of formlessness. Instead, Hegel insists on the harmonic unity of form, but for him this is an objective expression of spirit rather than a subjective apprehension. Hence Adorno is keen to emphasize the rational and objective aspects of Hegel's thinking over the sensationism of the Romantics, while maintaining a place for the relation of freedom and resistance, of expression and that which subtends and eludes it, whether this additional factor is subjective or objective.[6]

In this transformation it is also history that is found anew, just as nature is discovered as what is 'natural', for in the reconfiguration of nature the notion of time as combining development and change is uncovered, along with the notions of revolution and crisis, and questions about the aim or direction of history. This is a key point in that the emergence of nature by way of history, and vice versa, indicates that neither is pre-eminent, and that each is formed by way of the other and so remains linked to it. Such a model is intrinsic to the formation of the work of art and also to its experience, which are now seen to be intrinsically inter-linked as changeable and non-totalizing processes. Kant's notion of the sublime stands on the threshold of this doubled transformation, to a degree that surpassed his own understanding of it, as is witnessed by the way the sublime changed in the decades after his writing. For in this doubled transformation of nature and history the artwork evokes a further revelation: as Adorno writes, it is not just that the natural is newly revealed in the historical, and vice versa, but in doing so a third element is uncovered, which is an apperception of the objective world in its historical status [AS: 49/28]. Thus, the dialectic of aesthetics holds an implicit forerunner of materialist thought, which only cements its relation to the dialectic of enlightenment, but it does so in a way that bears its own relation to the object, and a freedom to the object, as is found in the strange relation that is marked sublime. Referring to Kant's descriptions of wild elemental power – thunderstorms, erupting volcanos, raging oceans – Adorno remarks on the subjective resistance that arises in the face of such overwhelming power. There is a subtle interplay in Kant's descriptions, in which the power unleashed in these phenomena finds itself recapitulated in the force of resistance that it inspires and, conversely, the force of subjectivity finds itself reflected in the formless power of the elements. The dialectic between the two is insurmountable and recurs in the form of modern artworks, for, as Adorno states, it entered art at this time as the force of the new itself. The form of this resistance is to be understood as both the (apperceptive) moment in subjectivity that is able to experience its own overwhelming, and that within the artwork that resists its domination in terms of meaning or work. It is thus that the sublime is on the threshold of modernity, as well as of the discovery of natural-history in a form that betokens its nascent dialectic. But Adorno goes further and finds that in the moment of freedom, 'this feeling of resistance against mere existence actually contains the utopia where mere existence does not have the last word' [AS: 52/30]. This utopia arises only in and as the moment of excess, a feeling that is without conceptual form and that fails to present itself fully or to persist in its appearance, but it is also a feeling that seems both subjective and objective. The sense of this excess is amply reflected in the fact that it is not a feeling of domination over nature but one that arises by way of the dominance of nature, so that the dignity of the subject does not arise at the expense of the dignity of nature. Of equal importance is the fact that this feeling, while dialectical, is characterized primarily by its tension and oscillation, as a movement back and forth between attraction and repulsion, impotence and resistance.

As a result, aesthetic experience is itself dialectical insofar as it is caught within such a tension, rather than being found in any harmonic balance, which has the consequence of implying that if all art since that time 'has necessarily and indispensably also had to be dissonant, then this fundamentally dissonant character of all modern art in a comprehensive sense is actually an expression of the dialectic that Kant encountered in natural beauty' [AS: 54/31]. This dissonance is particularly felt in the way that the apparently disinterested stance of Kantian aesthetics is reformed, not to base it on an instrumental approach but to register that desire is never absent from aesthetics, even if it is never fully actualized, let alone satisfied. Instead, as Adorno makes clear, desire remains latent in the relation to the object through the attraction and repulsion that its dissonant status reveals. This reformulated position means that the sensual is intrinsic to the aesthetic relation as it is that in which this desire is felt, even if it is not experienced as fully actual. Such a feeling can be found in minor forms like confusion or irritation, which register the inability not to be affected and break the taboo on interest. This point is noteworthy precisely because of its subtlety, for what is being suggested is a form of interest that is not instrumental, a desire that does not seek to consume or possess, which is in part confirmed by the refusal of the object to align itself with the instrumental approach. As was seen in the sublime, the resistance of the object and that of the subject come to reflect each other in the oscillations of their relation, which appears as the dissonance of desire, its activation without fulfilment, without domination. The attraction that the artwork activates cannot be erased through the Kantian prohibition on interest, any more than the Hegelian subordination of natural beauty simply releases the artwork into spiritual meaning. In both cases the natural-history of the artwork, as was perhaps initially found in the primal mimetic relation, is suppressed at the cost of the dialectic of aesthetics, either in terms of its objectivity (Kant) or its subjectivity (Hegel). Such suppression also avoids the fact that the attraction to the work is coupled with a pain or suffering, insofar as the desire is not fulfilled, alongside a repulsion that comes from the awareness of the work's apparently autonomous force:

> I believe that there is no sensation of beauty that is not accompanied, in a certain kind of pain, by something of that separation between the desired and the desirer that is originally expressed in the experience of beauty, but perhaps even from the pain that lies in the concept of beauty because, in order to be perceived as beauty at all, it is pushed away from desire, withdrawn from desire, and thus takes on that character of inauthenticity, of a special aesthetic sphere, of everything that is commonly thought of under the name of aesthetic semblance [*Scheines*].
>
> AS: 56/33

This thought needs to be developed carefully to avoid a psychology of art, for what it refers to is a pain that is inherent to the aesthetic experience itself, with the implication that aesthetics has thereby expanded to take in the sphere of sensual desire and suffering. In this way, the pain at issue is specific to the relation to aesthetics, such that it remains bodily and cognitive, since it is a very particular kind of suffering that is associated with the actualization of a desire that can neither be fulfilled nor left unfulfilled. Hence there is both the pain of separation and the pain of appearance itself, the work or object is too remote and too close, so that its appearance is as a form of dissonance that cannot be settled and thus it persists as a disturbance. Adorno goes on to suggest that this aesthetic quality of the object is that in which the suspension of instrumentality takes place, and that its experience bears this liberation from action insofar as it is marked by a form of resistance. Aesthetics would then imply a removal of the object from appetitive desire, whose energy is diverted into an experience of the work as outside the sphere of immediacy, as only negatively available. In effect, this proposal suggests a reversal in which aesthetics is not derived from psychology but vice versa; that the relation to the object in aesthetics is in part constitutive of psychological relations, which grants a different sense to the notion of sublimation. If aesthetics involves the transformation of sensuality into ideality, then it does so only to the extent that its sensual dimension is not erased or overcome but sublated, so that it is maintained in its negation, and the sublimation of the drives perhaps derives from this relation to objects.[7]

Adorno is not simply being perverse in reversing the conventional relation between aesthetics and psychology but is trying to grasp how the aesthetic relation may unfold and what this may mean for the place of psychology. This reversal is part of the history of the dialectic of enlightenment, in which it is primarily the relation to nature that is problematic, such that it is to be grasped by way of its transformation in the history of rationality. From this perspective, psychological interpretations remain derivative of a broader relation to objects and to nature in general, which arise out of the nexus of mimesis as part of the emergence of reason itself. There is an element of the speculative to this history of rationality, and despite its broad anthropological support it is necessary to understand why this approach arises and what it implies about the place of reason. On the one hand, there is the imperative to reassess the development of reason from within a history of materialist relations so as to avoid any sense of its status as given or inevitable. On the other hand, as has been shown already, there is the necessity to realize that the relation to nature is never overcome, that it remains constitutive, albeit negatively, to the development of reason. And it is in aesthetics that this doubled tension is made apparent, since it does so in a way that addresses object and subject equally, and in terms of their relation and non-relation. The object of aesthetics is both more and less than an object, and its experience is both more and less than a relation, and as a result, aesthetics remains unstable and a source of dissonance, not just in relation to reason but also in relation to itself. The reference to a reality external to it, without which aesthetics cannot persist, is that by which it risks undermining itself, as the very utopian moment of resistance that has been described is that in which the work and its experience risk voiding themselves in becoming instruments of desire, or commodities.

The form of sensuality is thereby reconfigured alongside this sense of a sublated relation to the object, and the form in which it appears is as dissonance itself. That is, as Adorno insists, the place of dissonance does not just refer to the suffering inherent in the work and its experience, because 'the moment of the sensually pleasing does not simply disappear, rather it is in its turn sublated and preserved in the artwork, although now in the form of the dissonant' [AS: 64/38]. As a result, dissonance bears the form of a negative dialectics as it presents sensual happiness in its absence, but as such it still (negatively) presents happiness and precisely through its appearance as that which is exceptional and unforeseen, together with its appearance as that of anguish. The experience of dissonance is then 'infinitely multi-layered' as it is a 'moment of pain and happiness at once' [AS: 66-67/39-40]. This characterization explains why the rejection of dissonance takes place, as there is a discomfort with this oscillation in the experience of the object. Summarizing these points leads Adorno to specify his understanding of the dialectic of aesthetics in relation to his earlier work by saying that art is an aspect of natural behaviour that is older than rationality, but that has given way to rationality. This converges on the ideas about mimesis in *Dialektik der Aufklärung*, and thereby shows that the dialectic of aesthetics is in some way a precursor of the dialectic of enlightenment, but one that persists alongside it in much the same way that the expressive aspect of language persists alongside its more rational content. Or, as he says, 'art is a mimetic behaviour that is held, preserved in an age of rationality' [AS: 68/41].

It is as such that art is able to preserve those remnants of nature that have been excluded or repressed by rationality, so that they can return in artworks. Thus, the imitative aspects of art lie not in its imitation of natural objects, but in the 'attempt through its gestures and its whole attitude to restore a state in which there was actually no difference between subject and object' [AS: 70/42]. The nature of this state is difficult to determine since it is not simply that in which subject and object collapse into each other. Although the artwork exists in a space distinct from the world, a space in which the ordinary rules of reality are suspended, it is also a space that is constituted by a surplus of meaning, of the appearance of the work in itself. These two aspects are inter-linked and the success of the artwork to some degree depends on how the tension between them is coordinated, insofar as the meaning of the work will begin to orient it back towards the world, while the space of the work will form its own kind of meaning, which is not identical to that which it expresses by its appearance. Hence this interaction corresponds to the two aspects of the genitive in the meaning *of* the work, in which is found the difference *between* subject and object, which is now no longer strictly between them, but part of their imbrication as subject-to-object and object-to-subject. As a result, and despite its distance, the work exists in and as a space that is not remote at all as it is only distinct to the small but fundamental degree of being distinct. This fact of being sheerly distinct also informs its quality of likeness, its appearance as itself, and it is by way of the inter-relation of these aspects that the respective orientations of subject and object are displaced, but thereby oriented to the broader dialectic of natural-history that the work unfolds and in which its critical and utopian moments subsist. For this degree can be understood as that of abstraction, which is made concrete in the artwork's appearance, and it is as such that it bears a sense of the absolute, of autonomy, of being whole in itself. For Adorno, this point bears an important conclusion, as it means that the artwork rids itself of the illusion that the other world that it presents is real. The artwork is not only an aspect of secularization but actively works through the demythologization of thought by rendering itself as what it is and not as an alternative reality that surpasses our own. As he writes, 'the semblance is freed from the lie of being real' and in place of this lie, the work bears a relation with the truth that keeps on unfolding [AS: 78/47]. Because of this unfolding none of the preceding descriptions of the relation between art and nature can be taken as definitive as the resistance of the artwork contests any form of this relation.

Instead, and integral to its status as a part of the dialectic of enlightenment, the dialectic of aesthetics work in such a way that the fact 'that nature is saved in art is inseparable from the fact that art is able to dominate nature to an ever-greater degree'. Adorno calls this imbrication 'the actual dialectical point of the relation between nature and art', and the tension between the control of nature and its liberation is what 'really distinguishes the artistic process and above all defines the sense of the artwork' [AS: 85/51]. In fact, Adorno insists that the significance of this approach is that the most advanced artworks are those that bear this tension to the highest degree, suggesting that it is only by way of its technical control that the liberation of the material can take place. Within this approach there lies a semblance of the sublime in that the experience of domination releases the sense of the work more fully, not through it but despite or contrary to it. Such a notion is key to the formal and abstract approach to artworks that characterizes Adorno's thinking, but it is coupled with their capacity for dissonance, which indicates how the dialectic of aesthetics inheres and diverges from the dialectic of enlightenment in both its dialectics and its rationality. The historical corollary of this relation is that artworks can lose their tensed relation to their times, or be otherwise out of phase, which makes it important to consider how the temporal acuity of the work is realized. With the outline of the dialectic of aesthetic natural-history in place, Adorno then sketches out its effects along the dimensions of expression, in terms of its purity or convention; status, in terms of its isolation or universality; and basis, in terms of its contingency or necessity. These dimensions are all aspects of the way that the natural-history of the work is unfolded and each leaves the work at risk of change or stasis, obscurity or reification. But as these dimensions arise out of the material, or at least the attempt to allow the material to come to a point of manifesting itself, they are not fixed or even. The attempt to objectify the logic of the material and the mediations sedimented within it is thus subject to the irresolvable dialectic of the material, which is necessarily part of the experience of the work as well. The dissolution of the difference between the subject and object thereby takes place according to the mimesis that is part of this dialectical relation, as will be shown. And the temporality of this differentiation and dissolution occurs across its pastness and futurity as well as its moment, that is, across its transience and changeability, and its punctuality and repetition.

II Music as Critique

Studies of Adorno's aesthetics have proliferated in recent years in anglophone scholarship, but they have largely avoided his extensive research in music, which is not only perplexing but also misguided.[8] Adorno's writings on music are at the basis of his understanding of the materiality and temporality of the artwork, and his approach to the dialectics of aesthetics is informed by his understanding of music, rather than the reverse. Furthermore, over the forty years of his research into music he gains a crucial understanding of the historical and social factors affecting the composition, reproduction, and reception of artworks, which grants him a broad insight into the changing fate of the avant-garde. When, in his sixties, he recalls his childhood encounter with a broken guitar he is not only remarking on the formative effects of its dissonance but also restating its importance for contemporary composition, which is not just a reference to music but also to philosophy.[9] He is thus emphasizing the ever-present challenge of responding to this dissonance, which implies that it reformulates itself as the techniques and materials of art change, and that this change requires a concomitant change in thinking if it is to be matched. It is to this change that aesthetics is ultimately attuned, such that it implies an irreversibility to the cultural and historical dimensions of thinking. Adorno's recollection of the broken guitar in the epigraph to this book is not a nostalgic image but one of a persistent imperative in the face of which there can be no turning back: 'Whoever devotes themselves to the older out of desperation with the difficulties of the new will not be consoled, but will be the victim of their helpless longing for a better time, which in the end was not even there'. As a result, this aesthetic imperative takes shape under the burden of what it confronts in society in general, 'where blatant disproportions have arisen between the development of technical forces of production and the human modes of reaction, the ability to use these techniques and to control and apply them sensibly' [MS4: 258/648]. These lines come from a talk on the difficulties of composition that was given shortly before his account of his childhood holidays in Amorbach, and it can be seen that the same issue is at stake, which he phrases rather modestly as one of achieving 'an appropriate relation to the state of the technique: either by the composers using and shaping it according to the state of their own consciousness, or by pushing their self-criticism so far that they reach that state. There are no general instructions on how to do this'. Furthermore, 'technique has its own weight; any attempt to merge it with subjective experience threatens to dilute it' [MS4: 260/650]. That is, the relation to the work is condemned to an insecurity that cannot be alleviated without bad faith.

Adorno's long perspective is valuable as he was able to observe the changes in music from atonal to serial to aleatory styles, and on to examples from *musique concrète* and early electronic music. And, following comments by Heinz-Klaus Metzger, he was forced to rethink some of his earlier ideas on the status and possibility of aesthetic experimentation. This vantage point then allows for a considerable insight into the ways in which these differing forms of music approached questions of history or material in their works, as well as what was and was not innovative in these approaches. The place of avant-garde works of art thus casts light on issues that are not just aesthetic, as they refer to the place of the individual in relation to society and to tradition, and the burden placed on any activity that would seek to compose or renovate. The challenge of responding to the material in itself, as much as that is possible, while also rendering it objectively compelling, is coupled with the difficulties that the material itself has come to bear on the subject. As Adorno remarked three years earlier, 'Serial and post-serial music is based on a fundamentally different apperception, provided that one can say of music at all that it is based on apperception', consequently, 'acoustically real hearing may not grant the highest musical criteria' [QF: 494-95/271]. The problem that arises in contemporary music, and that reflects not just the history of conceptualism in modern art but also the demands on social engagement more generally, is that its form no longer accords with a conventional mode of auditory thinking. Principal in this regard, insofar as he is discussing music, is the relation of the time in which the work is felt to unfold to that of the movement of time in general (so called), but the nature of this relation is such that it is no longer possible to treat it as given, and it is this transformation that affects the subject position inherent in apperception. The difficulties in a particular branch of aesthetics thereby open onto a broader problem in the relation between thought and history, in which the transformations that are felt to be underway are such that each must change in relation to the other. For, as he notes in a Hegelian point, the recognition of these limits implies the possibility of crossing them, which means that in coming up against these challenges to thought, thinking has begun to meet them, but in exceeding its own grounds it is placed in the most precarious situation, a fact that also affects the changing shape of Adorno's own thinking on the nature of innovation.

The difficulty thus involves a relation between subject and object that is not external and indifferent, but that is also not based in an apparently given lawfulness. Adorno's 1961 address to the Darmstadt Summer School approaches this issue from a number of different perspectives so as to draw out his notion of *musique informelle* without however defining it, a notion that assumes the same relation in regard to previous music that his understanding of negative dialectics does in regard to Hegelian thought.[10] For example, in terms of the problem of repetition:

> As self-developing, music absolutely negates repetition, according to the Heraclitean idea that no one steps into the same river twice. But equally it only becomes developing through repetition. Thematic work, the principle that concretises the abstract course of time in the musical substance, is always just dissimilarity of the same. Development that leads to the new only occurs through a relation to the old, which is set a priori in such a relation, and repeated in whatever sublimated and unrecognisable form. Without this highly formal constituent of similarity there is no articulated music; identity in non-identity is its lifeblood. Such dialectics are driven to extremes in serial music. Absolutely nothing may be repeated in it, but absolutely everything is, as a derivative of the

one, repetition. It is up to informal music to rethink this double sidedness in its abandoned problem, to set up its own organisation according to it.

QF: 506/284

A similar problematic can then be rephrased in terms of material, as well as temporal, innovation, but in all cases the relation of part to whole is transformed so that although the integration of subject and object assumes a necessity, it does not do so within an *a priori* framework:

> In the most advanced and acoustically sensitive compositions today yawns a discrepancy between the blocks that are joined together, layered as it were, which are often surprisingly through-composed in themselves, and the overall structure; as if there was no mediation from the unprecedented articulation of the details to the equally splendidly constructed totality, as if the two were connected according to principles of construction, but that these construction principles could not be realised in living phenomena. Mediation is absent in the banal as well as the strict sense. In the banal: there is a lack of links between the individual sounds into which everything is drawn together. In the strict: the events do not want to go beyond themselves, the structure remains largely abstract in relation to them.
>
> MS4: 271-72/659

The problem of the avant-garde thereby manifests itself, for in this innovation of the material the work itself risks indifference (a problem that he finds equally in John Cage and Pierre Boulez, despite the difference of their works). Nevertheless, if formal construction can lead to such apparent informality in its lack of mediation, then its other possibilities must be considered. The basis of the informal artwork lies in the fact that it must still be thought through, but in such a way that this must occur by way of the material, which is changed in being so considered, and rendered objective such that its sedimented social and historical senses are actualized anew. The difficulty of this model is that it seems to depend on nothing but the material, which gives rise to the situation of convergence and indifference that is found in the music that Adorno discusses, where serial and aleatory approaches fall short insofar as 'the extremes of absolute determination and absolute chance coincide' [MS4: 270-71/658]. It is thus that the role of thought is highlighted, in both its relation to the material and its obligations in regard to it. For if music is to organize itself according to the double sidedness of this problem of innovation, then it has to internalize this tension and develop from out of it, such that its whole emerges out of this internal critique. As a result, thinking itself is changed in this process, which is the demand that aesthetics raises.

Equally, this analysis of the form of the musical work casts light on its aesthetic character; its status as a work that bears a necessity in itself, and yet that arises as an illusion or semblance in relation to the world, and it is to this actuality that thought is required to respond, which indicates something of the burden implied by a thinking of the avant-garde. As he explains, the movement by which music emerges is not wholly subjective or objective and so the basic material of the work is neither its tones nor the relations among them, but rather its illusion or deception (*Trug*), as which it exteriorizes itself and thereby achieves a universality [QF: 522/301]. There would seem to be a Münchhausen-like quality to this appearance, which is evidence of its facticity, its simple appearance as what it is by which it demonstrates itself, however illusorily, and thus within which there is a quality of concrete estrangement; the work is not just what it is but something more, even if it not entirely possible to define what this 'more' involves. However, this situation has to be countered by the other part of its double sidedness, which is that the work is only able to develop through the intervention of the subject, or rather, the work 'demands the constitutive share of the subject in its organisation' [QF: 527/307]. This intervention is necessary because the subject brings an element of vivacity or animation to the work, without which it could not become something objectively lifelike, something able to become. This apparently organic element does not renaturalize the work but, recalling the discussion of Kant, instates a sense of resistance and interrogation that grants the work its autonomy. Hence for as much as the work cannot resemble the subject due to its estrangement from it, it also cannot not resemble the subject. So, despite the estrangement in which the work exists, it cannot become absolutely estranged without failing to be a work, and so its distance also contains an element of semblance, a semblance of estrangement, as its very situation begins to approximate it to the subject. This revision of the subject-object relation is then part of the revision of the compositional form of the work. Quite concisely, the dissonance of the work, in and through which the actualization of musical consciousness takes place, implies that 'artistic aporias express the aporias of politics', and exactly to the degree that an aporia is a point of impassability, a failure or contradiction in relation as such [QF: 535/316].

The statement upon which Adorno concludes his long survey thus bears a very precise sense: 'The shape of every artistic utopia today is: to make things of which we do not know what they are' [QF: 540/322]. If this is the imperative of aesthetics, then the demand on thought is to come to a point where it can approach such a thought; it too has to change so that it can think such a notion. For the notion of things 'of which we do not know what they are' is not simply of things that are unknown or mysterious but of things that exceed our thinking by a very specific penumbra of temporal and material exposure or becoming, and it is in this sense that they give shape to the notion of an artistic utopia.[11] What is imperative on thought is to find a way of thinking in which this utopia can be recognized, which then reveals itself as not simply aesthetic.

Part One

The Development of Dialectics

1

Kracauer and the Dialectic of Natural-History

Adorno's idea of the dialectic of natural-history (*Naturgeschichte*) is one of the key figures of his thought, but despite his attempts to explicate it by way of the thinking of Benjamin and Georg Lukács it largely remains a tacit figure. To help bring it to a better degree of tangibility I will examine some of the background of his thinking in the period prior to his lecture on natural-history in July 1932. While the significance of Benjamin's writings for Adorno's thought on this issue is beyond question, there are other equally important factors in its development, principally the work of Kracauer and Adorno's own notion of musical material, without which an understanding of this dialectic will remain one-sided. In addition to providing a better perspective on Adorno's version of dialectics, which is central to his revision of Hegel's thought, this background will demonstrate how the particularities of natural-history bring out a deeper revision of the relation between the abstract and the concrete, which is at the heart of the issue of dialectics per se. It is with this theme in mind that I will begin by looking in some detail at Kracauer's method in his early writings as this is central to the development of Adorno's own method of thinking. In particular, it is the issue of how dialectical thinking relates to the concrete that poses the most serious questions for Adorno's thinking. It will become apparent that the problems faced by this rethinking parallel those of the problems faced by the first post-Hegelian generation, one hundred years before Adorno's early work, with the crucial distinctions that Adorno was not only working after the immense disruptions caused by war and revolution but was also following the changes brought about by modernism more generally.

Kracauer's early works on urban culture derive initially from his architectural interests in forms of space and their material appearances and ornamentation, but they also focus on the structural changes to behaviour and experience that take place through the dominant urban tropes of distraction and coordination.

In this way, his works are an extension of the analysis of second nature that Lukács began to develop with his theory of reification, which Kracauer subjects to a more varied and fragmentary gaze, finding that the habitual experiences of modernity are less unified in their objectification, but no less damaging. This point becomes important for how Adorno will respond to the reification of experience in his analysis of musical material, where it is a question of the formation and status of habit as it is sedimented in the material as second nature, which then becomes the mode through which abstraction and concreteness participate in the appearance of artistic control and the loss of aesthetic specificity. Second nature as it is conceived by Lukács lacks the complexity of the form that Hegel studied, and it has often been thought that Adorno follows Lukács by way of his own concern with reification. However, the analysis of musical material offers a very different perspective on the relation of abstraction and concreteness in the formation of habit, and it is from this perspective that Adorno can perceive the significance but also the limits of the nascent sociological research that Kracauer was pursuing. It is only by becoming aware of the relation between thought and the material that the internal dialectical mediation of the material can be grasped, both historically and aesthetically, and thereby release the full potential of natural-history as a dialectic of enlightenment.

In this regard it is useful to recall that abstract and concrete are to be understood in terms of their relation to the object, as the abstraction from or concretion to an object. From this view it becomes easier to understand the two-way movement involved in habit as second nature, in which there is a removal from the contextual specificity of the action alongside an immersion of thought in the matter at hand. Just as habit makes possible the coordination and entrainment of manoeuvres, it also makes possible the intensive awareness of expert understanding. In a sense, what is found here is similar to what Hegel states at the beginning of *Wissenschaft der Logik* about the non-existence of being and nothing as separate terms, since it is not so much a question of abstract and concrete as such but of abstraction becoming concrete in habit, and concreteness becoming abstract in expertise. It is important to note that concreteness is not identical to material or sensible particulars, as Hegel indicates by demonstrating the existence of concrete universals. Intrinsic to this distinction is the role of mediation, for abstraction is that which removes something from the network of mediations out of which it is constituted, while to be concrete is to be a mediated complex, which is how it can apply to universals as well as particulars. This point is significant to move our thinking of habit and second nature away from sheer materiality and to recognize that reification involves any sclerosis or isolation of the mediated networks of interaction. Conversely, to be abstract is to work through the contradictions of the concrete in such a way that it reveals its essence, which is to say that the abstract is not a mere generalization or idealization of the concrete but unfolds its concreteness into its complete actualization in the concept. It is thus possible, as is the case with the concrete universal (e.g. subjectivity), for abstraction to lead to a concreteness that does not remove difference (abstraction) from its unity (concreteness).[1]

To provide a preliminary example of Kracauer's approach to this issue, it is helpful to examine his report on the Angerstein murder case from 1925. In December 1924 Fritz Angerstein killed his wife and seven other people in a fit of violence. Kracauer attended the trial seven months later as a reporter for the *Frankfurter Zeitung*, a trial that attracted an enormous amount of attention and became one of the showpieces of Weimar criminal justice. The case did not attract attention just because of its brutality but because it seemed inexplicable, as Angerstein was apparently a perfectly ordinary man, a loving husband, and a reliable worker. No evidence suggested that he was capable of such acts and, in his testimony, he struggled to recognize them as his own actions. While he accepted responsibility for the murder of his wife, he could not explain the other killings. Consequently, much of the trial was concerned with determining his motives, and it became clear that Angerstein had led a deeply unhappy and repressed existence caring for his wife, who been ill for most of the thirteen years of their marriage and had suffered six miscarriages. To try to understand Angerstein's character, criminal psychologists were employed, much to the scepticism of the press, and revealed something of the dissociation that had driven him and had led him to say that he had killed his wife because he loved her, while leaving the subsequent murders as anomalous aftershocks. Kracauer makes much of this disparity between the acts and the actor, and the impossibility of reconciling the nondescript perpetrator with the astonishing excess of the crimes. During his imprisonment Angerstein showed no violent or malicious tendencies, making it difficult to recognize him as the agent of his deeds, and it is thus that the psychologist Richard Herbertz stated at the trial that Angerstein did not commit his crimes; rather they happened to him, these were deeds without a doer. Kracauer was impressed by this viewpoint and details how the long-repressed feelings of anger and injustice exploded, like the irruption of a monstrous figure from the unconscious, before which Angerstein could only stand as confused and surprised as everyone else. However, despite this diagnosis, Kracauer feels that the crime remains inexplicable as the reasons for it remain undiscovered:

The fact that the deeds that are in the name of Angerstein lack personal reference points, without thereby leading to a deranged mind, that they have no sufficient reason in the consciousness of their perpetrator: this makes them a genuinely agonising riddle and gives them the uncanny strangeness of mere things. Depth psychology may have rightly stated that they have been brought to light from the craters of the unconscious life of the soul; the riddle of how this is possible has not also been solved.

Such may be the case, and in retrospect it is perhaps easier to perceive the gaps in the psychological account, but there is a sense that what Kracauer is seeking is something more fundamental, not just an explanation of how it was possible but also why it happened at all, what was it about human nature, as it is called, that brought about this monstrous irruption? It is here that Kracauer concludes his article, but not before making a surprising diagnosis of his own:

> the more people become objective in their relations with one another and allow released things to have power over themselves, instead of holding things to themselves and humanly permeating them, the easier it can and will happen that the disfigured humanity that has been repressed into the abyss of the unconscious will rush, goblin-like and gruesome, into the abandoned world of things. Only in a human world does the deed have its doer.[2]

By recalling Lukács's account of reification, alongside a Freudian vision of the unconscious, it is clear that Kracauer is taking an explicitly political approach to the case, but the result is that this position substantially reduces the complexity of the details he has so far sketched out. The Marxist notion of commodity fetishism that lies behind Lukács's thinking on reification is by no means irrelevant to an understanding of the Angerstein case, but the transition from it to the conclusion is too perfunctory. Kracauer was not alone in the way that he adopted Lukács's thought on this point, but the sudden appearance of this doctrine passes over the careful exploration of the problems in Angerstein's testimony, which would have revealed, given greater analysis, more than a verdict in which objects become subjects just as subjects become objects. For what would have become apparent would be the mechanisms of their transformation, the intricate dialectical interchanges by which natural-history changes itself by itself, and thus the reasons for why such changes come about. Of course, in the space of a feuilleton there is no real scope for such an analysis, but what Kracauer's account does indicate is the distinction he draws between a humanity disfigured by modern life and that which potentially beckons from a world where people and things mutually support and nurture each other. But it is precisely the complexity of abstraction and concreteness in these acts that must be addressed before any such estimation of the possibilities of an unreified society can be gauged.

If it is a question of subjects becoming objects just as objects become subjects, then we find the scope for considering people, including oneself, as tools or obstacles, just as, conversely, objects begin to assert their own demands and impulses, leaving the individual at their mercy. It is then possible to see the madness into which the individual can be drawn, alongside the loss of humanity that would make violence and exploitation not only likely but inevitable. This account illuminates the reification associated with commodities, but it loses sight of the rationality of this movement by which the persuasiveness and depth of its effects can be understood. While the hand can be understood as a tool, it is also necessary to see that the tool is an extension of the hand; rationality as well as instrumentality move in both directions, and it is this double sense that should be understood as the complex of concrete abstraction associated with second nature. Habit is a form of selection and, insofar as it is communal, it is evaluative: it allows for a standard of assessment related to the forms of life of that community, and it is as such that it encodes a specific form of knowledge, or tact. Habit is also the basis of freedom in Hegel's thought, for in releasing us from a continual negotiation with daily tasks we are able to consider them reflexively, which is a point of crucial significance in relation to artistic practices. Intrinsic to the designation of habit is the fact that what seems immediate (and natural) is a mediated complex of (sociohistorical) values. But equally, what seems acquired and generic can become creative and unique by virtue of the way these mediated forms are inhabited. In this combination we find the dual movements by which apparent rationality reverts to mythology, while apparent mimicry yields speculative knowledge. These points will come to be developed more fully in Adorno's response to the rationalization of Schoenberg's twelve-tone technique, as well as in his own model of philosophy as interpretation.

I Natural-History of Ornamentation

In 1929, when Kracauer started studying the new class of Angestellten in Berlin, this group had been around for a generation, but their appearance still constituted a phenomenon worthy of consideration because of the way that they were now changing the life of the metropolis. At this time Berlin was the most technologically advanced city in Europe and the Angestellten were the group in which the results of these advances could be felt most broadly. The word itself is not unusual, although it is not easy to find a simple translation, precisely because the appearance of this group in other urban settings was marked by different socio-economic pressures and so gave rise to slightly different manifestations. In German, *anstellen* is a verb meaning to employ, and so the Angestellten are those who are employed, which means that it refers not just to office workers, clerks, and white-collar workers, as it also includes workers in shops, warehouses, and transportation. The key point of distinction arises in the difference between employees and labourers, where the former are paid according to a monthly salary and the latter by the job. That is, the employee enters into a contract with their employer that means that they are paid a regular amount regardless of the actual work conducted each month, while labourers are paid for their work on a job-by-job basis. The nature of the employment contract is one of formally recognizing a relation and guaranteeing it with a level of security, and the consequence of this contract is a combination of freedom and constraint for both parties. For the employee, they have the security of knowing that they will be paid a set amount regardless of the different levels of work that may transpire from month to month, but on the other hand the contract involves a commitment to uphold the employer's code of conduct. Thus, the employee is bound by their relation in such a way that what they do is to some degree of lesser importance than how they do it; they are recruited to play a role insofar as they now exist, for the terms of the contract, as representatives of their employer. For the employer, there is the security and flexibility of a regular source of workers, but this is coupled with a greater necessity for training and organization in order to bring the employee into line with the structure and behaviour of the business.

Evidently, this contract has elements that derive from the way that military, religious, or civic organizations operate, which would have been the basic models out of which it emerged, with their emphasis on a moral *esprit du corps* that appears as a duty to uphold the organization. Over time, through training, bonuses, and promotion, the employee comes to identify with the business, but also to experience a dissociation in their non-working hours, which now appear ancillary: an off-duty period that is merely used to recharge in order to carry on with work. Hence the need for these hours to become as fulfilled and organized as working hours through the activities of out-of-work clubs and societies, as well as entertainment, holidays, and the expected family commitments that are geared towards developing the next generation of employees. Their designation was formally codified in the Angestelltenversicherungsgesetz of 1911, which guaranteed the rights and insurance of employees, and was extended in 1924 to include pensions. In doing so, the definition of this class became concretized, which also distinguished it, legally and socially, from that of manual labourers, a separation that was the first such definition in European law and remained in place as a legal distinction until 2005.

It is to this new formation in society that Kracauer applies himself in 1929, at a point when he was about to move from Frankfurt to Berlin and when, amid rising unemployment and inflation, he was to be promoted to the position of cultural editor of the *Frankfurter Zeitung*, having been a full-time employee of the paper since 1921. Kracauer is thus not an outsider to this social group, but his position as a critic and as a new arrival in Berlin is enough to place him at a certain remove, and it is this remove that becomes of pivotal importance in his response. As is found in his programmatic essay of 1927, 'Das Ornament der Masse', which details the relation between performers and audience in contemporary forms of entertainment, this distance is echoed in the strategic position Kracauer takes in response to the appearance of social formations in time. It is important to remember that as a former student of architecture, the ornament has a very specific sense for Kracauer, for it is that in which time takes place, that is, in which history becomes concrete in the seemingly superfluous aspects of larger structural developments.[3] The ornament then gives expression to and thereby allows for an insight into the specific historical currents of the period as they take form and are made real. There is then a movement between time and space, history and materiality, which is not entirely natural or intentional in its appearance but combines the two in a relation that also keeps them apart.[4] This is the sense of the quasi-dialectical relation that Kracauer sketches out at the beginning of his 1927 essay and, although this has often been discussed, it is worth examining its language carefully:

> The place that an epoch takes in the historical process can be determined more strikingly from the analysis of its inconspicuous surface expressions than from the judgements of the epoch about itself. As the expression of tendencies of the time, the latter are not a conclusive testimony about the overall constitution of the time. The former, because of their unconsciousness, offer an unmediated access to the basic content of what exists. Conversely, this knowledge is linked to their interpretation. The basic content of an epoch and its unconsidered stirrings illuminate each other reciprocally.
>
> OM: 612/75

A number of points become problematic on a first reading of this passage, since any mention of an 'unmediated access to the basic content of what exists [*Grundgehalt des Bestehenden*]' suggests some kind of intellectual intuition, which would abdicate from the rigours of the dialectical analysis that is being suggested, as does the idea that these surface expressions are 'unconscious'. However, the significance of this passage becomes clearer when it is placed next to the subsequent description of mass ornaments like that of the large dance spectacle, which exists purely as an end in itself, separate from its constituents, so that its form is invisible to those constructing it: 'The more its coherence loses itself [*sich entäußert*] in a mere linearity, the more it withdraws from the immanent consciousness of its builders. But this is why it is not struck by a gaze that would be more incisive, indeed, no one would notice it, if the spectators, who are aesthetically related to it and represent no one, were not massed in front of the ornament' [OM: 614/77]. Here again we have a contractual relation in which the two parts are bound by a seemingly formal and contingent exchange, which is wholly without content or purpose other than its own perpetuation. So, even in their mutual oblivion, the entertainers and the audience illuminate each other reciprocally, and it is on the basis of this relation that Kracauer's own gaze as a critic is grounded.

The rationality that Kracauer detects in the precision and repetition of the dancers' movements is, by virtue of its emptiness, an expression of nothing but its alienation, its lack of sense, which becomes its organizational form. The audience, no less than the dancers, are drawn into this hollowness by which their free time is structured, both are organized by the same merely formal structure. As he writes, 'the capitalistic production process, like the mass ornament, is an end in itself [*sich Selbstzweck*]', which is not say that it is solely geared towards profit, as he then remarks, but that capitalism organizes life so that it remains its organizational force; whether in the workplace or outside it, capitalism operates by producing and maintaining the circumstances for its own perpetuation [OM: 615/78]. Underlying the drive towards profit, the impetus is towards a formal reorganization whose emptiness and purposelessness, for the individual, guarantees a persistence of form by promoting the alienation upon which it is based. Alienation becomes the measure of the world, the metric of the quasi-dialectical relation that appears in the form of a contract of mutual oblivion. For the critic, alienation is the key to the illumination of the forms of social life in their current specificity, as concrete ornaments of history, but as such it can become subject to its own form of alienation unless the force of its dialectical gaze is rendered thorough by pursuing the rationalization of these forms further, as Kracauer importantly notes, but also by realizing that this alienation is not just the mark of lost meaning but of the immanent loss of organicism *tout court*. That is, the loss of the whole that alienation remarks is the loss of any sense of the natural as a pregiven world, whether this is understood in opposition to history or reason, which gives rise to the demand to rethink the form of relation that this loss implies.

Kracauer's response to this problem comes in the form of the fairy tale, which like the pursuit of reason is concerned with the 'introduction of truth into the world'. Confusion can again arise over this point, since Kracauer is not reverting to a sense of naturalized folk knowledge any more than a sense of theological fatalism, instead, *echten Märchen* 'are not stories about miracles but convey [*meinen*] the miraculous advent of justice'. As Horkheimer and Adorno would explore fifteen years later, there is a dialectical reversal here between a reason that has become irrational by allowing itself to be naturalized rather than pursuing its own rigour, and a history that conveys a rationality that surpasses the conservatism of its context by way of formal innovations. For the importance of the fairy tale lies in its structure, its sudden appearance and lack of explication, by which it simply arrives as a singular manifestation of itself, which is its truth. The unfolding of the fairy tale is nevertheless convoluted and unexpected, but through its turns it arrives at a peculiar demonstration of justice, a process that Kracauer is clearly seeking to follow, but that also leads his essays into the same risk of perfunctory demonstration. In the fairy tale, 'mere nature is sublated [*aufgehoben*] for the sake of the victory of truth', as if by dialectical fiat there is a formal sublation of what exists into its truth, 'natural power is defeated by the impotence of the good' [OM: 616-17/80]. But saying does not make it so, fairy tales must do more than merely mean justice; instead, their form must be rendered thoroughly dialectical through their alienation, and part of this development is found when it is realized that the audience and the performers of the mass ornament are the same shifting masses, the same class. In this case, the rationalization and emptiness of the entertainment becomes a mutually displacing demythologization of the natural, where the mass becomes both the spectator and the spectacle. This self-serving subsistence is then quickly exposed as a lie, as both aspects find that their positions have been prearranged by the machinations of capital, and it is this realization that their mutual illumination reveals: their subjection to capital in the face of a possibility to exist otherwise.

The problem clearly applies to the Angestellten more generally, and its root lies in the fact that these mass arrangements are only externally coordinated; while their formality has removed them from the naturalized morality of the military corps, this approach has failed to free them from capitalistic machinations not because it has gone too far, but because it has not gone far enough. Hence the mutual displacement must become internally coordinated as well, reason must provide the basis for an independence from nature in each individual so that its mass formations will bear a sociohistorical meaning, 'then society will change', as Kracauer concludes, performing his own fairy-tale-like resolution to the problem that he has just shown to be an infinitely remote possibility [OM: 623/86]. The mass ornament becomes problematic precisely because it is mass, which permits of too great a separation between the organic and the rational, for while this indicates the separation of the rational from the mythology of the natural whole, in doing so its own appearance as a mass is simply that of a mass of parts, an aggregate, which in its lack of immanent reason prevents the possibility of any realization of this mass to itself, and so it remains mute and trapped in a mutual illumination of emptiness with its audience. As one of the surface expressions of history the mass ornament offers an insight into its appearance but, in its extremity, it prevents this insight from being dialectically realized, insofar as its separation of the organic and the rational is aporetic. From this extreme Kracauer can only turn back and conclude with the miraculous flourish of a future change. Methodologically, this essay falls into the same trap of merely external relations in terms of Kracauer's gaze upon the phenomenon, which may be formally illuminating but fails to yield the sense by which its alienation can be pursued to the point where it might reveal itself in a relation that is removed from both the whole and its parts.

A suggestion of how this relation might be understood arises in the way that the ornament only exists for itself, that is, it is unconcerned with any purpose outside its own formation, and thus turns away from its ostensible audience and disregards them, which if it were to occur mutually would allow for a reciprocal divergence that would constitute a new form of relation. The potential of this point is taken up most extensively in *Die Angestellten* and is signalled early on in the text when Kracauer remarks that the lives of this new class 'is more unknown than that of the primitive tribes at whose habits the employees marvel in films' [AN: 218/29]. To be absorbed in that which has no interest in oneself is to be subjected, and this situation is played out across Kracauer's study as the employees find themselves in an unequal relation with their employers despite being offered what appear to be considerable rewards, as had happened with the mass ornament. The new businesses that had arisen in this period had given rise to new jobs, but although this had formed a new demographic group it carried over the same problems that had previously existed, for this new class was subject to the same force of proletarianization as before as they experienced the same constraints and insecurity. Because of the growing numbers of this group, power lay with the employers who were able to hire and fire at will, and the new working environments inherited the same problems as the work was often unskilled and repetitive, leading to an empty and unchangeable existence. It is in the face of this emerging problem that employers began to use a more sophisticated selection process, as Kracauer goes on to show, in which pseudo-scientific methods were introduced to give the impression of a rigorous and impartial system of recruitment. As the skills necessary for the job were often quite basic, other methods of selection were necessary to conceal their arbitrary nature, methods that were grounded in spurious qualifications and psychological evaluations that concerned themselves with the level of moral aptitude and commitment. One's job was now seen to be a vocation for which one would be chosen on the basis of more or less opaque processes of evaluation. In this way, the potential employee was placed in a situation of having to trust the employer implicitly, while the reverse was not necessary, and yet in dressing up the selection in terms of psychology the employee could feel that they were being personally valued even if their work was entirely impersonal. Thus, a sense of loyalty is generated that is entirely unsupported by either the work or the activities of the employer, instead, the class defines itself by its qualifications and employment and, ultimately, its salary, in order to show that, despite other evidence, it is not working class. Much like astrology, job selection and the concomitant employment status becomes a process of self-mystification masquerading as rigorous and legitimate (a masquerade that remains in place in contemporary data mining algorithms).

Kracauer's method then becomes one of disenchantment, dispelling the self-deceiving oblivion into which these employees have woven themselves by recasting their histories as dialectical fairy tales, which take their specific circumstances and unfold them into their general sociohistorical background before returning the employee, now transformed, back to their individual situation. Reading through the inconspicuous surface phenomena of these employees' existence, Kracauer finds the possibility of reversal, for insofar as both employee and employer are focused on the commodity of the selection process rather than each other they become estranged from each other, breaking up the totality that they purported to create. As the holder of a doctorate and the bearer of an unusual appearance, Kracauer is particularly aware of these vagaries of selection, and so he takes especial notice of the contradiction found in the syntagm of 'a morally pink complexion'. The meaninglessness of this formulation is matched by its self-evidence, making it a perfect example of the way that historical forms present themselves by confusing categories:

> This combination of concepts makes everyday life, which is filled with shop window decorations, employees, and illustrated newspapers, transparent at a stroke. Its morality should be coloured pink, its pink underlined morally. This is what those who are responsible for selection want. They would like to cover life with a varnish that conceals its far from rosy actuality. Woe betides, if morality should penetrate through the skin, and if the pink was not quite moral enough to prevent desires from breaking out. The gloom of unadorned morality would bring just as much danger to what exists as a pink that would start to flare up immorally. So that both are sublated [*sich aufheben*], they are bound to each other.
>
> AN: 229/38-39

In a sense, Kracauer's entire thesis is condensed in this formulation, for in its accidental catachresis the wrong state of the times (as Adorno would phrase it) reveals itself, along with the possibility of its transformation, which is not the same as its resolution.

The point is reinforced in the next chapter as Kracauer examines the processes of automation that have taken place in modern businesses, which have the result of reducing the significance of individuality in the employees as their skills and training are no longer important when their role is reduced to maintaining the correct function of machinery. But a problem arises with this scientific approach, for 'on the one hand it is supposed to rationalize the operations and on the other to create the cheerful mood that it has rationalized away' [AN: 236/44]. A double task that it is clearly impossible to satisfy, so, having reduced the role of individuality, these businesses then attempt to valorize this condition, in an odd and disingenuous move, suggesting that the resulting alienation is actually a benefit that many employees enjoy, since it grants them the free time to pursue their own thoughts. In just the same way that qualifications became more desirable as they became less meaningful, the call for a good attitude and a positive approach is accompanied by the evacuation of its possibility as well as its necessity. The role of the individual is progressively undermined by the disregard that the employer takes to them, which is bound to a requirement to fill this gap with one's own sense of meaning or purpose. The employee finds themselves subjected to a gaze that both supervises them generally while overlooking them individually, exposing the hollow of their dissatisfaction, which it is now their own responsibility to fill. The pervasive anomie that arises in relation to this process of rationalization does not in any way lessen its perceived desirability, as Kracauer concludes, '"The machine", a works councillor said to me, "should be an instrument of liberation"' [AN: 238/46]. The emptiness of this phrase is as resonant as that about complexions, since it both adequately represents the iniquity of what exists, its utter falsehood, as well as its slender, almost incidental suggestion of transformation, for which it has absolutely no grounds.

After studying the processes of recruitment and rationalization, Kracauer moves on to the bureaucratic organization of the business, and it is important to recognize that there is a logic to this approach. While it follows the architectural logic of drawing us into the organization and showing us what it is and how it operates, there is also a dialectic operating here. The problems that arise through the selection process, relating to the alienation of the worker from their role, are not resolved in relation to the actuality of the job but displaced, leading to other problems that do not find their resolution but only another form of alienation in relation to the organizational structure. At each point, solutions are put forward that only mask the problem and compound it with a further source of alienation, leaving the employee at a remove from themselves, their work, their colleagues, and their class. Kracauer's rethinking of Marx and Lukács on alienation is thus given a spatio-temporal embellishment that demonstrates the milieu of the employee, their situation between the extremes of their alienation and the materiality and ideality of their existence. This space keeps expanding, as Kracauer shows, by absorbing the labour exchange, works council, and employment tribunal, all peripheral spaces that are made part of the sphere of employment. The individual then finds themselves trapped in this milieu, without any possibility for defusing or escaping its extremes, and only finding stability through a detachment from its aims, which becomes ever more difficult, as one unemployed woman says when asked about her experiences looking for work: 'There's nothing else left to do [...] and besides, it doesn't matter what you do if you're not productive' [AN: 264/66]. The irony is that the emphasis on productivity has made it an illusion, since it does not matter if one is productive or not if the key is to appear so. For example, the significance of selection procedures and their pseudo-rationalization is undone by being shown to be unnecessary as the work is unskilled, and then by showing that scope for training is limited to empty activities, and promotion is counteracted by the introduction of managers from outside the company who are nominated on the basis of family connections.

What is of interest here, over and above the evidence uncovered and the insights that Kracauer draws from them, is his method, which seeks to discern the concealed points of contradiction and unfold them according to their own terms to expose their alternatives. This is not to find the points of sublation where the contradictory terms resolve themselves into a higher form, but instead, as we have seen, to reveal that these antagonisms circle around without the possibility of relief or release. In Hegelian terms this result would be a form of material bad infinity, indicating the dislocation of spirit from itself, which is for Kracauer the inevitable situation in the flattened world of Neue Sachlichkeit where idealism has been replaced with ironic resignation. Insofar as it remains a critique of its times, Kracauer's perspective remains subject to its limitations, but his approach goes beyond a mere diagnosis of the contemporary malaise to become an account of the scope of dialectics as such, when there is seemingly no longer any room for transcendence, and it thereby becomes an ontology of the false condition. That is, the falseness is adjudged not simply to be a circumstantial rupture of the dialectic, but that upon which it comes to ground, critically and fundamentally. This reading is of course the key problem of post-Hegelian thinking: that of seeking to understand whether the state of what exists indicates a merely provisional break in the movement of spirit, or whether it is actually evidence of a flaw in the thought of the dialectic as such, a problem that can only be broached by examining its historical status.

The place of the Angestellten is thus to be understood as a screen, interface, and mediator between the other classes by which it is defined and defines itself, and as such it remains bound to this milieu. In being defined by their salary, these employees have nothing else with which to demonstrate their existence, and so they are drawn into meaningless consumption. But insofar as their existence remains insecure, they do not have the means to satisfy their aspirations, and so they persist in dissatisfaction, without the community or the traditions of the working class or the bourgeoisie. The Angestellten are marked by a material proletarianization while suffering under a bourgeois spirituality and so find themselves separated from either class and, as such, they are not only without political ideology but also political interests. It is this last point that becomes the underlying argument in Kracauer's account, for in its rootlessness this new class becomes vulnerable to exploitation from all sides.[5] So, while his approach is attuned to the actual circumstances of the Angestellten, this is not to the degree that it becomes a merely empirical analysis, or one that simply uses these details to support or develop a theory. As he remarks in the preface to the book: 'The basis of the work is made up of on-the-spot quotations, conversations, and observations. These should not be taken as examples of some theory, but as exemplary cases of actuality'. For something to be an exemplary case is for it to lead beyond the specifics of its situation so as to be representative in some way, but, as he goes on to add, his work

> is a diagnosis and as such deliberately refrains from making proposals for improvements. Prescriptions are not appropriate everywhere and least of all here, where it was initially important to become aware of a still barely recognised situation. Knowledge of this situation, moreover, is not just the necessary presupposition for all changes but also includes a change itself. Once the situation in question is thoroughly known, it must be acted upon on the basis of this new awareness. In any case, one will have no trouble finding in the work a series of remarks that go beyond the analysis.
>
> AN: 213/25

There appears to be a degree of equivocation here, for the work would seem able to accomplish its transformation into praxis without any direct guidelines, but this move would leave it subject to various interpretations, which nevertheless must be acted upon. In simply presenting a thorough analysis there is the claim that such knowledge, by virtue of its fullness, gives rise to its own actualization, without it becoming a tendential prescription. If we then turn to some lines towards the end of the book, where Kracauer criticizes the irrelevance of left-wing intellectuals, we can see a slightly more detailed version of this account. As he writes, the radical intelligentsia

> is usually inflamed only by extreme cases – war, crude miscarriages of justice, the May riots [1929], etc. – without taking the measure of normal existence in its unremarkable terribleness. It is driven to the gesture of rebellion not by the construction of this existence itself, but only and always by its most visible emissions. Thus, it does not really seize on the core of what is given but confines itself to the symptoms; it castigates obvious deformations and forgets about the sequence of small events from which our normal social life is constituted, and as the products of which all these deformations can alone be understood.
>
> AN: 304/101

While criticizing those intellectuals who do not perceive the everyday iniquity of existence, Kracauer falls into an equally problematic trap by believing that these small events can reveal themselves in being reconstituted. Even if he claims that 'existence is not captured by being at best repeated in reportage', because reportage, 'as the self-declaration of concrete existence [...] merely loses itself in the life that it cannot find'. Nevertheless, 'life must be observed for it to appear', which means that 'it is to be found solely in the mosaic that is constituted from single observations on the basis of knowledge of their content' [AN: 222/32]. Thus, the analysis yields its own transformation merely by way of its construction, as an effect of its montage of details.

The direct analysis of empirical sociology becomes indirect and provocative by refraining from an explicit goal, while the idealist speculations of theory are muted by allowing the materials to guide their own construction. That is, the construction arises out of the thorough understanding of the details, immanently and by necessity, which then gives rise to their transformation. The lines of affinity with Benjamin's Trauerspiel study are evident, but so too are those with Adorno's inaugural lecture on the actuality of philosophy. While Adorno was critical of the lack of dialectical mediation in Kracauer's mosaic approach, the combination and development of its parts allows for a better understanding of the negativity that must inform this method, and the formal necessity that imposes itself on thought and leads to its reconstruction [NL2: 394/63]. Only in this way, for Adorno, does the montage lose its conceptual blindness and reveal not just its material conditions but the outlines of actual transformation. Otherwise, there is the suggestion that reality on its own will redeem itself, once it is fully understood, and that its reconstruction will lead to its rectification, naturally and inevitably, which disregards the depth and the manner of its conceptual distortion, and that materiality is thus both conceptual and distorted. As such, there is a need for something more than a faith in reconstruction: a critical approach that can examine the means by which change is possible but not actual and that can divert the former into the latter.

This point is developed further in Adorno's comments to Kracauer shortly after he read the book in 1930, where he makes an indirect criticism of its style by commenting on the 'divergence between aesthetic intentions, which conceive of the object as generated through language, and political ones, which think of it as given and refer to it'. As he explains, this divergence occurs in the relation between the form of the work, as one of improvising on the spot, and the *a priori* nature of its experience, which Adorno feels is not adequately encompassed by the documentary approach that Kracauer adopts. In conclusion, he asks whether it would not have been more appropriate if the author had kept strictly to what he had immediately grasped (*umittelbar Erfaßte*), rather than trying to accompany these surface impressions with detailed economic research, which is by its nature contingent and equivocal [BW: 207/139]. Kracauer responded two weeks later to say that he rejected the characterization of his approach as split. Instead, he writes, his insights 'developed from a theoretically grounded reflection on the empirical' and that his original intuitions had to be repeatedly revised after the fact. As a result, he feels that, methodologically, the work 'constitutes a new kind of statement, one that does not juggle between general theory and specific practice but represents its own structured way of seeing'. Although he considers this approach to be a form of material dialectics, this view should be tempered with the understanding that its materiality 'relieves' (*ablöst*) dialectics from the philosophy of totality on the basis of the most 'minimal intuitions' [BW: 215/145]. This characterization seems to fall foul of Adorno's criticisms, insofar as Kracauer admits that in doing so he gives the abstract connective elements of the analysis a validity that cannot be accounted for theoretically.[6]

In this instance, it may appear odd that Adorno would opt for recommending an account that consists entirely of direct experiences, unmediated with social or economic details, especially as he was at that point composing his Habilitationsschrift on Kierkegaard, which develops such a materially dialectical viewpoint. But the crucial formal distinction that he raises about the position and status of Kracauer's impressions is not alleviated by the idea that Kracauer raises, of removing dialectical thinking from the sphere of totality by way of the materiality of minimal intuitions, since it is exactly the question of the formal relation between these intuitions and the theoretical reflections that they are meant to punctuate that remains undeveloped. Only in this development can the antinomy between the givenness of data and the constructions of language be overcome without merely juggling between them. Adorno's criticisms arise from the feeling that Kracauer has oscillated between the two positions without satisfying the demands of either, when it would have been better to go more deeply into one perspective and thus emerge into a more dialectical relation between the two. Significantly, the example he gives, of improvising *a prima vista*, which needs to be read in terms of his later thought of musical interpretation, is one where the act of reading and performing a musical work is understood quite strongly as an original interpretation. Sight-reading, or playing a piece without former awareness but merely 'on first sight', is then an informed mode of improvisation that takes up what is given and gives it a new form that is also its own form, insofar as it is not grounded in prior viewpoints. To render sociological data in this way grants it a form that derives from its initial experience and so delivers it in a form that is materially true to its appearance. Accompanying this impression with explicit details only diverts from this formal singularity by conveying other, mediated and contested viewpoints.

What Kracauer has failed to grasp is the dialectic that already inheres in the material by way of this initial experience and is conveyed by way of its form in its apprehension, a dialectic he overlooks in seeking a more explicit interplay between the empirical and the theoretical. And, by missing this critical development in the work itself, he is led into further complications in attempting to create a theoretical relation between the material and its form, which cannot be grounded as it does not derive from the material itself. Tellingly, Kracauer takes Adorno's comment about improvisation *a prima vista* to be a criticism, referring to a weakness that needs to be counteracted by the intervention of theory. However, Adorno is drawing Kracauer's attention to the strength that already inheres in his approach, which obviates the need for any extra accompaniment. Kracauer, perhaps inevitably, does not see this and, indeed, the formula that Adorno sketches out is only realized in the latter's work in *Minima Moralia*. Without a view for how theory emerges out of the material in question, that material remains socially and politically detached, leading to the passivity and accommodation that seemed to take place in Kracauer's thinking. His aversion to idealism comes from a denial of the role of totality, which is not just a totalizing schema of thought, for he fails to realize that totality is not always totalizing as it can also be the whole that arises within the historico-material milieu by which it reflects (on) itself, for better or for worse. In this way, as Adorno would later conclude, Kracauer's analysis is unable to comment on why the Angestellten come to deceive themselves so thoroughly about their lives and their work and so the appearance of their ideology is only described, with the suggestion of change being no more than hinted at by virtue of the form of the enquiry [NL2: 400/68].

To understand the problems that Kracauer encountered in his analysis of the Angestellten, which were crucial for the development of Adorno's understanding of dialectics, it is necessary to turn back to his work on detective novels, which was completed four years earlier. This study is a key transitional point in Kracauer's thinking, but it remained unpublished until 1971 due to problems in its conception that revolve around the relation between sociology, religion, and philosophy.[7] Kracauer's approach to the detective novel is guided by two axes: firstly, that of *ratio*, as a secular process of rationalization exemplified in the actions of the detective; and secondly, that of a Kierkegaardian understanding of the world as being comprised of the different spheres of the aesthetic, ethical, and religious. The detective, as an agent of reason, is not just the one who brings order and restores justice (as contemporary studies had already recognized) but, in Kracauer's nuanced understanding of the role and status of reason, is also perpetually confronted by the limits and contingency of a reason that in its secularity is merely imposed on the world [DR: 157, 182ff]. Kracauer's reading of Kantian idealism as a form of solipsistic control makes the exercise of reason profoundly ambivalent, for insofar as it seeks to bring order it is necessarily constituted by that which is unordered. As a result, the actions of the detective (and the novel itself) indirectly reveal a reality, and thus the possibility of a justice, that exceeds the law. The detective then becomes a very vulnerable figure: on the one hand a passive observer who only comes to life through the appearance of criminality, and on the other hand subject to transformation in their search for justice as they are led into activities that go beyond the law and consequently reveal an affinity with the criminal world. As such, they are merely unconscious vectors of justice, unable to realize the step beyond the contingency of the law that would bring about a genuine resolution of the disparities between the aesthetic and the ethical in the religious.

Kracauer does not subscribe entirely to this Kierkegaardian model even as he maintains a space for the transcendence of the religious in its secularized form as mystery. His understanding of idealism lies at the root of this tension, for in conceiving of totality as an externalized form of solipsistic reason, the whole is understood solely in terms of rationalization, so that the elements of *unwesenheit* that are suppressed or excluded from this model become markers of a reality that is axiomatically exterior to reason [DR: 107]. Hence the elements of contingency and criminality that permeate the world are beyond the scope of theory and are thus signs of a utopia that cannot be realized, for the sense of these mysteries is only as indirect; they cannot be brought to actuality without dissolving themselves. While he would later retreat from the theological implications of this model (as he acknowledges in response to Adorno's *Kierkegaard*, which is itself indebted to the method and insights of *Der Detektiv-Roman* but develops a critical and dialectical analysis of the status of subjectivity and rationality), his study of the Angestellten still resists any move beyond its mosaic of observations. Kracauer's rejection of the form of the mysterious is indicated at the very beginning of *Die Angestellten*, seemingly in reference to his earlier book, where the idea that information about this new class can be found in novels is first asserted and then denied [AN: 217/28]. But with the move from a Kierkegaardian to a Lukácsian analysis in this study, the element of transcendence becomes an aporia, as it is no longer admitted but is just as emphatically resistant to being excluded, which puts pressure on the sociopolitical implications of his account, since he can neither discuss nor relinquish the possibility of a transformation of society. Thus, in adapting Kierkegaard's approach, Kracauer is left with the challenge of exposing the aesthetic distortions of the ethical, which is to say, the sensible, concrete ornamentations from which actions cannot be separated. However, this approach also imposes a demand on the form of his observations, as they cannot be presented directly but must develop indirectly, which in turn imposes a requirement of interpretation on the reader through which these elements of the concrete can be intimated outside the systematic and determinative approach of theory.

So, within the analysis of the detective novel, the act of crime becomes problematic because, although the detective may link the crime to the criminal in a causal relation, the presence of its irruption remains unexplained. The law and its enforcers can only control the outbreaks of crime by imposing a rational order on them, drawing them into the spheres of fully determined activity. But the act itself, in its existence and provenance, remains an anomaly and so the detective, like the criminal, has to pass into the supra-legal sphere of law-making, of the extension and execution of order, to explain its place and status. Crime is evidence of acts of law-making, and thereby of the unfixed and historical (rather than eternal) status of the laws; it is not simply an irrational element that needs to be eliminated but a perpetual reminder of the inability of reason to fully impose itself on the world: 'figures of legal enterprise do not recognize that in transgressions against morality the banished ethical can manifest itself, that murder does not have to be murder alone, but may also mean the sublation [*Aufhebung*] of conclusive human statutes by the higher mystery' [DR: 123]. Crime is then strictly meaningless in that it exists outside the sphere of reason and any explanations or justifications only emerge as ideological constructions after the fact [DR: 164]. In a problematic Kierkegaardian move, Kracauer seems to want to combine the cases of Angerstein and Abraham, as it were, by showing how the materiality of the aesthetic opens the way to the ethical. Crime is therefore manifest as the reverse contour of natural-history. For, just as reason risks becoming diverted into mere rationalization, so too can traces of actual reason be discerned within such highly commodified forms as the detective novel. Equally, the irruption of crime into history is at the same time a fracturing of history into fateful encounters, such that the sense of the whole that was projected on the basis of thought is made to open to what is not historical, without there being any harmonization or assimilation between the two aspects.

Kracauer's insight is to present the dilemmas of consciousness in concrete and spatial terms, as is evidenced by his discussion of the spheres through which the detective moves, for in doing so these dilemmas are removed from any concern with subjective interiority, a critique that Adorno would take even further in his *Kierkegaard* by showing how the bourgeois *intérieur* was constituted by its denial of exteriority, of history and society. In doing so, Kracauer finds a materialist reversal of Adolf Loos's polemical equation of ornamentation and crime, for rather than seeing ornamentation in design as a form of artistic atavism that should be removed, he finds in criminality the very ornaments of the natural-historical dialectic, the material forms by which it demonstrates its punctuation of rationality.[8] The 'spatial omnipresence' of criminal acts 'is required, because with them the outside stands in for the lost inside. Sin, which is a determination of being in the higher spheres; danger, which symbolically threatens from outside; mystery, which intervenes from above: everything that shatters temporary security is represented [*vertreten*] uniformly in the lower regions by embodiments of the illegal' [DR: 122]. Hence for as much as there is a movement by which the irrational is subdued by the rational, there is an equivalent movement in the opposite direction, which leads to a conception of reality as restless and contradictory, although Kracauer retains a sense in which this tension is suspended or superseded in mystery, which leaves an aporetic and secular messianism, inaccessible and incomprehensible. Moreover, his account is hampered by the emphasis on exteriority alone, in that it unfolds an empty space of merely external relations with a lack of dialectical interiority, which may be part of the sphere of rationalization he is addressing but is also echoed in his own lack of engagement with actual literary works, for there is no real discussion of detective novels in the essay, only the abstract sweep of theory, a division that is not remedied in *Die Angestellten* but only inverted.

The reversal that Kracauer is seeking from empty exteriority to some sense of unrationalized meaning cannot be accomplished without the labour of the concept, for in refusing the conceptual gaze he also refuses the possibility of its transformation into what it is not. It is only in the movement in which the concept is forced beyond itself in seeking to address its exteriority that it ends up reversing into that form, just as the conceptual becomes material, or the natural becomes historical. And, insofar as this reversal is intrinsic to its dialectical form, the concept cannot remain fixed but is instead fractured into transient phenomena that both express and represent it. These concepts are thereby aspects of immanence, rather than imposed totalities. Something of how this process is to work has already been seen in the transformation of sense that occurs when we read the relation between ornamentation and crime literally and reversibly, for in doing so the concept of each is pushed to the point of having to realize a connection to that which seems incredibly remote, and that is only doubled by the necessity for each side to do so. What is left is a sense of crime and ornamentation that have become transformed without losing recognisability, but also without being identified. The dialectic of their constitution is thus material but unfixed.

II Advanced Historical Material

The significance of Kracauer's work comes to be grasped when it is seen to be that against which Adorno develops his own thinking of dialectics and interruption, of how these minimal material intuitions can be made meaningful without totalization. This development is hinted at in one of his letters to Kracauer, where he remarked that the material dialectics that his friend had espoused was similar to a notion that he was working on in his Kierkegaard book, that of an intermittent dialectic, 'that does not proceed in closed definitions of thought but is interrupted by the reality that does not fit in, catches its breath in it (Kierkegaard's expression), as it were, and arises [*anhebt*] fresh every time' [BW: 218/147]. This formulation in part recalls Benjamin's thinking in the foreword to his Trauerspiel study and provides an early glimpse of the negative dialectics that will arise in Adorno's later works. But to understand the nature of the interruption that it raises, it is important to examine the debate on musical material that Adorno was currently engaged in with the composer Ernst Křenek, for it is out of this understanding of materiality that his criticisms of Kracauer arose, and it is also out of this sense of materiality that his renewed notion of the dialectic can be said both to spring and to fall.

Musical material is in the broadest sense that which the composer works with, not just the sounds but their relations and forms of organization, as well as the traditions of which they are a part. As a result, they form a natural-historical complex in which 'natural' sounds exist by way of their historical traditions, and vice versa. This notion is important as it indicates how musical composition arises out of a historical and natural complex, which is itself indicative of the form of the society from which it has come. Musical material is then an index of social and political change, and it is as such that the composer needs to approach it if they are to grasp the full extent of the interchange between its natural and historical elements, which are neither static nor harmonious. This notion enables us to come to a better understanding of the nature of change and innovation in the arts in a way that is not reductive to either the individual or the social. What this notion indicates is not just its indexical relation to its environment but the means by which the latter can be changed, since the material does not subsist in an inert form but changes in relation to its social and artistic background. Hence each formulation of musical material is an intervention as well as a response to its background, but in doing so this intervention is manifest only indirectly, by way of the refractions of its forms, and so both the forms and their methods often remain obscure.

The significance of this notion is that it is a model for social change in general: musical material in its abstraction and concreteness provides a way of conceptualizing change in a more broadly historical sense. It is with this notion in mind that Adorno responds to Kracauer's work, which may have been able to expose the fractures in social and political forms but failed to see how far these fractures were dialectically constitutive of the forms themselves, and so did not grasp how they could be reconfigured as points of intervention that are historically and materially active. However, the refractive index of these points of intervention, their historico-material obscurity, is also the basis of their diabolical potential (as was recognized in Thomas Mann's *Doktor Faustus*) where *diaballo* is understood literally as a throw of unusual trajectory and unknown distance, which is indicative of an inconceivable and perhaps destructive futurity, of interventions whose implications are unforeseeable. This idea designates the possibility for structural forms to emerge that redefine our understanding, as with the tritone in the history of music, which established a new form that was perceived as dissonant in relation to traditional intervals and was thus referred to as a *diabolus in musica* but that unfolded new possibilities of musical harmony. In addition, this change remarks the emergence of a new form of materiality and a new mode of intervention, which allows for different formations of musical material in general, as is evidenced by the role of dissonance in the development of modern music, particularly in the early work of Schoenberg.

When materiality becomes historical it becomes changeable, impermanent, and when history becomes material it becomes obscurely determinative. So, when Adorno refers to forms in which the musical material is the most advanced of its time, which is a central part of his debate with Křenek, he is referring to those in which this dialectic comes to the point of its greatest tension in terms of both its resistance and its passage, for within this tension lies the possibility of the greatest historical resonance. Given the model of change sketched out above, it may be possible to say that a musical work is 'better' than another insofar as it responds to the most developed form of musical material available. In doing so, it consciously pursues the tensions inherent in the material, rather than following tendencies that are no longer current and have perhaps become superseded or obsolete. This is not a question of fashion or style, but of the explicit handling of materiality in its most developed form since, in the converse case, where previous forms are followed, there is a sense of unconsciously holding on to social and historical patterns that are no longer meaningful and relevant. The same argument can be made about other artforms like painting, drama, or novels, in which forms that were resonant in an earlier historical period cannot achieve that resonance in a later period. There is thus a sense of irreversibility to natural-historical material, which in its changes imposes a demand on the artist to respond to it in its depth and complexity, rather than to ignore or reject it, which would be the case with kitsch, for instance. The most developed musical material is thereby revolutionary to the degree that, as an avant-garde, it presents the most conscious manifestation of the tensions and demands of the material, and it is in this way that it imposes itself. And, by rendering the material in such formal terms, form also becomes part of the material to be addressed, which leads to the development of new kinds of structure and harmony that have different possibilities of balance or closure. As a result, a different but concomitant set of demands are imposed on the audience in their response to the work as it now needs to be responded to by way of its natural-historical complex, which calls for a different mode of listening or reading, such as those that are found in the methods of improvisation and recapitulation that Adorno pursues.

Refusing to recognize that aesthetic material is not static, inert, or given, is not just to dismiss the ways in which it is socially and historically constructed but also to relinquish the possibility of taking up its critical potential as a refractive index of the times. Central to such a possibility is the fact that its critique is dialectical, which is to say that it operates by way of the unfolding of its natural-history so that it is not possible to render its potential directly or immediately. The place of the work is both within and without its milieu, and so its critique occurs by way of its refraction – of thought, discourse, or history, for example. In consequence, the explication of natural-history draws out a whole that is not complete or transparent, and in realizing its possibilities it only unfolds further opacities that demonstrate that its universal remains concrete. Thinking and responding to the artwork are tied to the concrete, and to the necessity of an unknowable decision in relation to it. There is thus an ethical burden to such a response, alongside the creative potential of recapitulating and improvising in relation to the work, which come together in the materialist approach. For, as Horkheimer writes, 'materialism opposes to cognition, through the irresolvable [*unaufhebbaren*] tension between concept and object, a critical self-defence against the belief in the infinity of spirit. This tension does not remain the same everywhere'.[9] Hence individual artworks matter to the degree to which they respond to this tension in the material and thereby expose it to both its cognitive and material possibilities, that is, in its natural-historical breadth, as Adorno explains in 1929 in relation to the innovations of Schoenberg's twelve-tone technique:

> It is constitutive of all of Schoenberg's music that, although it is more closely linked to material evolution than any other, it can never be understood as the mere execution of material necessities, but instead receives its material in historical dialectics: Thus, Schoenberg's twelve-tone technique is no natural order of tones that would be written in the stars beyond history; nor is it a rationalised positive technique like Cubism that would forget the specific differences in the material. Rather, it is the rational execution of a historical compulsion that the most advanced consciousness undertakes to purify its matter from the decay of the disintegrating organic; twelve-tone technique is not valid without history, but has its identifying ground in the state of the material that Schoenberg found and produced; it is not something that now seeks to transform this disintegrated material all of a sudden into an order that would necessarily be empty, but rather erases the last deception of order in it in order to create space for the freedom of constructive imagination; it is not a positive composing process at all, but the historically current *preforming* of the material that must be carried out; it does not explain itself mathematically, but historically and does not aim at a mathematical-formal musical region, but wants to make the freedom of the composer possible.
>
> AK: 168

In removing material from the reified history of its givenness as merely organic, or natural, artistic form also draws out the rationality that inheres in its order and necessity, just as the rationality of this form is thoroughly inflected by the pre-existing formations of the material, out of which its form thereby arises as a historically specific immanent reflection. This means that the apparent imposition of a rational order on the material is diverted by the material's own order such that the work reveals both 'complete thematic construction and complete invisibility of the thematic construction', a contradiction in which 'the moving productive force of Schoenberg's stylistic development is concentrated' [AK: 171]. In this thorough pervasion of the material by its formal dialectic there is 'the free execution of what is historically necessary' and an original reformulation of history, for in the work history 'is sedimented as the moving ground from which compositional freedom grows' [AK: 170, 173].

As sedimented, the history composing the material is opaque and is open to as much decay as it is innovation, and it is the demand of this opacity that imposes itself on the artist (or audience), which is the only basis upon which the notions of progress or reaction may be gauged, and whose efforts are then both free and necessary in relation to this demand. And so, in terms of neither the work nor the artist is there a given sense of the operation that may be uncovered by these efforts, instead there is only the dialectic that holds them together and keeps them apart. It is precisely this natural-history that confronts the artist (or audience) in the opacity of the material, but this opacity is not plumbed if one seeks to stand outside the work, seeking to maintain the position of a mere observer in relation to the work, rather, in moving closer to the work, we not only find our position becoming more free in relation to it but the work itself is released into a new historical configuration, 'whoever submits to the work and seemingly undertakes to do nothing but follow it to wherever it calls adds something new to the historical constitution of the work, like the answers and fulfilment given to its questions and demands, that does not follow from the historical structure of the work alone' [MMU: 135/149]. It is this model that Adorno had tried to explain to Kracauer with the notion of improvising *a prima vista*. Moreover, this reconfiguration becomes the imperative of the work, in terms of the necessity for demythologization that removes the work from any sense of original or conventional meaning, and the necessity for change that characterizes critical theory, by which thought, discourse, and history can be refracted.

There are problems with Adorno's thinking of this notion, in that there is as yet no real consideration of the social dimension of natural-history, and no consideration of the role of the audience to the work (I have added this second point).¹⁰ Furthermore, there is a correlation between the recognition of Schoenberg's significance and a privileging of the most advanced currents of contemporary composition as the basis of aesthetic intervention, which seems to suggest a methodological circularity, or at the least a contingency to the estimation of the avant-garde. Greater attention to the first two points, about the roles of society and the audience, will soon cast this correlation in a different light for Adorno, as will the development of his aesthetics more generally, which will broaden the analysis of material to studies of non-musical works. But the emphasis on the contemporary is, as he makes clear, necessary because of the indexical nature of its dialectical tension, and because of the demands this indexicality places on our response to this tension. We can discuss artworks from previous periods, but if we want to understand how to proceed in relation to the problem of constructing new works, then this needs to take account of the breadth and depth of what is currently possible, and what this contemporaneity reveals about the speculative horizon of history as such. Nevertheless, the study of aesthetic material allows for an approach that moves past the analysis of particular works into something more general, which is yet concrete and specific. Equally, the separation of this notion of material from any that would construe it as natural, as holding an original and timeless sense, not only reveals the movements of its sociohistorical determinants but also that which refracts and is refracted by these movements, and that remains active in a manner that is never given. In addition, the form of this notion provides an outline of the nature of the whole that recurs in Adorno's thought, a whole that is, as we have seen, not whole and cannot be made so in that it persists through being refracted.¹¹ But as such the idea of the whole, which is also that of reason, is itself made (im)possible by way of the constraints of the material, so that reason is emancipated through and in these historical-material contingencies. The work thereby becomes the measure of thought, in terms of both the praxis and the alienation of the former, so that thought does not return to itself but rather the opposite; thought returns to the work in its abstract-formal occasions and recapitulations. That is, insofar as the work responds to the demands of its natural-historical material, the audience or artist in their encounter with the work recapitulate the form in which these demands have been expressed and thought thereby finds itself reconfigured as its idea.

It can be seen how closely Adorno adheres to the Hegelian understanding of freedom, but also how this is accompanied by an awareness of the ways that freedom is curtailed in contemporary society, so that the thought that emerges follows that which Marcuse would loosely formulate thirty years later: 'No method can claim a monopoly of cognition, but no method seems authentic that does not recognize that these two propositions are meaningful descriptions of our situation: "the whole is the truth", and the whole is the false'.[12] Or, as Adorno would put it,

> Hegel himself had conceived universal history as unified merely through the force of its contradictions. With the materialist turn in dialectics, the heaviest accent fell on the insight into the discontinuity of what was not held comfortably together by any unity of spirit and concept. Yet discontinuity and universal history are to be thought together [...] Universal history is to be construed and denied.
>
> ND: 313-14/319-20

As a consequence, what is often seen as the greatest weakness in Adorno's thinking – its apparent equivocation in the face of praxis, and its absorption in a form of aesthetic theory – must be considered in a new light. What becomes significant is the fact that the status of his thinking cannot be ascertained simply: its movements between sociology, aesthetics, and philosophy are precisely what gives it a unique and novel configuration of theory and praxis, which cannot be reduced to a conventional relation. The importance of Adorno's thought lies in its singular form, by which it both inherits dialectics and reconstitutes it beyond the distinction between idealism and materialism and, insofar as it does, alters its relation to politics, art, and history. The questions that have been raised in response to his thought, in relation to the apparent limits of its scope, aims, or methods, lie in a flawed perception of its form and of the whole it exposes, which can only be addressed by reconsidering the status and position of his thinking. Only in this way can his relation to Hegel or Marx be understood, as is found in his initial formulation of natural-history.

Adorno's lecture, 'Die Idee der Naturgeschichte', was delivered in July 1932 to the Kant Society at the University of Frankfurt and followed discussions among the faculty about the impact of Heidegger's work. Adorno had been teaching courses on philosophy and aesthetics for two semesters (most recently, on Benjamin's Trauerspiel book) and was also starting work on revising his Habilitationsschrift for publication. His decision to focus on the idea of natural-history was 'to sublate [*aufzuheben*] the usual antithesis of nature and history, so that wherever I operate with the concepts of nature and history, no final essential definitions are meant, rather I am pursuing the intention of driving these two concepts to a point where they are sublated [*aufgehoben*] in their pure disintegration'. As such, the terms are themselves already mediated, in that they are markers of a broader engagement between the thought of Heidegger on one side, of the mythical status of ontology that 'bears human history as fatefully arranged pregiven being, which appears in it and is substantial in it', and, on the other side, a thought of history as change and innovation, of that 'traditional mode of conduct that is characterized above all by the fact that the qualitatively new appears in it' [ING: 345-46/111]. The latter thought is clearly complex in itself, but it seems to bear resemblances to the Marxist understanding of history and the artistic relation to history he had discussed with Křenek. There is thus a wider set of concerns here, and ones that reflect on the actuality of philosophy in a more concrete manner than his inaugural lecture (which, because of its greater obscurity and depth, will be discussed later) and, taking up the problems that this earlier position had raised, he terms the discussion of natural-history an attempt rather than a systematic statement. A dialectical confrontation is being sought between the two most significant strands of contemporary thought, of ontology as naturalized history and history as materialist innovation, which already renders the terms of the argument in a general and conceptual form that leaves them as less transient and contingent, even as these are the very issues at stake. It can be seen that this complexity makes the discussion more compelling, since its terms become more incisive as they are drawn together and, in doing so, provoke thinking into going beyond itself.

Consequently, the lecture develops in three parts by first examining Heidegger's ontology, then the works of Lukács and Benjamin on materialist history that first articulate the concept of natural-history, which Adorno then seeks to discuss on its own terms in the last part. There is an imbalance to this model, as Heidegger's mythical thinking of being largely serves to show the problematic against which the ideas of Lukács and Benjamin can be developed, which gives Adorno the scope to suggest his own formulations. Even at this early stage, Adorno approaches Heidegger polemically and while his reading is somewhat deficient in its details, the overall characterization of being as mythical and fateful cannot be overlooked. Where Adorno applauds Heidegger is in his rethinking of the relation between history and nature, which overcomes the problems of both idealism and theology (and their variations in the phenomenological thinking of Edmund Husserl and Max Scheler), as he explains: 'Every separation of natural stasis from the historical dynamic leads to false absolutizations, every isolation of the historical dynamic from the natural that is irresolvably posited in it leads to bad spiritualism' [ING:

354/117]. But replacing the analysis of the concrete unity of history and nature with the generalized categories of ontology only leads to the occurrences of the concrete becoming mere facts of being. If we are not to think of being as natural, then it must undergo the transformations of material history to the full extent of its dialectical complexity, which would prohibit any understanding of being as ontological, as that which underlies or resides within history in its unity, as Adorno writes.

As a result, Adorno turns to Lukács, specifically *Die Theorie des Romans* and its description of a world that has become, historically, remote and incomprehensible, as its meanings have subsided into conventions that offer neither conceptual nor sensible substance. In such a scenario, history has become materialized (static, given) just as materiality has decayed into a form that is empty and lifeless. This is, as Lukács writes, the world of second nature, which he would later discuss under the forms of reification and alienation, but the significance of this account derives from the way that it imposes itself on us: natural-history is not simply the name for a new methodology, Adorno states, but is primarily an experience of transformation, 'a change of perspective', which in turn reveals 'the problem that defines what is here understood by natural-history' [ING: 356-57/118]. This problem, Adorno explains, is that which Lukács had discussed in theological terms as a redemption or eschatological resurrection (a position that his later Marxist works would not contest), and in contrast to this account Adorno turns to Benjamin's Trauerspiel study.[13] This transition might seem peculiar considering the profoundly theological framework of Benjamin's study, but the aspect that Adorno wants to focus on is the fact that the problem of this change of perspective, which is not just subjective but is also the objective transformation of dead second nature into its historical renewal, is understood as a problem of interpretation, that is, as a problem that is at stake in reading (a point that was also central to his inaugural lecture, as will be seen). Where Lukács had shown the transformation of the historical into the natural, Benjamin, through his allegorical reading, finds the point at which enigmatic nature is transformed into the historical in the form of transience (*Vergängnis*). As a result, the problem of natural-history cannot be grasped in terms of general structures 'but only as interpretations of concrete history' [ING: 358/119]. For what is expressed in allegory is an image of nature in its transience: allegory is the form in which history expresses itself in its passing. Expression itself is historical, and so nature in appearing does so allegorically, as an image of itself; it is its own historical expression, as can be seen by looking at the characterization of the seasons, or, in confronting the development of a tree, for example, whose formation is both a literal and metaphorical image. But these aspects cannot be synthesized, only coordinated contingently and in passing, which then provides its own image of specific and concrete transience. As such, the sense of the historical begins to change under the force of this understanding of transience, so that what is at issue is precisely its sense, the form of its signification, which means that 'the moments of nature and history do not merge into each other, rather they break apart and interlink at the same time in such a way that the natural appears as a sign for history and history, where it is most historical, appears as a sign for nature'. Thus, signification is no longer a question of hermeneutics or meaning but of the transformation of history into 'original history' (*Urgeschichte*), as Benjamin calls it, which contains the seeds of the radical sense of natural-history that Adorno will develop [ING: 360/121].

In the last (and briefest) section of the lecture Adorno tries to counter the problems that his reading has generated by saying that he has not introduced a new ontology of history, or historical ontology, nor has he simply erased the differences between nature and history. Instead, natural-history must be understood in terms of the contradiction of the material and the mythical through the analysis of specific instances in which this antithesis is operative, which are then unfolded in their dialectical inter-relation. Adorno's subsequent discussion thus leads into an early form of the dialectic of enlightenment, in that he elaborates the dialectical structure of myth and second nature (understood as semblance), which is interesting as a precursor of his later thought but unfortunately displaces the analysis into questions of rationality rather than continuing to pursue the problem of history. Although it is persuasive to follow the analysis of myth into its rational and irrational elements, just as it is intriguing to uncover the innovative and material aspects of second nature, it is only when he mentions in passing that these modes of appearance can be apprehended in such ambivalent experiences as déjà vu or anxiety that we can gain an idea of the status and impact of natural-history in its concreteness.

However, there is an additional example that Adorno makes during this period that does cast light on the idea of natural-history, and it is necessary to recognize that Adorno speaks of it as an *idea*, but that (in the Benjaminian reading that he gives) its appearance, in its truth, is related to its appearance in language, which explains the importance of the act of interpretation as an actual transformation in the mutual dialectical expressions of nature and history.[14] This example occurs in a contemporaneous passage from one of his brief articles on music, in which he attempted to sketch out a natural-history of the theatre by examining its various sites – the stalls, the circle, the foyer, and so on. In his article on the gallery, he writes the following:

> Up there, at home nowhere else, in a thick cloud of smoke, with girls, hats, and drinks, the harbour people had quartered themselves for the long evening voyage with confiscated faces [*konfiszierte Gesichter*] that would have stood out better on any stage than in the auditorium. The way they joined in with the performances, hooting, clapping, and cheering over the heads of the decent people, it was as if the masquerade on stage and the masked people in the gallery had conspired to finish off those in between: either that those from above would make their entry onto the stage, or that the whole theatre space would be seized by the stage of eccentrics in their freedom.
>
> QF: 311/68

This account comes from a recollection of a visit to a music hall in Marseille, and to some degree we must recognize a certain conventional framing of this account as that of a northern European in a southern European context.[15] Adorno is not unaware of this convention, and his musical experience makes it possible to read through it to the idea that is at issue, which is (against Kracauer's idea of reciprocal illumination) the convergence between the people becoming art in the gallery and the art becoming people on the stage, with the inevitable critique that arises out of their lack of harmonious resolution and the turn to praxis that their transformation implies.

The essay as a whole appears to be no more than a series of rather whimsical sketches on the sociohistorical constitution of theatrical space, starting from its origins in public ritual and moving through the various regions of the space as they are determined by money, class, and aesthetics. But in doing so the theatre itself becomes recognized as metaphysical, not just in parallel with the space of churches but more specifically, as the last part of the essay makes clear, as a collection of spaces that are coordinated to the formation and exposure of a moment of artistic experience. Despite its illusion, the theatre draws out a region in which the ephemerality of art is preserved as its sounds are turned back on itself in the curvature of its domed ceiling, and as the music rises up to the false sky it 'traces the circumference of the dome that previously moulded it' [QF: 320/77]. Here is a sense of a culmination that is neither complete nor teleological but reveals the form of its contours in their exteriority, much as the last aphorism of *Minima Moralia* will do.

III Philosophy Interpretation Praxis

The nature of the artwork is critical to understanding natural-history because the latter can be grasped in its truth by way of the concrete formation of the artwork. As has been seen, Schoenberg's approach to composition (which will be examined in more detail in the next chapter) is important to Adorno because his works are not merely an example of the dialectic of innovation and tradition but are an expression of the reformulation of history in art, of an actual intervention in the reified relation between the material and the conceptual. Aesthetics then becomes the form in which critical theory emerges in Adorno's thinking, which means that critical theory can never be thought through without aesthetics. This point is also important because it forms the basis of his Habilitationsschrift, which is oriented by the question of the status of Kierkegaard's works, since this question reveals the problem of philosophy's own status in relation to that of artworks. The deliberate and self-conscious artistry of Kierkegaard's writings appears to blur the distinction between philosophy and art but, as Adorno develops his reading, this blurring is found to be false. Instead of a merging of philosophical thought and artistic form, there is an impoverished grasp of the demands of each, which in turn reveals the differences between the ways in which truth emerges in philosophy and art. Kierkegaard's work thus indicates the necessity for thinking through the problem of form in order to understand the variable natural-history of its truth-content. In exposing this flawed understanding, Adorno is able to perceive the conventional grasp of the subject-object, form-content distinction that underlies Kierkegaard's approach to art and thereby reveal the necessity to rethink philosophy beyond these conventions.

Adorno submitted his dissertation towards the end of 1930, and it was warmly accepted by Horkheimer and Paul Tillich who conferred the right to teach in February the following year. It was in the summer of 1931, after Adorno's inaugural lecture, that the so-called 'Frankfurt discussions' took place, as his peers sought to take account of the demands raised by the work of Heidegger alongside the contrasting claims of materialism, positivism, and theology.[16] These discussions followed Adorno's own debates with Křenek (on the interpretation of musical material), Kracauer (on the aims and method of sociology), and Benjamin (on the possibility of materialist historiography), which culminated in his most important publications of this time: 'Zur gesellschaftlichen Lage der Musik', which appeared in two parts in the first issues of the *Zeitschrift für Sozialforschung* in the summer and autumn of 1932, and *Kierkegaard* itself, which after extensive revisions was sent to the publishers later that year.[17] In happier times, this beginning might have been the foundation for a secure academic career, but it was only after a twenty-year hiatus that such a position would be found. Although Adorno's experience of exile was not as bleak or as disruptive as that of Kracauer, Bloch, or Benjamin, the survival and persistence of his thought is itself testament to a form of praxis. It would be surprising if the resulting thought did not express something of this experience in its material form.

In discussing Kierkegaard, Adorno has two aims in mind: firstly, to show how the paradigm of the existential thinker is a form of subjective idealism that is ultimately grounded in ontotheology, which is to say that the condition of alienation becomes axiomatic and is thereby removed from its historical and material specificity, a critique that inevitably reflects on the work of Heidegger. Secondly, despite this problematic constitution of subjectivity as interiority, Kierkegaard cannot separate his thought from the world it excludes, which returns precisely by way of the denigrated category of the aesthetic such that it can now be read by Adorno (in terms that recall previous discussions) as literal ornamentation, an actual figuration of the materialist history of subjectivity. Alienation is then no longer simply given for postlapsarian existence but bears traces of how it might be reversed, which the form of aesthetics in its fragmentation and obscurity reflects by virtue of its negative coherence. That is, by following through on the immanent construction of the aesthetic its status as critique is uncovered, a critique that does not require a sacrifice of subjectivity in a leap of faith but exposes the materialist constitution of subjectivity, whose micro-forms bear the possibility of being actualized as modes of reversal of the state of what exists.

An example of this modality can be found in the compositions of Schoenberg, which present possibilities for rethinking the world in terms of the relation between thought and materiality despite their difficulty and prima facie distance from the world. It is by way of the apparent incomprehensibility of these works, which makes them seem as far from art as from nature, that the form of thinking is reconstrued in terms of the change of perspective that Adorno highlighted in his lecture on natural-history. It is not just that tonality and harmony are reconceived by Schoenberg, but that in doing so a new form of rational expression is apparent that reconstrues the idea of the work in relation to its history and materiality. As a result, what is found in these compositions is not merely barbaric or opaque but a new form of work that gives evidence of the world of its constitution as much as of the tradition from which it has twisted free. The historical dialectic of art is reconfigured in a way that derives from the material without being reducible to it and is rationally pursued without being wholly determined by reason. Tradition, as the historical continuity of art and subjectivity, is rethought as rupture and repetition, not so much dialectics at a standstill, which is what Adorno finds in the frozen *intérieur* of Kierkegaard's thought, but the iteration of a fracture, a kind of form that, as he later writes in reference to one of Schoenberg's early lieder, 'suddenly presents the whole between an outburst and a dead stop [*starrem Einhalten*]' [MS4: 199/204]. This style, which Adorno takes over into his own writing, allows for the variation of thinking; moments that in their iterative development from one sentence to the next illuminate their exterior without assimilating it.

The possibility of this modal reverse is obscured in *Kierkegaard* by the language of hope and redemption that arises out of the discussion of melancholy.[18] However, the inversions of form that it announces also suggest that the artwork no longer appears as a work but takes on the appearance of a thing: it seems no longer to be a work of art at all as it bears the semblance of a lack of semblance, appearing merely contingent and factical, the very materiality that Kierkegaard had hoped to remove. Hence in encountering such a non-work (and we should consider what this means for the form of Adorno's own thinking), we are no longer in position of being able to respond to it simply as an audience. Instead, the work is a figure of reversal, so that it no longer means in any allegorical or symbolic sense but is literal in its self-presentation. Its praxis is not found by putting its thought into action, as Kracauer might have suggested, for it is its own praxis by virtue of the reversal that it brings to bear on those who encounter it, who come to recognize the inversions and intermittencies of natural-history that its lack of semblance presents.

This reversal thus has consequences for language itself as the distinction between form and content, which underlies the idea that words bear the subjective unity of objective characteristics, is voided by the contingency of their history: 'Through language, history gains a share in truth, words are never merely signs of what is thought under them, instead, history breaks into words and forms their truth-characters; the share of history in the word determines the choice of every word because history and truth come together in words'. The truth-content of words is not essentially given by history in a Heideggerian sense, but nor is it arbitrarily assigned, instead it arises through the transformation of their concrete sociohistorical substantiality (*Sachhaltigkeit*). Hence the task of the philosopher does not lie in unearthing a forgotten meaning, but with making interruptions and configurations that can allow the truth-content to emerge. But the dialectical basis of this approach is not there to enable the philosopher to reveal some prior or intended meaning for there is no simple mediation of historical truth-content by subjective intention and vice versa, instead, it is through the mutual rupture and displacement of history and subjectivity that truth-content emerges and thereby does so as a novel concrete formation. And so, in a recurrence of the motif that arose in response to the works of Schoenberg, the philosopher finds that, in the absence of the possibility of straightforward communication in a world of alienation, their task requires the 'radical difficulty' of their language.[19]

By analysing the form and development of Schoenberg's works, Adorno is able to show how their apparent difficulty arises in response to the reification of transparency and agreement in social communication, which only suppresses the actual differences and suffering that subtend it. Consequently, what emerges in Schoenberg's works, especially the early atonal pieces, is a rejection of the bases upon which this reification of communication subsists, which means that his works bear a social and philosophical importance as well as a musical or artistic interest. It is not simply a question of developing forms that refuse harmony and symmetry but of responding to the tensions in the musical material in a way that does not subvert them to subjective intentions but allows these tensions to emerge in their dissonance. In doing so, consciousness arises through the material without implicitly returning to the subject by way of its conceptual mediation. Here lies the syntactic significance of Schoenberg's innovations, which develop a different form of dialectic that reveals alienation as it is, while reconfiguring the very modality of expression:

> At the same moment when the entire musical material is subjected to the power of expression, expression is extinguished – as if it were only inflamed by the resistance of the material that is "alienated" from the subject and itself. The subjective critique of ornamental and repetitive moments produces an objective, non-expressive structure that, in place of symmetry and repetition, excludes repetition in the cell, namely the use of all twelve tones of the scale before the repetition of a tone, and at the same time refuses the "free", accidental, constructively unbound use of any tone [...] The extreme rigour of the immanent structure is coordinated with radical freedom from all material [*dinglichen*] norms imposed on the music from outside, so that it has at least in itself sublated [*aufgehoben*] alienation as one of subjective formation and objective material.
>
> MS5: 738-39/399-400

Only with this understanding of the material can it be reconceived in its transience, along with the demands and implications that are raised for its resulting form.

Adorno raises a point of caution here, for he is doubtful about whether the autonomous work of art that Schoenberg has developed can be reintroduced to the world when it has done so much to undermine its own status as an artwork, for the thoroughly rationalized construction of his compositions in the twelve-tone model presents a limit to the operation of musical talent.[20] To this end Adorno finds that the question of expression is to be reconsidered, as he finds in the work of Alban Berg, whose music 'by expressing the need or meanness of the individual without leaving it in its isolation, but by objectifying it at the same time, finally turns against the order of things, from which it arises as music, just as does the expressed individual as an individual, which, however, come to consciousness of themselves and their despair in it'. This self-discovery is not merely formal for in removing itself from expressive psychology, the music 'at the same time turns itself against the conventional formal language of music [...] disintegrates its surface connections, and constructs in a musically-immanent fashion a new language from the particles of musical expression' [MS5: 740-41/401-2]. While this is still too vague, the disintegration of surface connections implies a new way of thinking about syntax, and the form to which it gives rise, which no longer expresses and so cannot be read in such a way. A distance is thus being marked with the expressive model of ornamentation that had partly informed the earlier understanding of natural-history, and in its place a sense in which disintegration becomes the form for this negative dialectic (as the next chapter will show), such that the language in which these decayed surface connections appear is indicative of the force of what can no longer be found through expression.

This last point recalls Benjamin's 1924 essay on Goethe's *Wahlverwandtschaften*, which Adorno felt was possibly the best piece he wrote, in which Benjamin discusses the notion of the expressionless: that which occurs in a work but is not expressed and for the sake of which the critic is drawn to respond to the work.[21] But the aim of Adorno's thinking is slightly different, for while Benjamin is concerned with redeeming the work by salvaging that which has been lost within it, Adorno takes a less eschatological approach in which the materiality of the work bears an unintentional excess that it is up to the critic to draw out in order to expose what conceptual domination has not been able to suppress. Where Benjamin is focused on the work and its lost sense, Adorno is more concerned with the mechanisms by which the work is categorized and what falls outside this grasp. This is the programme that is developed in his inaugural lecture, which has generated so much confusion. The key aspect of this approach is the notion of interpretation (*Deutung*), which Adorno feels it is incumbent on philosophy to develop if it is to demonstrate its actuality. This issue is important, he states, because philosophy must consider whether, in the face of the ever-growing sphere of scientific understanding, 'there is still any adequacy between philosophical questions and the possibility of their being answered', or whether it finds that in the absence of an ability to answer these questions it has become 'liquidated' [AP: 331/29]. The questions that Adorno is referring to are metaphysical questions, the ones that logical positivism expelled because of their apparent lack of scientific rigour and grounding, even as this expulsion was made in the name of a scientific absolutism that was itself unquestioned. It is important to note that Adorno is not seeking to reinstate these metaphysical questions in the manner of an irrational *Lebensphilosophie* or generic ontology, instead, the development of empirical sciences necessarily raises questions about the status of the object and the subject that these approaches cannot answer. And by making use of a poeticized scientific ideal for such flawed thinking to provide additional support only gives it 'a bad ornamental covering', which is, as he writes, a worse option than leaving philosophy to its liquidation [AP: 332/30]. (As is apparent, Adorno is not using ornamentation here in the later more enhanced understanding that he would derive from Kracauer, as detailed above, but is using it in a more ordinary, less dialectical, sense to criticize the formalism of the Viennese school.) By contrast, a closer examination of the methodology of science will make its limits apparent and thereby make it possible to understand the role of philosophy. It is from this examination that he claims that the approach of science is one of research, in which the collection and analysis of information is not accompanied by any analysis of the status of this information, since it is treated as fixed and defined.

This critique is close to that which Horkheimer was developing at this time, which insisted upon the covert idealism of scientific empiricism in which its concepts and objects were treated as given.[22] But Adorno also recognizes that the whole within which this coordination of concept and object is organized is an aesthetic figure that is itself to be interrogated, and as such the aesthetic aspect of his thought is not merely ornamental (in the ordinary sense) but necessarily arises out of the immanent critique of philosophical discourse, which then creates an imperative in terms of the form that this discourse should take. As a result, the form of philosophy that he proposes is one of interpretation, which is precisely what can address the historico-material constitution of the object and the creative intervention of the investigator. An interpretation is not final or totalizing but creatively reconfigures what is on the basis of the relation it has to the investigator, and in this way the object is revealed to be other than a given or static entity but is rather formed in and through processes that are not entirely transparent or closed. Adorno is keen to show that he is not rejecting science, nor is he advocating a merely relativist multiplicity of interpretations, for while philosophy can never separate itself from scientific research, it must nevertheless interrogate the material findings of science from a position that is not idealized or fixed if it is to find its actuality. In this way, philosophy remains linked to its material basis while also reflecting on the situation of its interrogation, with a view to opening both aspects up to possibilities that have not been made historically apparent:

> There remains the great, perhaps everlasting paradox: that philosophy must ever and always interpret, with the claim to truth, without ever possessing a certain key to interpretation; that nothing more is given to it than fleeting, vanishing hints in the enigmatic figures of beings and their strange entanglements. The history of philosophy is nothing else than the history of such entanglements; that is why so few "results" are given to it; thus, it must always begin anew; that is why it cannot dispense with the slightest thread that earlier times have spun and that perhaps completes the lineature [*Lineatur*] that could transform the ciphers into a text. Accordingly, the idea of interpretation by no means coincides with the problem of "meaning" [*"Sinnes"*] with which it is mostly confused.
>
> AP: 334/31

Passages such as this have sometimes caused dismay for their apparent vagueness, and the abdication of philosophical responsibility that they seem to imply, but they arise out of the twin imperatives of historical materialism that the position of the interrogator is finite and creative, and that the object is concomitantly unfinished and non-transparent. Interpretation is thus neither passive nor arbitrary but responds to the fact that while not everything is possible, everything remains at stake, and so the possibility of change inheres everywhere.[23]

The apparent resemblance to Benjamin's Trauerspiel study in the reference to ciphers should then be considered in more critical terms, and it helps to provide some background on this point. The Trauerspiel book was published in early 1928 just as Adorno and Benjamin were starting to become philosophically closer, and the most important of their meetings took place in September the following year when Benjamin presented the first drafts of his *Passagenwerk* to Adorno and Horkheimer. This meeting was memorable for all parties, but was perhaps most significant for Benjamin, for in presenting his thoughts on the Arcades he was seeking to rethink the Trauerspiel study for the nineteenth century, which meant turning aside from its melancholic theology to a more dialectical and materialist perspective on historiography.[24] This transition had important consequences for Adorno, since for all its brilliance the Trauerspiel book was only an intimation of the kind of approach that was necessary in order to interpret history in the way that he sketched out in his inaugural lecture. With this perspective in mind, it is possible to see how his *Kierkegaard* was not so much following Benjamin's work, as seeking to develop the materialist critique that had been suggested but had not been forthcoming in the Trauerspiel study.[25] Even though Adorno would later come to see its faults, at the time of writing *Kierkegaard* he was concerned with showing how the insights of the melancholic could be transformed so that they did not lead to aesthetic withdrawal and theological longing. The hope, if there was one, lay with the material interpretations that it laid out, which showed how melancholy could become transformed without losing its insights, that contemplation could demonstrate the imbrication of mythology and reason in such a way that their dialectic would enable the translation from interpretation to actuality.

In much the same way that he had found with Kracauer's work, Adorno saw the constellational format of Benjamin's writings as foreclosing theoretical examination in that it failed to explicate the dialectic already inherent in the material through conceptual interpretation. As he goes on to explain, interpretation of the fragments of the world is not done to infer a world of redemption beyond them, but to indicate how these fragments can be read in such a way that their enigmas can be dissolved, and it makes sense that the example he should then give in his lecture would be that of the commodity-form. In this configuration, the historical, social, and material forces of reification become concrete in such a way that their ideological form can be exorcized. The function of interpretation is to illuminate the structure of the enigma like lightning and sublate it by rendering its contradictions tangible as both critique and resolution. And, insofar as these enigmas are not ones that conceal a hidden reality that would promise redemption, the task of philosophy is instead 'to interpret unintentional [*intentionslose*] reality'. These non-intentional aspects are concealed in themselves and so contribute to their own mythologization, which yields the imperative for the dialectical transition that supports Adorno's programme of thinking, for in his formulation of the task of philosophy, interpretation finds itself converging with materialism:

> Interpretation of the unintentional by combining the analytically isolated elements and illuminating the real by virtue of such interpretation: that is the programme of every genuine materialistic knowledge; a programme to which the materialistic process becomes all the more just, the further it distances itself from any "meaning" of its objects and the less it refers to an implicit, perhaps religious, meaning.
>
> AP: 336/32

Just as it rejects the idea of a concealed reality waiting to resurface, so too does this sense of philosophy turn aside from symbolic instances of totality through which it might attempt to absorb and rationalize these non-intentional aspects. Inherent in such a model is the idea that the particular merely stands in for the general and that its conceptualization will reveal its greater meaning as part of this totality. But without this symbolic redemption, and without the urge to configure the intentionless as meaningful, which would only justify its place in an ultimately rational order, the praxis of interpretation returns its conceptualization to the concrete as that which bears both rational and mythological possibilities.

So, that which traditional philosophy 'expected from meta-historical, symbolically meaningful ideas is accomplished by inner-historically constituted, non-symbolic ones', and this means that the thought of history is itself reconfigured. For without this idealism, 'history would no longer be the place from which ideas arise, independently stand out and disappear again, instead historical images would themselves be ideas, the context of which constitutes intentionless truth, instead of truth occurring as an intention in history' [AP: 337-38/33].[26] And, as this is the programme for philosophy, we should find it in Adorno's own practice, which is to say, not just in the micro-analyses of texts and artworks that yield the idea of natural-history but also in the non-independence of his thought, which does not pretend to occur ahistorically and *ex nihilo* but arises by way of his interactions with other thinkers and writers, and through which its ideas resist generalization and translation. This line of thought culminates in an intriguing demonstration when Adorno rewrites Marx's criticism of philosophy for only interpreting the world, by saying that interpretation, when grasped dialectically, is praxis. To be more precise, when interpretation is understood by way of materialism the resolution of an enigma does not remain in the closed area of knowledge as a 'praxis is granted to it'. Consequently, the praxis that materialism seeks is in fact found through interpretation, which alone has the capacity to interrogate problems to such a degree that they resolve themselves into actual change, which is what is understood by dialectics, and it is through such dialectics that genuine philosophical interpretation is possible [AP: 338/34]. Hence the transition from interpretation to praxis that Marx had apparently called for is revised by making interpretation a form of praxis when it is undertaken by way of a materialist dialectics, which is to instate praxis within theory at the same time as interpretation is embedded into the material, and by way of this mutual imbrication there arises a dialectical reversal through which the unintentional truths of the concrete can come to reveal themselves.

It is understandable why such a strategy would frustrate both Marxists and Kantians, and Adorno is quick to recognize that what he has suggested is impossible as a programme for philosophy because 'it does not allow itself to be worked out in completeness and generality' [AP: 339/34]. And, confirming this verdict, he goes on to say that he regards this weakness as a virtue, since it is better that philosophy remain true to the concrete historical complexes of actuality, regardless of its consequences for the form of philosophy, than it is to maintain that form simply through an unquestioned fidelity to idealized models of ontology, anthropology, or other generalized, invariant concepts of totality. To suggest such an approach in response to the new mode of philosophy developed by Heidegger is even more provocative, as Adorno's colleagues were thinking of responding precisely by way of a more robust, systematic alternative. But at the heart of Adorno's challenge is the insistence that the form of philosophy is not incidental, that it reflects the immanent constitution of the work, and so must be taken as part of its approach if it is not to be overlooked and then risk its foreclosure through its own unexamined contradictions. To explicate the sense of this approach, he attempts to specify in more detail how these historical images will operate, and as he had stated that the term constellation might lead to confusion, he suggests instead that they should be understood as changing trial arrangements (*wechselnde Versuchsanordnungen*) [AP: 335/32]. On its own this phrase does not add much (despite its resemblance to serialism), but it comes into focus in the later discussion of burglary as it seems to reflect a model based on the circular combination locks found on safes [cf. ND: 166/163].

This development in Adorno's argument is perhaps not as helpful as it might be, but it provides an intriguing indication of how he understands historical images. Initially he draws a distinction, apparently drawn from Heidegger, between the philosopher and the sociologist in which the former operates like an architect in relation to the object of their work, in that they approach it by developing blueprints of the structures in their field. Contrary to this broadly Kantian position, the sociologist operates like a cat burglar (*Fassadenkletterer*) who approaches their object with stealth and only takes what they need.[27] In both cases the structure of the field is taken as given, as one to which the scholar is seeking to gain entry, even if, as Adorno adds in relation to the work of the philosopher, that structure is collapsing as its foundations have decayed, which risks the loss of all that it once contained. Adorno's sympathies seem to lie with the cat burglar insofar as their approach seeks to rescue the remnants of the structure before they are lost forever (even if they do not know what to do with them once they have been rescued), but this reading is qualified by the point that grounds this extended metaphor. The problem with sociology (and the idealist or empirical philosophy upon which it draws) is that it fails in its allotted task as its keys are either too large or too small to gain entry to its field, that is, its terms are either too general (and so vacuous) or too specific (and so worthless). In contrast, Adorno's historical images offer a key that is appropriate to the scale of its objects, for they derive from an interpretive philosophy that can 'construct keys before which reality springs open. As to the measure of the key categories, these are now specially prepared [*sonderbar bestellt*]' [AP: 340/35].

It is not clear if the blurring of the distinction between the philosopher and the sociologist is deliberate or accidental, which is problematic given the contemporary development of critical theory by way of an interrogation of the two approaches. Instead, what appears to be at work is a distinction that Adorno is attempting to draw between his own approach and that of either philosophy or sociology, insofar as the historical image operates creatively, constructing rather than finding its keys, and doing so on the basis of a particular use of the imagination. As such, he insists that his approach is distinct from that of phenomenological intuition or psychoanalytic archetypes, and instead uses a formulation closer to Lukács when he says that these images are not found but 'must be produced by humans and ultimately legitimize themselves solely through' the fact that reality gathers around them in striking evidence' [AP: 341/36]. Historical images are thus models that convey a renewed understanding of philosophy as an *ars inveniendi*, a creative practice whose organon is exact imagination, 'which remains strictly within the material that the sciences present to it and reaches beyond it only in the smallest traits of its arrangement, traits, of course, that it must originally give of and from itself'. The speculative practice of the imagination is thereby anchored in its material, which leads to the idea of philosophical interpretation as 'a demand always to answer the questions of a pregiven reality through an imagination that reorganizes the elements of the question without going beyond the circumference of the elements, and whose exactitude becomes controllable through the disappearance of the question' [AP: 342/37].[28] While this model confirms the image of philosophy operating in a manner akin to that of serialism, through its alternation of parts within a framework, it also has another aspect that was hinted at in the earlier description of the way that music outlines the domed ceiling of the music hall. For the rearrangements that Adorno is referring to in this discussion of historical images are not mere generalizations but a speculative praxis, which means that they do not just spring the locks of the problems of reality but also (negatively) indicate the background of their enigmas, in which the state of things can be viewed otherwise, rendering and legitimizing its materialism by way of its possibilities.

As a result, the notion of a combination lock becomes translated into that of the essay, as the attempt to respond to questions through their rearrangement, in which the material determinants of the question are reposed in their possibilities to see if they can be answered through this praxis. The essay is then both the method and the result, and as such is not isomorphic to the question but extrapolates it to the smallest degree by way of its reorganization. In this way it removes itself from fundamental questions about the nature of the reality at issue, except insofar as these become evident through the extrapolation of the form of the question. Thus, there is no sense of an essence subtending existence or history, no being or spirit that would ground and ultimately determine the material currents of life in their possibilities. In this way, the essay is intrinsically part of the reality that it seeks to explicate, and it is through this practice that alternate possibilities can be essayed. And, as this means that philosophical interpretation is part of the reality to which it responds, there is no scope for philosophy to step back from it to posit a totality to which it may give form. Instead, such philosophy is continually brought up against the ruptures of history and materiality, of which it is itself part, so that it is engaged in perpetuating their disruptions in order to break through the reification of what is existent. The proximity to a kind of Surrealist practice is evident here, although it is politically and philosophically more rigorous, and what it may lose in terms of a general totalizing vision it gains in terms of a responsiveness to the particular, but this means there is less scope for assessing Adorno's thought as a philosophy that possesses, by virtue of its existence as an independent body of thought, its own doctrines.[29] One final point in relation to Adorno's method here: it would appear to resemble a contortion of the method of immanent critique in which concepts are examined on their own terms and are shown to be contradictory, which leads them to transform themselves. I say contortion, as Adorno is not rejecting or inverting this model but turning it back upon itself, so that the movement of transformation is not found to lead to a more general or complete instantiation of the concept, as he points out, but instead forces it back into itself so that its problem restates itself otherwise.

IV A Balzac Reading

One of the most interesting attempts that Adorno made to sketch out this mode occurs in a late essay on Balzac, which shows how Balzac's novels embody a materialist critique that effectively anticipates Marx.[30] The significance of this overlooked essay comes from the fact that Adorno's dialectic can only be understood if we consider the two questions it raises: is it legitimate in relation to Hegel's thought, or does it arise out of a misunderstanding? And secondly, if it is legitimate, are its extensions of Hegel's dialectics merely extensions, or do they radically reconfigure his thought? Such problems lie at the heart of all post-Hegelian thought from Heine to Marx and onwards, but what becomes compelling for Adorno in Balzac's novels is the way that they deliver a materialist critique through literature, which does not undermine idealism but reconstitutes it on the basis of an ongoing attempt to think negativity *in actu*: as the negativity of the modern metropolis in its alienation. In this context the figures of mediation and critique, system and praxis, through which dialectical thought operates, are transformed through the literary understanding of history and *histoire*, which puts in question the very possibility of a structure to the movements of spirit. As he later writes, in a Benjaminian mode: 'The world-spirit is, but is not one, is not spirit, but rather the negative that Hegel shifted from it to those who have to parry it and whose defeat doubles the verdict that their difference from objectivity is untrue and bad' [ND: 298/304]. The fact that literature unveils this disintegration of history through its narratives shows how thought can pursue the whole without its totalization, and thereby deliver a critical reflection that is its own praxis. Furthermore, history is the area in which Hegel's thought is made to confront its greatest obstacles in the constant affront to reason that it exposes.

It is thus that Adorno's thought of natural-history presents his most significant contribution, since it reconfigures dialectics on the basis of a renewed understanding of the actual movements of the material and the ideal, which is then developed in his studies of aesthetic material and the dialectic of enlightenment. But to return to Balzac, Adorno introduces his argument:

> The totality-character of society, previously thought theoretically by classical economics and Hegelian philosophy, is called down from the heaven of ideas to sensual evidence. That totality remains by no means merely extensive: the physiology of the whole of life in its various branches, which might form the programme of the *Comédie humaine*. It becomes intensive as a functional context. A dynamic rages in it that society reproduces itself only as a whole, through the system, and that every last man is needed as a customer. The perspective seems to be foreshortened, and all too immediate, as always when art misses vividly evoking a society that has become abstract. But the individual atrocities with which they mutually, visibly, chase away the surplus value that has already been acquired invisibly, allow the horror to emerge graphically that could otherwise only be achieved through the mediation of the concept.
>
> NL1: 140-41/122-23

Literature accomplishes something very different from conceptual mediation but can still achieve a level of concretion and rigour that both comes from the matter and reconstructs its concept. 'The alienation that caused him to write, as if every sentence of his busy pen was building a bridge into the unknown, is itself the secret essence that he would like to guess' [NL1: 140/122]. And it is as a result of this latent pressure that Balzac's concern is often with criminals and artists, dandies and prostitutes, politicians and journalists, with those elements that exemplify the alienation by which society constitutes and undermines itself, and who display the contradictions of exchange value within themselves. The dialectic is hereby reconstituted on a microscopic scale as the concrete embodiment of its failure to resolve or even grasp itself.

Adorno is not new in his estimation of the significance of Balzac's works – the same response can be found in Engels and Lukács that Balzac was singularly attentive to the form of modern reality and the complexities of its representations – but what he brings to this understanding is an awareness of how the collection of Balzac's works achieves a unity in its movements that is constituted by its material accidents. As such, his novels perform the transformation of the concrete and the abstract through their interweaving of characters and events, while leaving this movement with no other ground than its irrationality. They can thus represent society in its iniquity and yet find in this same lack of reason the possibility of critique. Like Hegel, Balzac is conflicted in his response to modernity, being both fascinated and alarmed by its democratic potential and its material excesses, but what 'Hegel's speculation in the *Rechtsphilosophie* shrank from, like the positivist Comte – the explosive tendencies of a system that suppresses naturally evolved structures – bursts into flame as chaotic nature in Balzac's enraptured contemplation' [NL1: 145/126]. What Balzac's novels present is not a form of direct realism, but one that in its exaggerations presents the reality of the concrete, its alienation and reification, and so cannot be opposed to decadence. It is within this dialectical structure that Adorno's thoughts about the mimetic quality of the artwork will take place, alongside its natural-historical distortions.

The role and estimation of decadence is of key importance here, as it is on these grounds that Adorno distinguishes his reading of Balzac from that of Lukács, who in his later works was keen to separate his understanding of Balzac's realism from that of the expressionist appreciation found in his pre-Marxist work, *Die Theorie des Romans*. Moreover, the role of decadence is intrinsic to Mann's diagnosis of the problematic of contemporary creativity in *Doktor Faustus*, as it refers to the barbaric rupture of a supposedly natural order of artistic conventions and harmony, but that already appears to be evident in the decay of order found in Balzac's novels. In his early work, Lukács finds the essence of reality in Balzac's novels to be their 'demonic inadequacy', the 'endless series of fateful encounters of souls with each other'. As a result, his writings form a 'strange, infinite, confusing turmoil', but through 'this paradoxical homogeneity of the material, which has arisen from the extreme heterogeneity of its elements, an immanence of sense is rescued'. This vaguely Hegelian reading is complicated by the assertion that this unification only occurs at the level of the individual novels, and not in terms of *La Comédie humaine* as a whole and, furthermore, the unification that takes place in the novels, 'is not only realized through the repeated appearance and disappearance of figures in the infinite chaos of these stories, but has found a type of appearance that is completely adequate to the innermost essence of this material: that of chaotic, demonic irrationality'.[31] It is this characterization that Lukács rejects some twenty years later in his essays on Balzac in *Studies in European Realism*, in line with his changed understanding of realism, but that Adorno will seek to recapture in his own reading.

However, Adorno does not simply oppose Lukács's early reading to his later one but indicates the limits of each account (in terms of their emphasis on an apparent order or disorder), which provides a greater appreciation of the form of realism that Balzac was pursuing. The decadence of the modern is an indicator not merely of the iniquities of capitalism but of a transformation in the times, of a reformulation of the natural and the historical, which suggests a decay of traditional forms, and demands a renewed understanding of how to approach this ongoing reformulation within the framework of artistic works. The irrationality of Balzac's world is more profound than the apparent chaos of its organization and is not to be rejected on the basis of its seeming Romanticism. Instead, it is to be understood as the milieu in which the reformulation of the work takes place through its negotiation with the turmoil of the times. This turmoil is constituted by the morbid phenomena that Antonio Gramsci spoke of in 1930, which occur in periods of transition that are themselves found to be the mode of temporality of modernity, which is to say that the latter unfolds as an interregnum without end.[32] Thus, what is ongoing in these artistic endeavours is an analysis and reflection of the times, which thereby exposes their dialectical involvement in the times through what Adorno had called the key of their historical images. The novel in this view does not exist outside the world, but nor is it merely its expression; instead, the novel actualizes the very movement of natural-history in its transformation alongside that of the world in which it takes place. This process shows how the analysis of aesthetic material is also a critical intervention, as it creates the most diabolical (innovative, unpredictable) effects by drawing the apparent decadence of the times not out of but back into its turmoil.

Hence what becomes changed in Adorno's reading is the status of 'realism' as an evaluation of the representational relation that the artwork has to the world. In his later readings, Lukács describes Balzac's novels in straightforwardly realist terms as showing how 'the conception of life of those living in a bourgeois society – a conception that although false, is yet necessarily what it is – is shattered by the brute forces of capitalism' [SER: 47].[33] The basis of Lukács's later approach is not to delve into the problem of what these novels say about the nature of actuality and how, but to focus on how artworks depict social processes in order to realize their potential as instruments of proletarian emancipation. As he points out, Balzac is significant because, despite his conservative politics, he was able to see clearly into the mechanisms of exploitation and reification that capitalism uses, and it is this theme that determines the form of his composition. While his novels begin with the individual, this starting point is excavated to reveal the objective tensions that it bears, which reveal the social interconnections that underlie and inform these characters thereby giving 'a more correct evaluation of the trends of social development'. And so, although Balzac 'apparently reverses the logical and objective connection between the material basis and the superstructure', his approach is still successful because of his artistic skill and social criticism, especially in terms of the way that the novel develops through the variable fate of its characters and the implications this holds for an understanding of the social determinants of fate [SER: 51]. The nature of the reality thus addressed and exposed, and the ways that it is drawn into and transformed by the literary work, are questions that are for Lukács set aside by the objective clarity of Balzac's representation. As a result, he is able to state that, in the stories that Balzac provides about his characters, 'he shows the objective dialectic of their rise or fall', so that the fate of Lucien in *Illusions perdues*, for example, is determined by the commodification of literature to which his existence as a writer is owed [SER: 53].[34] Insofar as the characters are so determined, they are representative of the social totality, not simply or directly, but in such a way that their particularities are emphasized and concretized by the typical so that this general understanding itself becomes real, and thus 'it is always the totality of the social process that is linked with the totality of the character' [SER: 55]. In this way, despite the confusing complexity of Balzac's novels, within them the individual and the general are always inseparably united.

Lukács seems to be struggling to assert this model of totalization in his reading, for to do so he has to repudiate the elements of the accidental and irrational that he had earlier acclaimed and insist that the whole in Balzac's writing is organically united even through its multiple, uneven, and contradictory patterns. Indeed, Balzac's works combine to create a model of determinism for Lukács, so that the characters and plot are entirely determined by social processes and 'individual destinies are always a radiation of the socially typical, of the socially universal' [SER: 55]. While the intensive layering of details is registered, as is the pervasive sense of chance and contingency, these are only considered in terms of their orientation towards a revelation of social determinism. But the passion of Balzac as a writer, his intense curiosity and productivity, undercut this determinism by suggesting that what is apparent in his works is not yet fully formed, that the possibility of evasion remains.[35] Adorno highlights this tension to show that Balzac's realism takes place through these effects rather than despite them and, in this way, the 'realism' of his works also changes. Hence their critique does not exist passively in relation to the world, they do not merely collect and organize its data, nor do they simply reflect the totality of social processes that constitute that world. Instead, and returning to the point that Adorno made in response to Kracauer's attempt to think through the world of the Angestellten, the artwork stages a decisive intervention in the world by drawing out its configurations and interrupting them, which not only exposes their underlying tensions but crucially reformulates the dialectic of natural-history through which these tensions take place. That is, the artwork allows for this dialectic to be materially experienced in its resistance to closure and its evasion of order, which is not merely a model for reality, but an aspect of it. Central to this point is the understanding that social reality is itself no bearer of realism but is merely the reproduction of illusions, which means that the novel must consider a different set of demands, as 'it is precisely the faithfulness to the façade of a method purged of Balzac's deformations, in the culture industry as much as in socialist realism, which harmonizes with externally imposed intentions'. As a result, 'historical truth is nothing other than the self-renewing metaphysics that emerges in the permanent disintegration of realism' [NL1: 152/132]. Metaphysics is the mark of the experience that goes beyond the façade of what is merely given, indeed, it renews itself in its destruction, but it nevertheless remains grounded in what there is as its opening to its natural-historical possibilities.

Thus, the key to Balzac's significance lies in the disparity between his person and his writing, for in this way 'he gives thought the luxury of wandering away [*hinweg auszuschweifen*] from the person who is thinking it', which is the (dissolute) basis of literature. But Adorno goes on:

> The non-identity of spirit with its bearer is both its condition and its flaw. It shows that it is only in the midst of the existing, from which it detaches itself, that spirit represents [*vertritt*] what is different, and that it disgraces it by merely representing it. In a business based on the division of labour, spirit is the placeholder of utopia and hawks it off [*verhökert sie*], making it equal to what exists.
>
> NL1: 157/136

The historical passage of the world-spirit is compromised in its idealism and commodification, since it is, as Adorno makes clear, only in the midst of what exists and so is conditioned by both its opacity and its extravagance, and it is as such that there is history. This is not to say that history becomes irrational or chaotic, but that it occurs in the same way that thought does, through an unexpected departure from its ground, as he had earlier remarked: 'only those thoughts that do not understand themselves are true' [MM: 216/192].

This reading of Balzac is also important for an understanding of the status of Adorno's thinking in which, following Kracauer and Horkheimer, the dialectical inter-relation of sociology and philosophy is accompanied (in his own contribution) by the aesthetic reconfiguration of this dialectical inter-relation on the basis of the understanding of (musical) material and its necessary interpretation and recapitulation. To this degree, Adorno's thought occurs creatively without becoming merely relativist, and can register the ground of theory alongside its aporetic ruptures. His inaugural lecture was a first attempt to give shape to this formulation, however crudely and unsuccessfully, and its problem lay with its form, which would only be overcome in the writing of *Minima Moralia*. The problem with this lecture lies in the status of the creative dimension of thinking, how it presents its critical investigations, just as Adorno had found in Kracauer's work, except that it is a problem whose significance he has now fully recognized. In a sense, this problem is the very aporia around which critical theory is forced to stumble, since it is the problem of being unable to present the universals of its critique in a way that is effective insofar as these universals are that which it has found to be false. A different idea of universal needs to be generated that is grounded and constructive and thereby manages to be a whole without totality.

Adorno's lecture on 'Die Aktualität der Philosophie' was poorly received by many in the audience and this may have been because of its hybrid nature or its materialist inclinations, or both, as it seems to have satisfied neither Adorno's peers nor the established scholars at the University of Frankfurt. It is easy to see why there should have been this frustration, as the essay bears an uneasy combination of critique and speculation that leads to an obscure conclusion that leans heavily on Benjamin's understanding of truth as an enigma or rebus, which would have dismayed both the Marxists and the Kantians who were listening. Kracauer did not attend the lecture but read a copy of it and wrote to Adorno with his thoughts and, after complimenting him on the critical overview with which the lecture begins, he stated:

> The transition to materialism, however, fills me with disquiet. You are making use of a small backdoor that is not itself materialist. I mean the image [*Gleichnis*] of the rebus. Perhaps this explains the curious and, I believe, very private relation between Benjamin's interpretative arts and his Marxism, which is no less curious but is skewed in relation to materialism itself. In my opinion, this is not the way to unveil dialectics. Quite apart from the fact that it would be more correct to bring out the decisive impulses of university philosophy on the one hand and materialism on the other, instead of mediating them in this way. And then the conclusion! You defend the form of the essay, but this is in the end a form based

on size [*eine formale Grösse*]. In any case, it is less a matter of smallness than of the fact that every such investigation takes up the given reality, pushes it on dialectically, and thus changes it.

The lack of dialectical relation between the ideal and the material is, as Kracauer points out, only exacerbated by the conclusion, which presents the image of the rebus and the essay in their apparent reciprocity. While it might be noted that Adorno's understanding of the essay is not merely formal, as he goes on to show, Kracauer's point seems valid in terms of the mode of critique that it seems to make possible for, as he writes, it could have been treated more effectively:

> Instead of the programme, which was definitely not required of you, I would have used some small, actually dialectical investigation, and this would be broken off at the exact point at which the upheaval would be due. With that you might have aroused more genuine and long-lasting disquiet in the professors than by your actual procedure.
>
> BW: 280-81/191

Such indeed was the notion of intermittent dialectics that Adorno had earlier described, which had been missed in the attempt to deliver a programmatic statement. Adorno did, in a later letter, concede this point, although he claimed that the transition to materialism was an attempt to think its appearance otherwise than just as a demand for praxis, which would become an important point of distinction for his thought in terms of its negativity. Nevertheless, it is compelling to find such a level of mutual insight in these letters, as well as the illumination they provide about the difficulties of developing the novel dialectical procedure that concerned them both. Materialism cannot simply adopt a pre-existing philosophy, nor can philosophy develop the insights of materialism without being changed in both its aims and its methods, to the degree that the form of theory itself becomes changed. While Benjamin's work on the Trauerspiel, much like Kracauer's study of the Angestellten, had attempted to follow through on this idea it had lost sight of the demands of theory and the rigour of materialism, which the essay, at this stage in Adorno's thinking, can only barely accommodate. Given the demands that have been placed on it, form initially becomes materially operative at a small scale (as is apparent in music in terms of the study of dissonance and serialism), and only by proceeding from this point can the transition to materialism remain both consistent and dialectical, and thereby become critical for thinking.

Kracauer's claim that form is solely determined by its size is clearly far from Adorno's view, as is the idea that there is a sense in which the dialectical investigation should be broken off at the point at which its change 'would be due'. For in relation to the latter idea there are no grounds to the assertion that such a change has an inner necessity that would somehow be known to the investigator. This idea follows from Kracauer's belief in the natural isomorphism between critique and actuality, which would simply require their reciprocity for change to occur. However, if we are to see the form of the essay as that which is changed by way of its investigation, so that its size is not merely determinative but critical, then its formation participates in the actuality to which it seeks to respond to the degree that its thought is not merely broken off but also changes in its relation to actuality. As a result, the essay is not there just to render actuality critically legible but to bring it to the point where its natural-history and that of the work itself interrupt each other.

And then? This is the conclusion often drawn in relation to Adorno's thought, since it appears to come to a halt at this point, on the appearance of the negativity of its dialectic. This is partly due to the oppressions of contemporary society that make it difficult to consider the possibility of the next stage and also, more fundamentally, to the impossibility of preconceiving how things might take place otherwise. Thus, the rupture of thinking that occurs with this interjection is not just an aporia but also the very form of what happens, in its openness and uncertainty, and it is as such that the dialectic avoids presenting itself in a form whose positivity would engender doubt. The task is to leave the course of history hanging, as Kracauer suggested, so as to increase its disquiet and the responsibility of its suspended resolution, which is what the models in *Minima Moralia* are seeking and what, more broadly, Adorno's critical theory aims to find as its mode of praxis.

Later, he will further unfold this approach by stating that while artworks present a critique through the fracturing of their form, it is up to philosophy to explicate their truth and rationale [AT: 520/350, 531/357]. This is not to say that art exists in a subordinate position but that the dialectic of its appearance occurs across modes, and the same is true for philosophy. This requirement inheres in the notion of an intermittent dialectic, one that takes place between an upsurge and an arrest: it stops, to start again by way of a different mode. There is this, and then this, and by way of this pause there is a new syntax of relation, a formal relation of interruption through which commentary arises so that what is not expressed can be understood.[36] While the practical aspect of this demand is apparent in the conjunction of aesthetics and sociology with philosophy, its formal aspect is felt in the paratactic mode of writing and thinking that Adorno develops, which makes it possible for there to be a sense of dialectical understanding without losing sight of its material or diverting it into a totalized vision. The difficulty of his language lies in the way that this disjunctive syntax is worked through at the level of each thought and sentence to provide the basis of its capacity to bring about a change of perspective. Adorno sees an example of this approach in the rebus that Benjamin finds in baroque allegory, for in the combination of written, visual, and auditory elements in the rebus, 'writing and sound confront each other in a highly-tensed polarity. Their relation grounds a dialectic'. This dialectic is not resolved in its contemplation, as 'the gulf between signifying written images and intoxicating language-sound tears open the solid massif of word meaning and forces the gaze into the depths of language' [UDT: 376/217]. As such, there is no consolation for thought in the rebus, only its provocation, and yet this is not the simple provocation found in some Surrealist images, but a challenge that brings thought up against the enigma in the image: that it is not expressed but nevertheless remains an imperative to thought. A version of this point is also found in *Kierkegaard*:

> For the moment of the pause, when the dialectic holds itself, is the same in which its mythical ground, nature, reverberates in the depth of its tolling. Its appearance assures humans of their transience, like the caesuras in the course of time of the terminally ill. But its empty figure, the rhythm of mere time, with no other expression than that of itself, signifies the speechless intervention of reconciliation.
>
> K: 144/101

However, as we have seen, it is this latter aspect, as important for Benjamin as it was for Kierkegaard, that Adorno will express reservations about in his later works, not to dismiss the idea of reconciliation but rather to question its quasi-religious manifestation, which implies a necessity that cannot be guaranteed. In doing so, the syncope of the dialectic, in which there is no life as, literally, breathing has stopped, reveals an empty, formal expanse that is neither mediated nor resolved. If transience is the truth of natural-history, then it is also that which undermines the ability to think it, except by way of its gaps.

It is only by way of a formal innovation that Adorno can move away from the static enigma of this image, not to return to its conceptual mediation, but to counter its sheer presence by way of its persistent rupturing. This is the perspective that informs *Minima Moralia*, whose organization Adorno explains as working along two Hegelian axes: firstly, that of the aphorism, which remains Hegelian despite its isolation and distance from totality. For, as Adorno says, aphorisms follow the Hegelian duty 'to consider the evanescent itself as essential'. In this way they linger with the negative, rather than turning aside from it, and it is as such, in absolute rending (*Zerrissenheit*), that spirit attains its truth [MM: 15/16; PG: 34/27, 27/19]. This aspect is coupled with the second axis that Adorno follows, in which the sequence of aphorisms moves from the narrowest private sphere, through considerations of a broader social and anthropological scope, to philosophy, yet without pretending to be complete or definitive [MM: 16-17/18]. The series of aphorisms takes place without being teleological or transcendental; there is no totality to which they would refer even as their inherent subjectivity is shown to reveal a broader penumbra of concrete historical concerns. Consequently, reading through the content to the object remains dialectical without dissolving the former in the latter, and without assuming a reduction from one to the other. The position of subjectivity being so compromised in the sphere of contemporary capital, it is necessary to acknowledge the forces of this subordination alongside the possibility of an alternative. For just as society produces the individual and reproduces itself by way of individuals, so too is the reverse the case, even if evidence of this is far from obvious and precisely to the degree that individuals align themselves with the dominating concerns of society. Adorno construes the organization of aphorisms along these lines, in that their lack of explicit theoretical coherence leads to a denial of totalitarian structure and so leaves scope for its critique and evasion, precisely through the penumbra of its necessary material possibilities. Nevertheless, this formal disruption only partly expresses his insight into the transition from thought to praxis through interpretation. As the next chapter will show, it is through Adorno's analyses of the changing historical demands of the material that his thinking will be led away from the melancholy of the Trauerspiel, and to deepen and extend its dialectics into a form of dissonance.

2

Dialectics of the Avant-Garde in Music

I Style of Disintegration

The first part of *Minima Moralia* is dated 1944 and begins with a number of pieces that are quite personal or autobiographical, and that seem to reflect a reading similar to that which Horkheimer had developed in his early essays on bourgeois habits and attitudes. So, for example, there are pieces on family and marriage and on the status of the intellectual and the emigrant. Then, with aphorism sixteen, on the dialectic of tact, something that is closer to the more familiar voice of Adorno arises and reveals itself in a way that will prove to be important for his subsequent work. Tact is an inconspicuous element of social life, but precisely for this reason it takes on considerable weight. Moreover, Adorno makes clear that it is not just an issue of social and historical importance but one that also conveys an aspect of his understanding of dialectics. He begins by referring to Goethe's concern with tact as a crucial marker of and negotiation with the changing nature of society in modernity. As traditional social relations began to change under the pressure of urbanization and technology, a new form of interaction became necessary to navigate through this world of unclear distinctions. While it is possible to decry these changes, the development of tact as a new social skill itself became a form of investment in that society, even as its need emphasizes the lack of consideration of its causes. And so its dialectic begins to be formed, which has become deeper as the place of tact has become more and more displaced by the absence of regard for the importance of human relations. In place of the careful navigation of social forms, a consistent and obvious hierarchy imposes itself to provide the signposts that have become lost. In such cases, sensitivity to the individuality of relations would appear to have become unimportant, but it is here that the individual must make most use of tact in their navigations, which gives evidence of the persistent necessity for a form of human relation, even if it is illusory, at the very point where it appears to have been made redundant. It is this situation that emerges in Kafka's novels one hundred years after Goethe, and with a much greater degree of dialectical confusion, since here tact has become the means by which an inhuman system can be humanly maintained.

The significance of this dialectical tension is drawn out by the way that Adorno sees the importance of tact in relation to other cultural forms and the way that they assert themselves: 'Beethoven's regular reprises after dynamic developments, Kant's deduction of scholastic categories from the unity of consciousness are "tactful" in an eminent sense. The precondition for tact is the broken and yet still present convention. This has now decayed irretrievably and only lives on in the parody of forms, an arbitrarily devised or remembered etiquette for the ignorant'. This decay has always been the case, as convention has always been in the situation of being present and yet of also being flawed. However, its ongoing breakdown may seem to release individual expression but not the need for tact, which only appears more necessary now, for it is that which 'demands the actually impossible reconciliation between the unsupported claims of convention and the unruly ones of the individual' [MM: 39-40/36]. Tact lives on in the interstices of this relation, despite their decay, but in the absence of either side it becomes insensitive, a mere empty gesture that lacks concern; in itself it becomes tactless. But in its continued functioning we find not only the sensitive regard for the individual but also the desire to place them correctly in the hierarchy of the universal. Thus, tact reverts to a nominalism in the service of the universal, just as the lack of it exposes life to the assertion of sheer dominance and the false intimacy that masks it. Following on from the forms of ornamentation and habit, but rendering their historical concreteness more self-conscious, tact presents a mode of ambivalent adaptation in that it is used both to maintain a convention and to negotiate its transformation. Tact is then a name for the dialectic that emerges from this situation, as the skilful discrimination that is to be found in the manoeuvres of any thought or praxis that seeks to operate from out of the immanent contradictions of its material, whether it seeks to preserve or to expose them. In this way, tact becomes a name for the dialectic itself, insofar as it takes the measure of relation at the point of decay, that is, in both its necessity and impossibility, and thereby, as Adorno would later term it, as a logic of disintegration. It is as such that there is a dialectic *of* tact, both subjectively and objectively, which returns repeatedly in Adorno's notes on Beethoven, as well as in the writing of *Minima Moralia* itself, which gradually develops into a more abstract rendering of this dialectic.

The notes on Beethoven that Adorno began to make in 1938 are unique in his works for their extensive and detailed accounts of the materiality of this dialectic and its immanent development, and in doing so he becomes occupied by the antinomy of the universal and the individual, part and whole, which is so distinctive of Beethoven's works. It is precisely this aspect of musical composition that is critical for Adorno's own dialectic and for his concerns with the difficulties of development as such, given its material and sociohistorical constraints. Before examining this issue there is a further aspect of the dialectic that should be mentioned, which places the very issue of development in question and emerges under the name of innovation. In an early account of language that discusses the place and status of foreign words, Adorno refers to the antagonism between the supposed purism of language and the apparent disruption of foreign words, by which the subject seemingly comes to express themselves by way of their own impulses:

> If the language-forming subject faces language as something objective, then the subject poses its own urge against language by means of those words that are not subject to language and that it mobilises against linguistic convention, however rigidly conventional these words may be when encountered in everyday linguistic life. Foreign words become carriers of subjective content: the nuances. To be sure, the meanings of foreign words correspond to our own; but they cannot be replaced by these at will, because the expression of subjectivity cannot be purely resolved into meaning. Mood, atmosphere, linguistic music, all the postulates of Verlaine's *art poétique*, as they are subject to the differential principle of nuance, want to substantiate the claim of the individual to its rational indissolubility in language by demonstrating it through untranslatability.
>
> NL2: 641/287

However, as Adorno writes, while the introduction of foreign words may seem to go against the purist account of language, it also depends on an organic model of language development, which means that there is ultimately no difficulty in these apparently disruptive forms becoming absorbed by the conventional. Counterposed to this model is that of the inorganic shards of found language: hard, inassimilable fragments that seem more like names in that they are in fact not found, but made, and as such they escape the ideology of a language that is supposedly natural.

This form of naming seems related to that which Benjamin pursued, which dates the article in which this account appears, as does the relation to a kind of redemptive truth.[1] But this resistant language is also to be found in the discussion of late style (which is central to the reading of Beethoven), of the forms that emerge in the barren landscape of alienated humanity, for

> the more alien things become to people in society, the more alien the words must stand in order to reach them and to warn them allegorically that things have been brought home. The deeper society is pervaded by the contradiction between its natural and its rational essence, the more isolated must foreign words necessarily persist in the sphere of language, incomprehensible to one part of the people, threatening to the other; and yet they have their right as an expression of alienation itself.
>
> NL2: 643/289

Whether it is in relation to slang or jargon, archaisms or reconstructions, purist thoughts of language oppose themselves to an alternative that is nevertheless easily assimilated under the guise of *Bildung*, in all its senses. The thought of the inassimilable that Adorno has sketched out is concerned with modes of innovation that remain resistant and, by virtue of their opacity, disrupt this thought of the organic, and it is this thought that reappears in the thinking of aesthetics and philosophy itself. For insofar as these foreign words arise as made, they are as foreign to the writer as they are to the reader, and so they do not preserve the ineffability of nuance through the superficial decoration of language, which educational conventions would prefer, but declare a new form of knowledge, as disintegrated as the forms that these names allegorically evoke.

The use of an allegorical landscape to describe the appearance of these foreign words confirms the role that Benjamin's Trauerspiel study played in Adorno's thinking on this issue. The image of a decayed and inhuman landscape recurs from Benjamin's analysis of baroque drama to the readings that Adorno gives of Schubert and Beethoven and later of Beckett and Celan. This bare and inhospitable space is sketched out on the one hand in order to avoid the ideology of the natural, and on the other hand to demonstrate the counter-idealist sphere of materiality. In both cases there is a response to the inhumanity of the contemporary world and its lack of sensuous relation, alongside a dialectic stripped of both reconciliation and transcendence, and so while this image is central to the notion of late style, it is not limited to it. In Benjamin's words, the significance of allegory, which the Trauerspiel exemplifies, is that it presents the face of history in its morbidity and loss of sense as a petrified (*erstarrte*) primal landscape [UDT: 343/174]. Contrary to the movement of symbolism, which espouses a transcendent evasion of both nature and history, the allegorical perspective refers meaning back to the world in its ongoing decay and disintegration. Thus, there is a secularization of history and nature, and a concomitant revision of dialectics, which Adorno is beginning to examine through the forms of style and tact.

The first piece in which this examination appears is an article on Schubert from 1928, which opens with a comparison between Beethoven and Schubert. It is easy to think that this comparison, in which the move from Beethoven to Schubert is described as one from a volcanic landscape to its extinguished remnants, is simply a way of conveying the transition from Beethoven's heroic symphonies to the wintry melancholy of Schubert's songs. But the significance of this comparison lies more in the displacement that it makes from an analysis of Schubert by way of the personality of the composer to an estimation of the nature of the works as conveying their own distinctive landscape. The basis for this change in perspective lies in the fact that the status of truth in the work is not subjective, as its lyrical evocation has disintegrated: 'The lyricist does not immediately depict his feelings in the structure, rather his feeling is the means of drawing truth in its incomparably small crystallization into the structure'. In this way what is unveiled in the work is the image of truth in its historical objectivity as 'the history of the image is its disintegration', that is, insofar as the subjective and intentional dimensions of truth are revealed as illusions, the resulting decay reveals the crystalline fragments that remain as the material-content (*Stoffgehalte*) of the work. This model of truth recalls that which Benjamin developed in his essay on Goethe's *Wahlverwandtschaften*, but it is adopted by Adorno to show the implications of the fact that truth is not related to the intentions of the artist nor is it a transhistorical ideal. Instead, the historical objectivity of the work means that the image of truth that it bears is itself subject to decay. The work stages the encounter of objective material-content and the ephemeral context of the artist or audience, in which both aspects are forced to change, which thus affects the unity of the work itself as it becomes 'the scene of its own transience' [MMU: 20/16-17].

Alongside his discussions of musical material, which showed the emergence of the demands of the material, this thought of the concomitant decay of relation indicates the appearance of a dialectic of natural-history, but Adorno has not fully recognized its resonances yet. Instead, he refers to Schubert's works by way of the figure of a potpourri, a disorganized assembly of decaying forms that creates its own sense of transience and distances it from any organic model of artistic works. This figure is extended further in the hardened, crystalline form of Schubert's pieces, which makes them remote from any form of musical medley. To understand the sense of this removal of the organic, Adorno stresses that it is the absence of life that forms the object of Schubert's music, an absence that is of death but is more far-reaching than the melancholic caricature to which his themes are often reduced. Instead, this is an inorganic landscape in which death is objective, a landscape that is beyond any psychology of fear or anxiety. The encounter with these objective images distorts the landscape so that its eccentric structure, 'in which every point is equally close to the centre, reveals itself to the wanderer who circles through it without advancing: all development is its complete antithesis, the first step is as close to death as the last, and in circling, the dissociated points of the landscape are scoured [*abgesucht*] but not abandoned' [MMU: 25/22]. History is replaced with the coexistence of themes that are repeatedly encountered, which constitutes the mood of these pieces, their changing reflection of its objective unchangeability, whose harmonic shifts only reveal the inability to plumb the depths of the landscape that has been exposed. For in its absence of metaphorical transport this landscape is that of the earth itself as 'the physical manifestation of death', an earth that can never become a homeland [MMU: 30/28].

The relation of the work to history is taken further in an article that appeared a year later, 'Nachtmusik', which would attempt to sketch out the general implications of this point in terms of both the essence of the work and its interpretation. For if the essence of the work is linked to its historical relation, then it is possible for works to fall into a disintegration that would render them inaccessible to interpretation. Conversely, the act (and tact) of interpretation, which seeks to respond to the historical nature of the work's essence, might be able to bring it into a relation to the present that would, by virtue of its distance, shatter its naïve position in history:

> The freedom of the artist, a reproducing one no less than a producing one, always and only rests on the fact that he has the right to realise, beyond all the constraints of what is currently existing, what he recognises as the current truth of the work according to the most advanced historical status – recognised not in the sense of abstract reflection, but as the content-related insight into the composition of its always historically preformed material. What is eternal about the work is only what is manifested with power here and now and that breaks open the semblance of the work; the apparently unchanged natural qualities of the work are, at the most, the scene to which the dialectic of form and content of the work applies
> MMU: 55/59

Thus, the movement of historical disintegration works in two directions (which explains the nocturnal aspect of music that Adorno has highlighted): as the disintegration of meaning and access to the work, and as a disintegration of the moment in which it comes to appear. Equally, this approach denies both the eternal aspect of truth that a work might be said to expose and the apparently antithetical subjective nature that would align it with passing opinion. Against both idealizations, the historical basis of the material-content of the music indicates the objective and transient status of its truth, so that it is neither fixed nor arbitrary. The darkness into which the truth of the work falls is that from which it speaks in its own nocturnal voice, one that does not directly illuminate the present but reveals it and itself in a more hidden manner because of the disintegration into which both have fallen. There can be no simple revelation of the meaning of a work, for neither current nor historical circumstances make this possible, there is only a more solitary and partial echo that resonates with its truth. From this perspective it is possible to understand how to approach the difficulty of contemporary works, which emerge precisely in and through this darkness of historical materiality, by which their historical status can be assessed. As the essence of the work cannot be separated from its historical appearance, the stripping away of this historical appearance in favour of some timeless truth only leaves the work empty and senseless. So, it is only by way of its historical disintegration that musical interpretation in either of its senses can take place. Gradually, and by way of this modulation of the notion of musical material, Adorno has begun to reformulate Benjamin's idea of truth away from the eschatological account of history and towards a more nocturnal dissociation, which he would come to discuss not just in its inorganic expanse but also in the lateness that it would share with thinking.

Much as with his later remarks on *Kierkegaard*, Adorno prefaced the later reprinting of these two articles with criticisms of the disparity between their ambition and their lack of detail, along with the clumsiness and immediacy of their philosophical development. Nevertheless, their formative status in his thinking is clear, and the high tone of these works, as he calls it, is indicative of the programme he sought to sketch out for himself [MMU: 10/4].[2] Alongside the suggestions of redemptive recapitulation there is an awareness of the distance across which artistic interpretation must venture, and the possibility of reading musical material through a sociological understanding of historical materialism is made doubtful by the historical disintegration that is foregrounded in this allegorical reading of history. As a result, Adorno's early thought is already markedly different from the accounts of either Benjamin or Kracauer as it bears little scope for any real political or theological hope, despite the suggestions of such that appear in these essays. Indeed, the way that these suggestions are appended only makes them less substantial (as is particularly clear in *Kierkegaard*) and the rest of these works bear a countervailing sense. But this appearance does not mean that what underlies it is a form of hermetic pessimism, ensconced in the eyries of the obscure and difficult. Instead, the reformulation of history on the basis of the analysis of musical material conveys a wholly different model that is as remote from decadence as it is from progress. As has been indicated, in this model temporality is subject to a dissociation and retarding, which arises from the degradation of time in modernity and an avoidance of the ideology of organic development, and in its place the materiality of history exposes a time without natural order. Thus, the form of a dialectic of natural-history can be perceived here, a dialectic that in being drawn from an analysis of artistic works reconstitutes the notion of the dialectic as a mode of thinking. The place of the philosopher is the same as that of the artistic interpreter: they are both constrained to respond to the most advanced materials of their age, which means that the dialectic must be rethought from out of its most complex historically mediated forms.

It is from this position that Adorno approaches the works of Beethoven, which, just like those of Schoenberg, present a challenge to any philosophical thinking of music and any understanding of the relation of concept and object. Two articles announced the beginning of this project in 1934, which he would continue to work on for twenty years, and while these take up some of the notions that have already been developed, they also introduce a more sober reflection. As he notes in 'Spätstil Beethovens', the attribution of a change in tone to the late works of an artist all too often slips into a biographical fallacy, as if everything could be explained by the ageing of the artist, along with their suspected frailty and seclusion. Removing this frame means examining the works without assuming that their style derives from a subjective condition. The changes that can be perceived in Beethoven's later works – their resistance to interpretation, their complexity, their abandonment of simple harmonies – must be approached from an analysis of their forms and the effects of their changes on their mode of expression. But 'the formal law of the late works is such that they do not add up to [*aufgehen*] a concept of expression'. In their place are found 'extremely "expressionless", distant structures', and any trace of expression they may bear is 'more of history than of growth' [MMU: 13/9-10]. Consequently, the nature of late style, if the term still has meaning, has to do with the role and status of conventions as the only form in which a mode of expression remains, albeit one that is failing. So, rather than assuming that conventions are overcome or transformed by the triumphant assertion of the artist's subjectivity, something else occurs in Beethoven's late works, since the conventional forms remain, as Adorno's remarks on tact indicated, but in such a way that they now appear naked and obvious, and thereby fractured.[3]

This appearance of conventions is not a regression or ironic citation, but instead that which needs to be understood by way of the appearance of death, as had been found with Schubert. This point does not return the analysis to the biographical perspective for death is not subjective nor is it the substance of these works. To begin with, it is 'the relation of conventions to subjectivity itself that must be understood as the formal law from which the import of the late works arises', that is, in terms of the pastness of these conventions, so that it is in 'the thought of death' that this formal law is revealed. However, this thought necessarily has an effect on the work: 'If the right of art disappears before this reality, then it certainly cannot pass directly into the artwork as its "object"' [MMU: 15/11]. Thus, death instead enters the work objectively in the form of its ruptured sense, which persistently reasserts itself. Evidently, this thought of death recalls that which was discussed in the essay on Schubert, and the same rationale is at stake: to avoid a psychology of artforms. If the thought of death is not the expression of subjectivity, then it cannot appear in such a form but must pervade the work as the absence of subjectivity as such. Hence the force of subjectivity in these late works is that of its departure from itself, and in doing so it does not express this departure but avoids expression entirely, leaving only the empty ruins of the work. The late works are then marked, as he had formulated, by history itself, by the fissures through which the material exposes its impotence in the face of this reality [MMU: 15/12]. The disintegration of the conventions recapitulates itself at every stage, which is the form of the work. And so, these last shards of works are objective expressions of the failure to complete themselves, of materiality abandoned to its actual existence, and conventions revealed in their unadorned dereliction. Only in this way is the semblance of their appearance shattered and, concomitantly, that of their historical situation. For without the unifying thread of subjectivity there is no centre or harmonic restoration to these works, just the ruptures of a work that seem to erupt with no inner or outer horizon. In this way their fractures are both objective and subjective without drawing these extremes into reconciliation, for they remain apart as exposed ruins.

Thus, tracking the formal law through the immanent dialectic of its contradictions leads to the work fragmenting under its own pressure. Following this dissociation (rather than development) within the work then leads to its further recapitulation at the level of the works themselves, as is found in the interconnections between Beethoven's late string quartets, which no longer appear to be single works. Consequently, the reformulation of the relation of subject and object by way of this execution of the formal law leads to a loss of this relation; these are no longer works as such and thus no longer seem to be worked, so there is no place for a conventional positioning of a subject-object relation by way of them. As a result, these late works take on an abstract, inhuman, unnatural sense, appearing only as fragmentary ciphers unmediated by any totality: spaces, ruptures, aspects of bare conventions, sequences without resolution and with unexpected turns, which never amount to fulfilled sense but only suggest the possibility of meaning. It is in this way that, despite the loss of subjectivity, these works come to reflect the actuality of individuality, for they are neither complete in themselves nor parts of a whole [B: 223-33/154-61].[4]

This fracturing necessarily has an impact on the social dimensions of the dialectic (the relation of the individual to society) as the form of the whole is no longer able to mediate the existence of individuals in a meaningful way, that is, it is unable determine their existence as individuals in relation to society. Form, as that which has arisen through the dialectic of natural-history, is no longer able to support a mutually sustaining relation between society and the individual. There is neither the possibility of a full assumption of self-creating individuality nor of a satisfactory socially determined relation. These aspects do not come together harmoniously, but nor is there the simple assertion of one side over the other. In their place is found mere dissociation, a struggle to assert that is never resolved, leaving neither determination nor indeterminacy in their simplicity. These new forms then become the concepts of music's appearance and of a negative critique of society, as well as leading to a reconsideration of form itself. The form of the work thus enters a dialectic of resistance to form as such in terms of the tension between autonomy and heteronomy, which undermines the possibility of the music appearing as a work in itself. And, as the nature and status of the work changes, so does its relation to society and the world, such that what is or might be construed as subjective or objective appears otherwise: as elements of a relation that is now without relation, abstracted from their apparently autonomous or heteronomous background and merely adrift. Subject and object then become grasped only through their absence, or through the absence of their determining relations. Equally, convention itself appears in isolated forms, undercutting its ideological effects and allowing it to be seen as it is, which is to situate it in its finitude and contingency rather than its dominance. Hence the work begins to bear forms without relation and transitions without substance or direction. The surface of the work becomes disorienting and opaque, refusing easy assimilation by its denial of recognized forms and resistance to conceptual penetration. What remains within (if at all) remains without expression. The work can then appear as incoherent and incomprehensible even though it is thoroughly pervaded by thought, thereby rendering its thought foreign to access. Thus, the implications this transformation has for society and history are necessarily extreme in their denial of substantial grounding and the loss of harmonious formation through the erosions and contradictions of materiality. Hence while this change may make the negative impressions of utopia more apparent, as that which is not evident, it also makes it much less possible or tangible.

As is clear, these early readings are suggestive but suffer from their lack of detail, and risk losing their insights through a generalized conceptual vision. As a result, it is necessary to address the question of the relation of Adorno's philosophical thinking to that of his musical writings, especially when he makes statements such as 'Beethoven's music is Hegelian philosophy: but at the same time it is truer than this' [B: 36/14]. Music in general, and Beethoven's music especially, is not philosophy because it does not operate through concepts, but nor is Adorno pursuing a philosophy of music, as if philosophy were to apply itself to music and generalize its findings. Instead, music is a form of immanent dialectic that works through its material and so provides a model of such thinking for philosophy, and Beethoven's works are particularly valuable in this regard owing to the rigorous application of this dialectic. This comparison places a burden on philosophy, as it finds itself encountering a deliberate and materialist analysis in music, but it also has to contend with the distortions of the dialectic that follow from this analysis. The degree to which music can obtain 'truer' accounts of the movement of the dialectic casts doubt on the privileged generality of philosophy and shows the importance and implications of the materialist demonstration of philosophical thinking. For such demonstrations cannot proceed without the transformation of philosophy, which implies the insufficiency of any philosophy that occurs without these materialist demonstrations. Nevertheless, music occupies a more intransigent situation for Adorno, since its logic does not involve judgement but brings about a synthesis that is not based on the predication or subsumption of elements [B: 32/11]. In addition, this alternate form of synthesis is not grounded in an apophantic truth, as its sense does not appear nor is it apparent, and it is by way of this distance from conceptual logic that the dialectic of music unfolds, a dialectic that is perpetually at risk of falling into a conceptual form if we persist in approaching music from this point of view, however unintentionally. However, this dilemma also reveals that music and philosophy share a sense of work, what Hegel called the labour of the concept, or of the negative, by which the inner tensions of its logic are worked out [PG: 48/43].

Because music is not simply like philosophy but follows its own logic under its own constraints, the way that this working out of its inner tensions takes place does so with its own problems. Firstly, there is the problem of what happens when the piece appears to have fully worked itself out, which Adorno discusses as the problem of recapitulation. In the sonata form, which characterizes many of Beethoven's works, there is a specific structure in which the tonal materials are introduced in an exposition, which then passes into the development where the materials are contrasted and elaborated, and in the last part, the recapitulation, the materials are then harmonically resolved.[5] This basic structure, with its suggestion of a dialectic, poses a key problem as the recapitulation needs to appear satisfactory without being teleological or conclusive: so how can the work resolve itself when the very form of its closure cannot be presupposed? The second problem relates to this first one, as it centres on the issue of time. Within the sonata form there is a strong sense in which the past emerges after the future, as the recapitulation allows for a sense in which the beginning of the work can only be grasped by way of its return, which then rephrases the sense of the music's present. But how can we grasp the sense of this temporal complexity without turning to spatial or linear models, how does the music itself take the measure and moment of its movement? Thirdly, following the above sketch of what takes place in Beethoven's late works it is evident that there is a move towards a formal abstraction in these works, an abstraction that as we have seen involves a laying bare of its elements, but how can this abstraction be grasped without assimilating it to the abstraction of philosophical concepts? In all these problems the status of the work is at issue, and in all these cases it is in Beethoven's late style that the specific forms by which musical logic develops seems to be shown in itself. It is thus that Adorno can find in Beethoven's late works a simulacrum of Hegelian thought, but one that yet goes beyond it, as if the late style was precisely what Hegel did not manage to uncover. For in the last period of his compositions, Adorno finds Beethoven going beyond the heroic symphonies of his middle period into the forms that are necessarily exposed in the wake of them.⁶

As such, the late works seem to arise as an immanent critique of the syntheses of the middle period, and thereby show the equal degree to which the social integration that they had espoused has begun to fall apart as the harmonic resolution of individuality and sociality expressed in the symphonies gives way to a radical fragmentation that is not merely musical in scope. The materialist insight into the mechanisms by which society reproduces itself is conveyed through the immanent development of music, whose logic is precisely focused on the nature and status of identity and the relation of part to whole by which it is constituted. Music then becomes an objective model of social reproduction in which the presentation of identity can be suspended so that its constitutive transitions can be examined, and in doing so it reveals the objectivity of the obstructions that may disrupt these transitions. In this way the whole that would mediate the work becomes understood from out of its immanent development, rather than as a self-sustaining imposition, and within this reformulated whole the individual is reconstituted on the basis of its loss of relation at the same time as the universal becomes a form of resistance to the whole [B: 73/42]. When we look at the way that a piece unfolds under the pressure of its initial material, it is found that these inner tensions carry both a necessity and an excess, as the way that the form arises is as variable as the way that its actuality is immanently derived. The transitions that then arise in the development of this material are exposed to contingency by way of this excess, which means that each tension can develop otherwise so that the transition, despite its necessity, takes on some of the role of the accidental, of a rupture as much as a transition. Thus, the temporal 'development' of the piece is put in question, since what comes after is not only subsequent but also that which is rephrased otherwise by its contingency, so that what 'was' is no longer strictly before but found to be still present alongside its other accents. While there remains freedom and irreversibility in the development, there is a sense in which there is no progression but only coexisting alternates. Transitions have become suspended as movements of linearity or continuity, leading to an overall suspension of resolution that affects the recapitulation as well. The work cannot culminate in the essential destiny of its form; there is no natural fulfilment of the material but only its avoidance by way of the deviations of sense that its artefactual development provides. The status of the work and of its experience then becomes of critical importance for what it says about the relation of thought to history, materiality, and society.

II Hegel and Absolute Music

To gain a better grasp of the significance of Beethoven's late works, it is necessary to place them in the context of Hegel's contemporary discussions of music, which form the background for Adorno's studies but also concern themselves directly with the question of what this late style implies: the notion of music as absolute. The central points around which Hegel's argument is structured, which are the critical points of intervention for Adorno's thinking, are the status of music as an artform, as a work in itself, and its potential to become absolute or independent. In doing so, Hegel looks at how music is structured and how it develops, which is to discuss its natural-history in terms of its specific materiality and temporality, which reveals its proximity to thought but also its effects thereupon. However, the approach to music in the lectures on aesthetics is initially oriented towards its difference from other artforms, since the expression of spirit in and through art necessitates an approach that looks at the different ways in which spirit is expressed and made manifest.[7] Thus, Hegel moves from architecture to sculpture and then to painting to show how these modes display an increasing sophistication in their concretization of spirit. While architecture can display its forms in their objectivity and arrange them externally through principles of heaviness and light, it cannot bring out the subjective qualities of spirit, its depth and variety. Sculpture presents an advance on this model in that it can make spirit into its subject, but it cannot do so in a manner reflective of the interiority of spirit. This interiority only becomes apparent in painting, which is indicative of its status as a Romantic art, for in painting the inner life of spirit can be made manifest through the particularities of line and shade, colour and depth. However, painting is still limited in this regard as it is objective and static. 'But if the interior [...] is indeed to reveal itself as *subjective* interiority, then the truly corresponding material must not be of the kind that it still exists for itself.' Hence it is necessary to find a form of objectivity that does not persist so that it can reflect interiority in its own lack of stability. The importance of music arises because it is able to make interiority apparent through an obliteration of space and externality. 'This eradication not only of *one* dimension of space, but of total spatiality in general, this complete withdrawal into subjectivity on the part of the interior as well as its expression, is accomplished by the second Romantic art – *music*' [VA: 133/889]. Although it is worth being sceptical about this hierarchical model of the arts, Hegel's primary purpose is to show the specific necessity of each artform by differentiating it from the others, and to this degree his account is helpful. From this beginning a number of points are already apparent, for example, that music has an objectivity that is unstable and unenduring, that it is made manifest without taking up space, and in drawing out the subjectivity of spirit this subjectivity is made concrete as itself. These aspects will inform Hegel's deliberations and make music a strange analogue to thought, one that may not, within the scope of his argument, achieve the objective sophistication that is found in poetry, but still finds an appearance in which feeling can be expressed to its utmost. It does so to the degree that its existence remains subjective in its objectivity so that it is not fixed and external.

This appearance depends on the materialization of sound as vibration – that Hegel spells out in more detail in the *Naturphilosophie* – which makes of music an aspect of physics, the movement and resonance of material bodies. When a specific sensuous material is made to move it loses its 'peaceful separation' from others, and thereby its position, and begins to oscillate and it is this oscillation that delivers sound. In this development there is a negation of space as position, which is in turn negated by the form of the body itself, so that sound as an expression of this double negation occurs and annihilates itself in the same movement. It is thus in coming to be and passing away that sound 'becomes a mode of expression adequate to the inner'.[8] As an expression of the movement of bodies sound has an existence independent of humans, but in hearing these sounds the ear cannot remain distant and unaffected by them, for insofar as they are not spatial there can be no separation between sounds and hearing. But inasmuch as sounds are not fixed and enduring, what is heard through them is rather the passage of subjectivity in its appearance and vanishing. Hence 'only the completely objectless interior, abstract subjectivity as such, is suitable for musical expression', so the 'main task of music is therefore not to let objectivity itself resound but, on the contrary, the way in which the innermost self itself is moved in terms of its subjectivity and ideal soul'. There is a natural resonance between music and subjective feeling, as each finds itself corresponding to the other such that music becomes 'the art of feeling [*Gemüts*]', in both senses of the genitive, as each aspect directly addresses the other [VA: 135/891]. This resonance means that the distinction between the object and its subjective apprehension disappears, so when the sounding of the note passes away, it passes into memory, moving from the objective into subjective interiority, which is moved by it. Conversely, the objectless content of music, which constitutes its form, is such that it requires objective configuration for any content to emerge within it and so, while remaining a natural and direct resonance between subjective and objective, it requires an artificial and somewhat arbitrary configuration to render this resonance detailed and specific. It is on this point that Hegel believes that music can lose its way in becoming purely formal and instrumental in its configuration, which is only of interest to connoisseurs. As the art of feeling, music remains for him intrinsically related to the expression of spirit, and although abstract it renders the interiority of feeling to a superlative degree, which is lost as soon as music becomes more concerned with its own formal configuration regardless of its subjective resonance.

This last point might lead us to think that Hegel's account is historically limited and of little importance for understanding the strands of absolute music that recurred from Beethoven to Schoenberg, and that Adorno acclaimed so highly. Although Hegel may not have responded well to the more experimental traditions of modern music, the basis for his argument – the relation of formal configurations of music to their subjective resonance – is not lost, as Adorno attempted to draw out by showing that formal experimentation was necessary to respond to the reification of musical material in which its resonance could no longer be found. This point is developed almost by accident in what Hegel says next, for he goes on to remark that the turn to formal interiority may betoken a liberation of the soul, but the way that this occurs is limited. This is the case because the expression of meaning within a musical theme is exhausted with that thematic expression, so that any further development, repetition, or variation is superfluous. Hegel then complicates this point by stating that while there may be an interchange between different themes, this elaboration does not make the unity of meaning more profound or concentrated; 'it is rather an expansion, dissemination, divergence, a distancing and return, for which the content that has to express itself remains the more general focus but does not hold the whole together as tightly as it does in the forms of the visual arts'. Thus, the formal liberation in the development and variation of the music becomes centrifugal, for music 'is too close to the element of that formal freedom of the interior to not turn away more or less beyond what is available, what is the content'. Equally, in the recollection of the theme, there is a recollection of the artist as the one who expands and unfolds the theme, so that in this developing liberation there is a mutual propulsion and affirmation. As opposed to those works that are concentric, in asserting a return to themselves in accomplishing a finished whole, the free exercise of the imagination in music can become one in which liberation becomes an end in itself, which then enables the artist to develop the work in such a way that the transitions and transformations lead to 'the most heterogeneous' form [VA: 142-43/897].

While Hegel is registering the effect of such formal liberation, he also deems it less successful than music that bears content. But it is important to note the way that this point emerges, for he first makes clear that the range of sound is not merely subservient to meaning, as it might be said to be in poetry, for example, but is instead the mode and the essential end of the liberation of feeling. Hence while adverting to the priority of content, he nevertheless still finds the possibility of content occurring through the sensuous form and modality of sound, even if he claims that this is only for connoisseurs [VA: 145/899]. The difference from poetry lies in the greater degree of differentiation afforded by the use of words, whereas music can only occasion a sense of vague feeling, however effectively or impressively this may take place. What has to be understood is that the form of these feelings, as it is conveyed in the formal unfolding of the music, is directly and mutually resonant with the form of music itself and so is borne out by this reciprocal development, thereby conveying a different mode of expression perhaps unavailable to poetry, insofar as the latter has removed itself from the sensuous basis of its material. However, seeming to forget his earlier point on this mutual resonance, or perhaps displacing it by emphasizing the greater determinacy of the interchange between ideas and words, Hegel then states that it is only our own (prior) ideas that are aroused by the unfolding of music – rather than those that are produced by the musical treatment of the notes as the piece develops. It is as a result of this perception that he feels that the combination of music and text often fails as one aspect predominates over the other.

While music has the greatest possibility of freeing itself from any text or subjective content, it is at risk of becoming empty and meaningless unless it combines this ability with an expression of spirit, and it is only in this way that it can be considered an art. The problem is one of how to make this inner feeling resonate with the configuration of notes so that it can emerge anew. Firstly, it is necessary to recognize that 'inwardness as such is the form in which it can conceive its content, and it is thereby able to take in everything that can enter interiority and primarily clothe itself in the form of feeling', which means that music shares in both the expansiveness and the vagueness of feeling [VA: 149/902]. Although music is not independently external to the self, it arises as the objectification of its expression, much like inarticulate sounds and cries, such that it is in need of articulation and generalization in its form so that it does not appear as merely arbitrary sounds. It is thus that it takes on, in contradistinction to the externality and separation of spatial forms, the objectivity of a temporal form. Interiority, as it is expressed in music, is therefore not distinct from the feeling that arises within since 'the content is interwoven without separation with the interior as such' [VA: 152/904]. In this way the demand is either to bring to inner feeling that which arises within the music, or, conversely, to enable the musical expression of that which has aroused the spirit, but in either case this operation must proceed by way of the configuration and articulation of a sequence of notes over time. It is because music is evanescent that it can capture the equally transient movements of the soul, which in turn becomes carried away by the flowing stream of tones. As a result, the self is not only gripped by this element but also activates and is further activated by it. From the perspective of what Hegel has said so far it would seem that because feeling gives rise to expression in sound, the converse also takes place so that sounds, because of their rhythm or tone, give rise to particular feelings and perhaps action, such that, for instance, it becomes difficult not to respond upon hearing a series of regular beats. Although under-examined, this correlation seems to arise because of the close material affinity between feeling and sound, in that sound is merely the expression of feeling, that is, it is feeling in the sphere of sound. On the one hand, this affinity was sketched out in the *Naturphilosophie* when Hegel described how materiality leads to sound through vibration, and on the other hand, this vibration occurs in the self in the area of feelings – inner, transient, and inarticulate feelings that give rise to sound (to the same degree as was found in the physics) through their escalation.[9] While speech is the obvious analogue for this process, Hegel makes it clear that speech is of a different kind, due to its distance from its sonic materiality and its approximation to the generality of the idea. However, this positioning of speech should still be seen in terms of its relation to more fragmentary and impulsive ejaculations of sound, which can neither be controlled nor defined but thereby give form to inner feeling through their expression in such a way that the sound and feeling are, as he has pointed out, indistinct and inseparable. It is on the basis of this interweaving, which is not simply union or merging, that the converse effect can take place in which sounds can give rise to feelings and actions. Although this close affinity is undefined, it demonstrates the active combination of what is felt and what feels, which conveys a basic epistemology that is not separate from praxis, much like the information encoded in behaviours like habit or tact.

At this point Hegel uses an unusual example:

> the disorderly restlessness of a table d'hôte with many people, and the unsatisfying stimulation it causes is annoying; this running back and forth, clattering, and

chattering should be regulated, and since one has to deal with empty time beside eating and drinking, this emptiness should be filled. On this occasion, as with so many others, music comes to be helpful and also averts other thoughts, distractions, and ideas.

VA: 155/907

Prior to this example, Hegel had spoken of the way that music operates in relation to military entrainment, which is more obvious, but in this example of the noisy restaurant we find much more than just an image of bourgeois stuffiness. It is not sufficient to disregard this example because of its view that noise should be regulated, and emptiness should be filled. While it gives us an understanding of Hegel's perspective on noise and idleness, beneath this view there is the notion of how music fills and orders a space, which is not only to regulate activity in the restrictive sense but also to accompany it with sound in order to provide it with meaning. Activity, which on its own may appear disordered and meaningless, can become ordered and meaningful when regulated by music, as the feelings that accompany the activity are brought in tune with it through the music so that they present a combined and organized activity. Thus, it is music that allows for the sense of coordinated meaning, which is lost when feeling and activity are not consonant. Music provides this arrangement because of the way it allows for feeling and activity to resonate, which is what enables meaning to emerge, albeit one that is indeterminate. Music allows for activity that may appear unfocused to become focused by enabling a specific parsing of act and world.

In what ways it can do so, and with what differing effects, of course remains to be discussed, but what is also found is the latent discovery of the subjective unity of such occurrences, which comes about through their experience. At first, this unity is merely abstract as it is only the form in which there is a sense of an 'itself' to the experience, but this unity is undifferentiated and negative as it is only posited in the negation of the moment of the now that occurs in the passing of time. However minimally, this unity still indicates that 'the self is in time and time is the being of the subject itself'. This bare reflexivity is then enhanced through sound, for insofar as it operates through time, music's rhythms penetrate and grip the self and thereby put it in motion, since the definite configuration of notes provides for a concrete enrichment of the subject's sense of self as it is drawn on and out by the musical configuration [VA: 156/908]. It is on the basis of this formulation that Hegel insists on the priority of musical content over simple formal experimentation, for although music can rally the emotions it is only through its idea that this movement can be given force and direction. Nevertheless, insofar as music presents this interior motion as such, in the form of its subjective interiority, it has no lasting subsistence but can only be reproduced, which puts pressure on the formalization of this procedure such that it can be reproduced, in contrast to the virtuosity of the performance in which it is reproduced.

The configurational language of music is of crucial significance because it is through the connections with other notes that a note can begin to have a definite sound. However, this form of configuration is not part of the structure of notes themselves but arises externally and artificially, and so comes from the performer or listener in terms of their awareness of the overall relation of sounds. It is thus that music comes to be understood through a numerical system of proportions; the equal or inequal relation of sounds and their hierarchies and movements. Despite this quantitative, formal structure, music still manages to convey inner feeling and to such a degree that the latter comes to feel itself, as defined and articulated, through this musical relation. Hegel proceeds to examine the formation of this configuration by looking at rhythm (in terms of the coming to be and passing away of sonic material), harmony (in terms of the relations and proportions between the notes), and melody (in terms of the particular expression of spiritual content). Because notes are produced by making a body vibrate, this sensuous material becomes music only in the form of temporal duration and movement, as these trembling vibrations do not exist spatially but merely follow one another in time. Consequently, music occurs across time as both a continuous stream of the coming to be and passing away of tones and as an undifferentiated duration. But as such, it cannot express the feeling of the self in its self-expression, and so the differentiation of time arises in order not just to articulate the flow of tones but also to render it objective so that the self can reflect on itself, and it does so by punctuating this stream of appearing and disappearing tones with its own experience of moments, which thereby become discrete and concrete just as the music itself does. Rhythm thus occurs in the way that indeterminacy is overcome through the formation of a regular series of beats, so that it receives its determination from the way that the undifferentiated stream of sounds is punctuated [VA: 167/916]. Hegel then goes on to discuss harmony in relation to instrumentation and intervals (scales, keys, and chords), and then melody, which overcomes the substantive basis provided by the necessary forms of rhythm and harmony to give expression to the free sounding of the soul. In this way melody allows for the combination and supersession of both freedom and necessity, abstract and concrete, so as to give ideal expression to interiority. While there is a dialectic operating here, it must necessarily pass through its own dissonance and rending of harmony in order to arrive at this more complete expression of its idea. The true concept is not an immediate unity but one that is essentially divided in itself such that it has fallen apart into contradictions [VA: 183/928]. And it is only by way of the overcoming of these divisions that the harmony of the work can be grasped more fully, and its melody express itself in its completeness.

In the last section of the chapter Hegel makes what seems to be the culminating determination of musical form: the distinction between music as accompaniment and music as independent or instrumental. Within this division lies the final appearance of expression itself as that which is, in its combination with words, the expression of a feeling interior to the subject, or that which adheres within the musical form and to which the subject is drawn to immerse themselves. In both aspects, the formation of the experience as a whole takes place as a movement of externalization and return, bringing about a complex unfolding of self-expression that is no longer merely vague or interior but has become concrete and defined through the movement of the music between inner and outer, and material and ideal. It is with the varieties of this model of development that Hegel sides, in contrast to the apparently formal experimentation of solely instrumental music. But it is not the case that the latter is entirely absent of content, for its thematic independence may become the content itself, in the sense that its self-development becomes its focus. Or, the free expression of musical development may remain free and unrestrained by any notion of content or theme, in which case its intellectual formality remains unfocused.[10] The importance of this distinction between music as accompaniment and as independent derives from music's position as a mode of the self-expression of spirit in its feelings, and so the 'sense' of music is never absent, as it is always engaged in the self-expression of spirit, which then has a certain role and status in its mode of expression. It is no accident that this distinction arises as a critical point for Hegel, when (following the works of Beethoven) the notion of absolute music is itself arising in music criticism as the idea of music appearing on its own terms, without reference to any theological or social context. Consequently, the idea that music can become a work of art also arises at this time, when the theoretical and practical means of such autonomy become available. This notion will last into the twentieth century and will form the notion of a musical avant-garde, but of what it has become the avant-garde remains uncertain, as Adorno's works make clear. It should be noted that Hegel's last remark on the question of music's status relates to the issue of musical reproduction, which is to say that it occurs in the same manner as the argument around *Sittlichkeit* in the *Rechtsphilosophie*, as that of the formal mode of social reproduction so that music forms part of the way that society reproduces and reinstates itself, and so it is to the content-based expressions of music that this social and aesthetic reproduction is most crucially attuned.

However, the argument is not so clearly divided, as Hegel's apparent criticisms of Beethoven's use of Schiller in the Ninth Symphony demonstrate, as does his indication that the independence of instrumental music can become its own expressive focus, thereby allowing for a formal development of its idea [VA: 147/901]. What is at issue is not the presence of a text, but the integration of expression and formal development, whether instrumental or not. Nevertheless, the development of independent music in the early nineteenth century meant that there could be no return to earlier forms of artistic expression since these could now only be conceived as unsatisfactory given recent developments.[11] This argument parallels that which Adorno would adopt a hundred years later about the irreversibility attached to the notion of musical material and the importance of pursuing the significance of the latter by examining its most historically advanced forms. But it is interesting to see Hegel defending instrumental music despite his professed inability to understand it fully and his own preference for more tangible and vocal performances. What is at issue, as with his understanding of the role of dissonance, is the form in which music develops in itself, that is, the form in which it finds its own most complete expression, which necessarily means following through on the indeterminate and abstract movement of its tones, to some extent regardless of their accessibility. While music must remain the sound and form of expression by which feelings can come to reflect on themselves, this reciprocity does not prohibit or exclude a transformation in the status of such feelings, quite the opposite. There is the suggestion that with the development of more formal and abstract modes of expression, music may enable similar transformations in the feelings themselves, which means that it cannot be assumed that the form of feelings has itself been established and hence that music has become adequate to them. In this way, there is an open-ended possibility sketched out in the discussion of music that not only makes us rethink the development of music after Hegel but also his own suggestions about the pastness of art, and the role and form of artistic expression in the realization of spirit. Although he will go on within the structure of the aesthetics to say that it is poetry that becomes the fullest expression of the development of spirit, the discussion of music remains an alternative pathway in that music is the form of the expression of feeling, which persists alongside the concrete expression of ideas in poetry. The latter may provide the determinacy required for spirit to actualize itself, but it does not cancel or subsume the expression of feeling in music.

If we are to understand music as a kind of temporalization of spatiality, given the transition in both the *Naturphilosophie* and the *Ästhetik*, then this would have to be revised by the fact that the inner life and feeling that is expressed in music is not a real spatiality and does not give rise to a real temporality.[12] Instead, this inner life and feeling is its own movement, which is only partially captured in the scales and intervals that are imposed on it. To that degree music becomes the temporalization of the spatiality that it derives from, with all that this entails in terms of its movement and indeterminacy, its vivacity and transience. This temporalization is a very specific form that occurs as a resonance of sounds, of their reflection and transformation, and so despite its apparent vagueness it bears out its own form by way of this resonance, which becomes its material vibration and temporal form. Music is not fully objective, as it does not endure or occupy any place, and yet it unfolds its own non-subjective expression as an abstract living form. Through the overcoming of its doubled negativity (the negation of the negation of objectivity), music conveys its own version of *aufheben*. And for as much as this *aufheben* seeks harmonious unity, it also provides a concrete experience of the failure to accomplish this synthesis as music does nothing but allude to the possibility of such completion, which forever remains out of reach. Even if the work demonstrates its own conclusion, in doing so it is unravelled by virtue of music's transience and finitude; as soon as the resolution has been found, it passes away. While for Hegel this may indicate its limited and provisional status in relation to poetry and thinking, for Adorno, it indicates an alternative pathway for dialectics, a form of historico-material expressiveness that is neither totalizing nor essentialist. Although the self is able to experience itself as a self in its experience of music, it only does so through this experience, which is necessarily transient and finite, even in its enduring impressions and internal resonance. As such, there is a sense in which music individualizes the listener by grasping them in their specific situation, while also referring them to a horizon of sense that remains intangible. What is felt is the movement of *aufheben*, of a synthesis that remains open and so only relates from one tone to another, and from self to other, that is, in the mode of resonance. A tone on its own means little; it is in combination with others that it comes to mean, and then only by way of its differences and repetitions, around and upon which the structures of composition are configured. In this network the final summation of meaning remains elusive: there can be no complete determination or fulfilment but perhaps only the exhaustion of sense. And just as music and feelings are not simply given, so too are they able to generate innovations in each other; feelings constitute music but can also be formed by it as part of the manifold but uncoordinated historico-material self-reproduction of society.

It is perhaps thus that there can be found a similarity between *Takt* and tact, between the beat or measure that structures the indeterminate time of the musical movement and the subtle intervention that guides social interactions and keeps them within a certain sphere. It is for this reason that tact becomes the key term within Adorno's interpretation of Beethoven, as it is by way of this stroke that Beethoven's rhythms become so innovative and, in his later works, so challenging, for what it indicates is another mode of temporal determination, a changeable, irregular measure that punctuates time in an unusual manner, provoking not a simple rhythmic unity but an unstable and jarring impression.[13] Such irregularity is not complete disorder but is rather the mark of the changing temporal formation of experience in modernity, and of the resonance with this irregular and unstable measure by which music indicates its own non-natural and non-static position and status. Along with harmony, which provides the schemata or grammar of relations among tones, their differential inter-determinations, melody arises as the speculative force of reason and imagination, of exact fantasy, which goes beyond the framework of what exists by conveying new formulations and movements. Melody opens up the resonance of feelings in sound to an experience of itself that surpasses its basic structures and relations, and it is this that it can be said to elevate the inner life and convey novel emotions. Melody is thus the expression of freedom, not as merely arbitrary or accidental but as freedom won through the natural-historical relation of necessity and form, and thereby of their substantial modulation. For just as music has changed since the time of Hegel and Beethoven, so has the nature of this freedom and its modes and possibilities. And so too has the nature of the dialectic it uncovers, as has been seen by the prevalence of dissonant and irregular formations in modern music in which harmonic unities no longer hold the same status. Hegel seems to recognize this possibility in speaking of the way that instrumental music allows for music to develop entirely from out of its own sphere, without the distractions of text, and in saying as much he recognizes the possibility of the open-ended developments that this change brings about:

> The principle of music is made up of subjective inwardness. The innermost core of the concrete self, however, is subjectivity as such, not determined by any fixed content and therefore not compelled to move here or there, but only based on itself in unbounded freedom. If this subjectivity is to come into its own in music as well, it must break free from a given text and take into account its own content, the course and type of its expression, the unity and development of its work, the implementation of a main idea and the episodic involvement and ramifications of others, etc., it must be taken purely from itself and, insofar as the meaning of the whole is not expressed by words, restrict itself to purely musical means.
>
> VA: 214/952

As has been noted, within this framework, instrumental music is not inevitably lacking in content, as is found by the persistence with which listening appears to construe such content, but also because of the necessity to counterbalance pure formal experimentation by turning to the form of the musical development as its own content.

The importance of Beethoven's later works lies precisely in their reconfiguration of the nature of transition and continuity, of the nature of if and how something can follow something else, which is both a question of history and of transformation. In the works of the middle period there is a heroic force of freedom that arises through and against the obstacles that would resist it, and even if this freedom is ultimately defeated it still exists as a force. Hence the sense of this ultimacy is itself reconfigured, as well as the relation between what arises in the musical expression and what might seem to oppose or restrict it according to the forms of harmonic or temporal closure. But, in questioning this relation between freedom and necessity, the nature of relation as such (and the continuity or consequence it presupposes) is brought into focus, and it is in regard to these more problematic issues that Beethoven's later works develop, which is why they seem so strange and complex and fragmentary. Thus, the Romantic atmosphere of the works of the middle period in their unbridled subjectivism, which both Hegel and Adorno would resist (although from opposing sides, in that Hegel would focus on the realization of spirit through social mediation, and Adorno would focus on the impossibility of such realization), is changed in the later compositions to show how subjective force is itself transformed in relation to its temporality and materiality, as that which cannot simply overcome such obstacles, even in a Pyrrhic fashion, but is reformed through them into something that is neither subjective nor objective, neither conclusive nor inconclusive, but occurs through a different mode of consequence and relation, which might be considered paratactic, discontinuous, and thereby radically innovative. Such forms are not merely arbitrary, either in a materially chaotic or in a transcendentally wilful manner but arise out of the pressure of previous formations without being entirely determined by them. In this way, there is no complete loss of continuity but there is still space for unforeseen possibilities.

Music then becomes a mode of understanding temporality, of relations of transition, but also of experiencing and orchestrating such changes. Temporal relation, as that which concerns the sense of consequence, is historical and political in terms of how the past relates to the present and how the present relates to the future. And, in developing differing models of such transitions through music, temporal change becomes available to experience even through its ruptures and contradictions, surprising detours and ambiguous recapitulations. These points are particularly evident in Beethoven's late works, so that Adorno considers these pieces both as a challenge to modes of listening and in contrast to Hegel's thinking of dialectics. This combination is the focus of what Adorno calls structural listening, which is also remarked in the notion of a speculative ear (adopted from Kierkegaard), as he describes in a later work: 'Hegel's style is certainly contrary to usual philosophical understanding, but because of its weakness it prepares another: one must read Hegel by describing the curves of his spiritual movement with him, as if by playing along with the thoughts with a speculative ear as if they were notes'. This notion recurs through a number of Adorno's writings in the 1950s and 1960s as he comes to terms with the demands placed on listeners by the New Music then emerging, and it is significant that he turns to this metaphor to describe the difficulties faced by readers of Hegel (equally, this essay on reading Hegel is one of only two places, outside of his works on music, where Adorno mentions the speculative ear):

> Hegel expects two things from the reader that would not be ill-suited to the essence of the dialectic itself. They should slide along, let themselves be carried along by the flow, the momentary should not force them to linger. Otherwise, they would change it despite and through their greatest loyalty to it. On the other hand, however, a method of intellectual slow-motion has to be developed to slow the tempo in the cloudy areas so that they do not evaporate but can be seen as moving. Hardly ever are both procedures given in the same act of reading. It has to be broken down into its opposites just like the content itself. The Marxian

formulation that philosophy passes into history already characterises Hegel in a certain sense.

DS: 354-55/123

While Adorno aligns this idea with Hegel's own sense of reading, as found in the *Phänomenologie*, he goes further in making reading not just an experience of its own temporalization, and vice versa, but one that operates by way of its manoeuvring into and out of the work while holding to this contradictory and centrifugal tension, which then, surprisingly, becomes an analogue to Marx's eleventh thesis since it becomes a mode for an original form of temporal innovation.[14]

However, the two notions of structural listening and the speculative ear are not synonymous; rather the latter is brought out in a way that seems to support and extend the possibilities of the former. Structural listening arises as a theme in Adorno's attempts to counter the perceived regression of listening that he finds in the popular consumption of music, and to this end it focuses on an intensely focused listening with, or co-execution, of the work that would seek to follow it as it develops without adverting to any other perspectives. Such an intense focus, while essential for the informed reproduction and response to the work, risks an austere formalism that neglects the role of context and history.[15] But it is precisely the latter that the speculative ear can hopefully detect, insofar as it seeks to balance the microscopic with the macroscopic, without letting either take priority. Indeed, by combining the two approaches the close attentiveness to the development of the work is offset by the awareness of its greater ambiance and implications, to such an extent that each becomes inflected by the other without losing its distinctiveness. What is important about this combined model is that it attends to the temporality of the work as it unfolds in such a way that the sense of it as a whole is both grasped and suspended, allowing a sense of the whole to develop from its materials, just as the reverse takes place, so that the grounds and directions of its temporality are determined from this polarized and unresolved tension. As a result, there is an interchange between the sense of the whole and the sense of the differing movements as we listen, which creates a changed impression of both, so that sections that seem to follow or not follow might be found to do so or not, given this changed impression. This creates a different sense of continuity and progression, and thus of the piece as a piece, so that it is not clear whether it is in fact a whole or, if it is, whether it is a different kind of whole, given that what comes after and what comes before seem to change places in our listening comprehension.

A particularly helpful example of what Adorno means by the speculative ear can be found in the 1965 essay 'Form in der neuen Musik':

> Schoenberg defended his harmonic innovations, the most tangible phenomena of atonality, with the sentence: "I always decide according to the sense of form [*Formgefühl*]". In doing so, he noted the compulsive consciousness of objectivity, the norm of which is nonetheless hidden from itself, opaque; just as the state of the world no longer grants truth without risk, everything that is certain is condemned in advance as a lie. A sense of form means: listening to music wherever it wants to go; as far from an imposed will, from imposed architecture, as from foreign necessities, in which for the most part subjective arbitrariness that has become blind is entrenched; it is undeterred in the dark, no differently from the authentic linguistic structures of modernity. But this requires an extreme subjective tension. The speculative ear is the only organ of unconfirmed objectivity, a negative defence against its falsification.[16]

It is clear that this approach explicates some of what Adorno means in his emphasis on the priority of the object, of an adherence to the force of objectivity despite its opacity, but it also indicates how this mode of listening is not merely passive but actively reconstructs the work through the inter-relation of understanding and imagination. As he writes in an article on how to listen to New Music, from a few years earlier: 'The demand for an active behaviour on the part of the recipient instead of a passive culinary one meets with one of its essential desiderata. Except that such activity does not consist of diligent participation, of dull fiddling busyness. Rather, it is a silent, imaginative, ultimately listening activity, an achievement of what Kierkegaard called the speculative ear'.[17] This subjection to the object is an act of intense subjective effort in which the false objectivity of the object can only be suspended through the closest attention to it and, in doing so, its repressed historical possibilities are released. While this attention to the nature of the object releases its history as a new temporal mode of expression, it is this same attention that is found in the guidelines of how to read Hegel, which demonstrates the close relation between Adorno's response to (and reproduction of) music and philosophy:

> But intellectual [*geistige*] experience cannot be expressed in any other way than by reflecting itself in its mediation: being actively thought. Indifference between the expressed intellectual experience and the thinking medium cannot be gained. The untruth of Hegel's philosophy manifests itself precisely in that it presents such indifference as realisable through sufficient conceptual effort. Hence the countless breaks between what has been experienced and the concept.

Hegel is to be read against the grain, and in such a way that every logical operation, however formal it may be, is brought to its core of experience. The equivalent of such experience in the reader is the imagination. If he just wanted to state what a passage should mean, or even to chase its chimera to guess what the author was trying to say, the content of which he was seeking philosophical certainty would vanish for him. No one can read more out of Hegel than he puts into it. The process of understanding is the progressive self-correction of such projection by comparing it with what is written. The matter itself contains, as a law of form, the expectation of productive imagination in the reader. Whatever experience may be registered, he must think out from his own. It is precisely in the breaks between experience and concept that understanding must intervene.

DS: 368/138-39[18]

In that this understanding is developmental it bears its own metaphysics, as it points beyond what is into the sphere of possibility, and as such it bears a utopian form but also its suspension, since this is a gesture of leading beyond that can never be actualized. Adorno's understanding of philosophy and aesthetics is thereby marked by an experimentalism in both its aims and its methods, a point that will have considerable impact on its status, as will be seen.

III Expressions Formal and Dissonant

In 1934, two years after completing *Kierkegaard*, Adorno left Germany to go to Oxford to pursue his fourth dissertation, the book on Husserl that would later appear as *Zur Metakritik der Erkenntnistheorie*. Then, in 1938, he left Europe entirely and went to New York, where he would work on the Princeton radio research project, before leaving in 1941 for Los Angeles, where his growing collaboration with Horkheimer would lead to *Dialektik der Aufklärung*. After the large quantity of work he had produced in Germany, the mid-1930s were less crowded with publications, but many of the works that would appear after the war were begun during this period, including *Versuch über Wagner*, *Prismen*, and *Philosophie der neuen Musik*. Specifically, this period sees Adorno move into more sociological work, with writings on Karl Mannheim, Oswald Spengler, Thorstein Veblen, and Aldous Huxley, as well as empirical studies of the effects of radio on the reproduction and consumption of music. These studies provide greater insight and substance to the way that Adorno's ideas about dialectics developed following his conversations with Kracauer and Křenek, since they raise the question of how the strange form of listening that becomes necessary in order to comprehend Beethoven, for example, offers an analogue for a form of thinking that can operate forwards and backwards across the experience of a work, while plumbing the depths of its details alongside the range of its expanse. The larger Beethoven project was started in 1938, and Adorno would work on it inconclusively for twenty years, but the focus on a form of listening that was conducive to a reformulation of experience, concomitant to the encounter with the work, indicated not only how this capacity had dwindled in contemporary culture but also what could be found if it were reconsidered in terms of its dialectical logic.

When Adorno states in the introduction to *Philosophie der neuen Musik* that 'philosophy of music is only possible today as philosophy of new music', he is concentrating this idea that the philosophy *of* music is inherently concerned with its force of innovation, that music understood in this way opens it up to the forms of possibility [PNM: 19/13]. The same point should then be taken in reverse, in the sense that philosophy is reflexively reconfigured by way of this understanding of music to focus on its own forms of possibility; that it is inherently concerned with its form as that of an open-ended, non-reified, objective innovation. Consequently, this is a philosophy of new music, of the forms that have arisen in modernity and continue to do so, as those that bring about the greatest demands on thought. This point is central to Adorno's account of Schoenberg in the first section of the book, where he states that musical means have a historical tendency that 'expands and contracts in the course of history'. This is because musical materials are not natural or timeless and 'the more completely they carry historical necessity within them, the less they are more immediately legible as historical characters' [PNM: 38/31]. Such a thought has been consistent throughout his studies but now finds its mature formulation:

> the demands that the material makes on the subject stem from the fact that the "material" itself is sedimented spirit, something socially preformed through human consciousness. As its forgotten former subjectivity such objective spirit of the material has its own laws of motion. Of the same origin as the social process and always pervaded by its traces, what appears to be mere self-movement of the material runs in the same direction as real society, even where neither no longer know anything about one another and feud with one another. Therefore, the composer's engagement with the material is with society precisely insofar as it has migrated into the work, and is not confronted with production as merely external, heteronomous, as a consumer or opponent.
>
> PNM: 39-40/32

The dialectic of this inter-relation is explored through the development of Schoenberg's works, firstly in the early atonal compositions and their expression of the extreme solitude of the individual (which ultimately reverts to a mere monadic objectivity) and then through the total compositional practice of twelve-tone technique (which asserts a reconfiguration of time in the way that melody and harmony are reconceived from the point of the material).[19] Alongside the negative critique of society that arises in these forms there occurs a slender possibility of historical reformulation. The sequence of Schoenberg's works thus becomes significant as it indicates how expression is recorded in music in such a way that its transcript (*Protokoll*) becomes its law of form [PNM: 47/37]. That is, the formal law of the work does not exist outside or prior to the composition but arises out of the sedimentation of expression, which takes up the reading developed in the account of Beethoven but intensifies its focus on expression.

The theme of expression is important because of the way it extends the problematic uncovered in Hegel's discussion of instrumental music into the more contested arena of modernity, and in doing so it uncovers the question of dissonance as an intractable obstacle of expression. As a result, its modern formulation removes it from Romantic notions of an expressive soul and the concomitant ideas of intuition and sensual immediacy. Instead, Schoenberg's approach to expression is as that which is neither fully immediate nor fully sensual but arises from material suffering through its formal configuration. Expression then becomes a form of both knowledge and necessity, and the form that it takes arises from the extremes that characterize it. In refusing to subsume this expression to any universal, Schoenberg finds its appearance not in conceptual mediation but through the extremes of what has become buried within it; the suffering and inarticulacy that are its historical form. This unadulterated suffering takes shape as a paradoxical combination of convulsive paralysis (or, what Adorno had earlier referred to as an outburst and a dead stop), which grants a different structure to the work and places pressure on the forms of tonal harmony [PNM: 47/37]. The experimental or avant-garde nature of the work is thereby found both formally and thematically, as its extreme expression asserts itself against conventional structures and configures itself as such despite its extremity. Hence the apparent difficulty or remoteness of such works is in fact evidence of their historical concreteness and universality, of the isolation and alienation of the individual in modernity, along with the obscurity and provocation of its attempts to express itself. The dialectic of loneliness (*Einsamkeit*) that Adorno refers to is one in which isolation is revealed as socially formed, but that also comes to affect the form of the dialectic itself, which in its own loneliness is stripped of the ability to resolve itself in a universal whole. The apparent autonomy of the work is genuine in its formation, but it is also a critique of the form of unity and self-sufficiency that arises in the individual monad, which is no more than an appearance or semblance that becomes reified through the conventionalization and repetition of the work, thereby giving way to the false objectivity of Neue Sachlichkeit.

Adorno's preference for avant-garde works is not just an aesthetic choice but arises out of the sociohistorical necessity that these works activate, which makes them more than just artworks as they bear a philosophical necessity in terms of the reformulation of the dialectic that is implied in their expression. The avant-garde work is intrinsically critical both artistically and socially and thus demonstrates a remoteness from convention and an aspiration towards another form of life and expression, which indicates how its isolation is dialectically constituted and holds an element of untimeliness as well as illegibility. Because of the pressures that inform this isolation, it is only in the mode of despair that the standpoint of its relief can be adumbrated, however negatively, and so a dialectics *in extremis* emerges as an attenuation of the dialectics of mediation that had perhaps been viable in an earlier age. Hence the extreme risk of these works is a counterpart to their despair, as was also found in their apparent autonomy, as they cannot guarantee their expression or communication and so the 'radically alienated absolute artwork in its blindness tautologically refers to itself alone' [PNM: 50-51/40]. If hope is a kind of belief that one's expectations and desires may be fulfilled, then it is a temporal modification, a form of teleology in which the belief in a (hopefully) guaranteed future enables actions to proceed. The lack of hope is then grounded in the awareness that the future cannot be guaranteed, that there is no natural resonance between the world and one's actions that would permit such a belief in success. There is then a loss of futurity in the face of contingency and alienation, which leaves subject and object estranged from each other. And yet, as Adorno goes on to say, 'inversion necessarily takes place', so that although 'the aesthetic object is to be determined as purely that-there [*Diesda*], it is precisely by virtue of this negative determination, the rejection of everything overarching to which it is subject as its law, that it goes beyond the pure that-there' [PNM: 53/42].

The importance of twelve-tone technique comes from the fact that, as a system of contrasts, it actively instates this movement of reversals and thereby reconstitutes a dialectics in and through a context of extremes. So, in arising from the particularity of its material, the work no longer needs an imposed structure of conventional tones and chords but can express itself by way of its own formal impulses, which occurs in Schoenberg's discovery that compositional structure can arise out of a series of material combinations. However, through this complete reorganization of the material, the identity of its elements is modulated by way of its non-identity such that the 'music gains a completely new relation to the time in which it transpires', which then has an effect on subjectivity as well as tonality [PNM: 58/47]. In the earlier works dissonance was found to be rational as it articulated the actual relation of the constituent sounds, rather than their suppression or coordination through given laws of form. With the appearance of twelve-tone technique this rational constitution is extended into the relation of subjectivity and time, for music is not indifferent to time, but nor is it subservient to it; instead, the initial material expresses itself in its reformulation as its own form of temporal unfolding, its own sequence and development. This total organization forces a reconsideration of structure, as there is no necessary hierarchy between centre or periphery, beginning or end; all parts are equally related to each other, and so the work as a whole, in whatever form this now transpires, does not exist as a development at all. Its relation to time has become dissociated such that, as Adorno writes, 'music drafts the image of a state of the world that, for better or for worse, no longer knows history' [PNM: 62/50].[20]

Thus, the major problem of twelve-tone technique becomes evident, as its dominance of the musical material leads to a formulaic process that can lose sight of its dialectical necessity such that it simply becomes a preformed and static technique, a neutral spatialization. The reversal of enlightenment that would be sketched out in *Dialektik der Aufklärung* is then made apparent in the way that rationality reverts to myth, for even if the rules of composition arise out of the historical tendencies of the material, and emerge to counter its semblance as a work, in doing so they become congealed and irrational in their arbitrariness (a concern Adorno would later express in regard to serialism more generally). Such a reversal is always implicit, but is not inevitable, and its reification of historical possibilities only exposes the pressure to maintain the dialectical scope to do otherwise, a scope that the polemical edge of *Philosophie der neuen Musik* tends to overshadow. Schoenberg's compositions can then be seen to pursue a formal eradication of meaning through this organizational dominance, despite ostensibly doing so in response to the material expression of meaning. In its place, the material becomes that to which the composer responds as if it asserted a force of its own, and as such its form is left empty and opaque and thus dominating. Formal construction thereby becomes its own repressive system, which becomes all the more powerful insofar as it forgets how it arose from the concreteness of the music material and, in forgetting this, the technique forgets its own freedom. Where the artwork sought to struggle against ornamentation, it now becomes sheer (non-dialectical) ornament, to a degree where it is no longer a work of art at all but simply a technically produced objectivity, as his debate with Křenek had suggested. The aim of the work of art to become more than just a work is tragically, ironically, confirmed, which indicates how closely the dialectic of its expression runs the risk of its own annihilation. As Adorno concludes, this ever-present possibility means that it is undecided whether musical ahistoricity (*Geschichtslosigkeit*) 'is dictated by the horrible fixing of society in contemporary forms of domination or whether it points to an end to antagonistic society' [PNM: 81/65]. This eventuality is not accidental but necessarily implied in the expression of the material and to such an extent that there is never any guarantee that it can be avoided. The dialectic is itself placed under pressure as it cannot secure its own realization, since its historical expression bears the seeds of its own ruin from which there is no defence. This is not just to restate the Hegelian point that the results of experience can only come about by way of its labour, but that the form in which such experience occurs is never without its own failure to realize itself, so that this historico-material actuality affects the form and possibility of its conceptualization.

In this way aesthetics not only indicates the basis of the dialectic of enlightenment but also its own limits, the difficulties involved in thinking the artwork and its experience, dialectically or not. And, insofar as aesthetics deals with the vicissitudes of historico-material expression, then it also exposes the milieu of the abstract and the concrete as being unsurpassable. But this suggests that the pressure of Adorno's rethinking of dialectics leads to an impasse, and initially this would appear to be a result of the structure of his essay. On the one hand, the contrast between the works of Schoenberg and those of Stravinsky seems to generate a narrow reading of the expression of material. On the other hand, although the place of historical tendencies in the material was premised at the beginning of the essay, it is perhaps because of the way these tendencies were developed by Schoenberg (as he moved from his early atonal, expressionist works to twelve-tone compositions) that the appearance of a mythologized rationality seems inescapable. However, this was not the only pathway that could have been taken, so it is possible that the impasse is Schoenberg's rather more than Adorno's, in that serialism seems destined for sterility and meaninglessness as its technique annihilates the differences of tones and intervals, leaving the impression that the continuation of the sequence is merely arbitrary [PNM: 73/59]. The force of this account leaves little scope for Adorno to find a way out of the dialectic of mythologized enlightenment. Nevertheless, as he points out, twelve-tone technique is not the origin of this disaster, for it arises out of the expressive dilemma of Romanticism, of whether expression arises through the material in its particularity or through the technique in its formal construction. This was also the dilemma posed by Jean Paulhan in *Les Fleurs de Tarbes*, which played a major role in French discussions of literary creativity at this time, where the question was one of whether the poet should eliminate clichés in order to free their own expression, or whether clichés should be controlled by being designated in advance.[21] In both cases, whether in terms of music or poetry, it is a question of whether there is a pure creative expression that pre-exists the technique, and to which the latter should be subsumed, or whether it is in being organized and structured that the material permits expression. Paulhan refers to these approaches as those of terrorism and rhetoric, and he finds that each leads to the same impasse in which language refutes the strategies to reduce or control it. The same issue arises for Adorno in relation to the status of music after Beethoven, which shows that this is a problem inherent to the discourse of creative expression, for expression is that which seems to be separate from its medium. It is this distinction that gives rise to the sense that it bears a purity that is somehow disturbed through its expression, leading to a confusion between the sense expressed through the material and that expressed by it. Thus, it is a question of an antagonism that is material – 'between the given tonality that must always be reinforced and the substantiality of the particular' – and temporal, for 'if Beethoven developed the musical being out of nothingness in order to be able to determine it entirely as becoming [*Werdendes*], the late Schoenberg destroys it as what has become [*Gewordenes*]' [PNM: 77/61].

The key to the problem of creative expression lies in the contention that expression itself is unitary, from which arises the sense that it is pure. However, as Adorno explains in regard to Schoenberg's early works, the importance of dissonance is that the sounds are not merely dissonant in relation to the standards of consonance but are also dissonant in themselves. As such, they remain faithful to the origin of dissonance in the materiality of suffering, and vice versa, and so 'are no longer media of subjective expression' [PNM: 85/68]. The dissonant chord is one that bears a differentiation in itself and maintains this internal difference in its distinct relations and its changeability. This mode of expression yields a constraint of considerable importance by complicating the development of the music, since the unfolding of its initial notion according to the demands of the material is always in tension with that of the piece in its unfolding. This process is significant for the way that it shows how the music is not fully governed by either its origin or its ostensible aim, and its meaning is neither in its parts nor in the work as a whole but only in the moments of its expression. By virtue of these moments, as he writes, the composition is able 'to transcend the that-there [*Dies-da*] of the thematically posited', and as such the question of these moments is both posed by the composition and left unanswerable [PNM: 98/79]. It is this sense of expression that is unfortunately flattened out in twelve-tone technique, for although it explicitly creates a structure of variation it does so within a framework that limits the range of that variation by rendering the difference between theme and variation indifferent. Twelve-tone technique becomes a system of thorough organization that leaves its parts only externally related to each other and so presents a simulacrum of a society of administered alienation, which thereby prevents genuine change while still presenting the illusion of variation. Themes then have to be inserted artificially, by way of musical citations, so as to provide the basis for variation, but in doing so they merely expose the lack of real possibility attached to their citation.

The significance of Schoenberg for Adorno is that his works very precisely track this movement by which the rationalization of Expressionism becomes subsumed into its own mythology. Not only does this provide a concrete example of the dialectic of enlightenment but, because of the way that Schoenberg consciously struggles against its movement, it also shows how the dialectic becomes available for greater nuance and possibility in being made concrete in this way. And so, in a move that parallels Paulhan's account in *Les Fleurs de Tarbes*, the composer is forced into a situation of constructing their own language while being aware of its obscurity and artificiality, a language that seeks to respond to the particularity of the material and the sociohistorical context. And, insofar as this language cannot ever confirm itself, it becomes ever more brittle and arbitrary, which thereby comes to affect the composer's situation as well. Those who came after Schoenberg, particularly Alban Berg and Anton Webern, were placed in the position of either having to weaken the twelve-tone technique, as with Berg's more expressive, operatic works, or to strengthen it even further, as Webern did with his miniature formal experiments. In both cases the approach to the material begins to lose sight of the dialectic of expressiveness and risks becoming either rigidified or less innovative in its form, and so remaining trapped in a melancholic evocation of change without its actuality. Thus, unfortunately, precisely by following through on the historical tendency of its material, music can fall foul of its own subsumption and lose itself in forms that are lifeless and innocuous. It is only by way of the technique of twelve-tone technique that this subsumption can be avoided, even if it is always in danger of becoming overly didactic and polemical. What is at stake in this reformulation is not just the status of artworks in relation to society, and the mechanisms of ideology that seek to subsume them, but the nature of what is meant by progress or reaction, that is, the relation to history as such, and consequently the relation of reason to contingency. In Schoenberg's works particularly, the abstraction of the technique is such that it only determines the historical element of the material to a general degree so that it remains alienated, stripped of its apparently natural objectivity but no closer to the subject as a result. Hence, confronted by a music that has become its own language, the subject finds just the coldness of an empty self-determination without relation, much as Hegel had suggested in his warnings about instrumental music. However, for Adorno, Schoenberg's later works are saved by way of his ability to neglect the absoluteness of his technique, to forget its comprehensive grasp and return to the sonorous possibilities of the material; only in this way is the dominance of the technique over the material suspended, without abandoning it entirely.

As noted, however, the formal development of dissonance leads to a fracturing of the work, which is revealed in its incomplete rationalization and is indicative of the contradictions of society, but more importantly, it opens the work up to thinking, without which it would appear unitary and immaculate and only available to intuition and a semblance of identity. By contrast, the fragmentary work displays its partial rationalization as pathways of thinking through which the contradictions of society can be reflected, even if they remain unreconciled in being so reflected. But this failure is itself a cognitive experience: 'only when the contradiction is measured against the possibility of its settlement is it not merely registered but known'. The artwork thus bears its own knowledge in the form of its antagonism to reality and, as a result, knowledge is ruptured in its form because of its contingency and failure to resolve itself. This means that the artwork thereby presents a different mode of knowledge taking place in the world, since the knowledge-character of the artwork 'becomes radical in that moment when it is no longer content with itself' [PNM: 119/97]. Such an image of the artwork is self-destructive: it is an image of the work suspending its status as a work of art in favour of reality, for it is in this way that its critical content can be liberated. It is only in the fragmentary work that such a collapse of its status and position is made possible, and only insofar as its fragmentation implies this self-destructive collapse. In its objectivity the work presents the demands of the social context, and in the breaking apart of this objectivity, it negatively presents the forms of what is not existent in that context. This duplicity is central to the form of the work as that which is both totally organized in itself and yet counters itself by referring elsewhere; the autonomy and unity of the work is determined by this contradictory sense of organization, which becomes its own contradictory meaning and meaninglessness. The model of autonomy that Adorno is sketching out is not merely in counterpoint to the paradigm of expression but also to the tendency to respond to music in terms of a 'language' of music, with its own inherent structure and sense. In a powerful if unusual conclusion, Adorno claims that the origin of music, in reaching beyond meaning, more closely resembles crying, not as a sentimental expression but as the physical opening up of the face to the alienated world. The face, while part of the body, dissolves in crying and this gesture dissolves the tension separating it from the world. However, this gesture is only partly a reconciliation as it is also the step by which the alienated world is not just entered but also drawn back into the subject [PNM: 122/99; cf. AT: 410/276].[22] In this way, the externalization and return that comprises Hegel's thought is coupled to a more mimetic loosening, or dissolution, in which any return occurs by way of a return to the material. Thus, artworks rupture their own dialectic of form by necessity, by force of the need to respond to objective antagonisms, no matter how remotely these may appear to be reflected in the material. It is as a result of this failure in their form that such artworks risk oblivion, even as they present the most strident critique of forgetting.

This essay on Schoenberg can be considered the first extended formulation of Adorno's views on aesthetics and dialectics, and as is evident it conveys much of what would be developed in *Dialektik der Aufklärung*. This point is made clear by the epigraph that Adorno adds to 'Schönberg und der Fortschritt', which is taken from Hegel's discussion of the place of pure insight in Enlightenment thought. Pure insight is the distinguishing mode of Enlightenment thought, it is that thinking in which the concept alone is actuality, which it pursues in the certainty of its self-consciousness of this fact and independently of any other constraints. However, this pursuit necessarily yields its own dialectic, for 'pure insight is at first without content and is instead the pure disappearance of it; but through its negative movement towards what is negative to it, it will realize itself and give itself a content' [PG: 294/329]. Thus, the apparently formal emptiness of Schoenberg's technique becomes the means by which its content can be realized, which is a critical step in the realization of thought itself. The use of Hegelian ideas here is itself a relatively novel and significant development in Adorno's thinking, as they are being taken up in order to support the readings of Schoenberg's technique in its combination of thought and material, not only in terms of an analysis of the social and philosophical dimensions of the artwork but also in regards to the notion of expression more generally.[23] As such, this essay effectively presents the culmination of the thought of dialectics that Adorno had been developing over the previous fifteen years, especially in terms of the nexus of natural-history. As has been seen, the place and status of music becomes a way of examining the development of thought in its relation to the abstract and concrete, and material and ideal, and yet throughout this approach the musical analysis has not been a mere example but a way of indicating how music operates by way of its own logic, which has as much bearing on thinking as the reverse. The problem of instrumental music that remained at the end of Hegel's account is the critical pivot around which the dialectic of form is reformulated, along with the experience of temporality and the kind of relation that emerges out of the reification of history. Moreover, the position of the artwork comes to put in question the nature of knowledge and its status in the world by way of the collapse of its autonomy as a work.

While the key aspect of expression is reformulated by way of dissonance, the relation of dialectics to dissonance is not fully worked out despite the strong role that the latter comes to play in Adorno's thought and the implications it bears for a thinking of dialectics. The two modes are not easily compatible, for although dissonance reveals a way of thinking about how identity is unsettled from within by the manifestation of difference and instability, it does so without any intrinsic movement of unfolding, whether this would imply resolution or not. Instead, dissonance operates through the rupture and suspense of form, without any implicit direction or goal; it is not linked to any mode of development, but simply persists. In saying as much, Adorno is separating dissonance from a sense in which it opposes consonance so that it can instead 'hold all possibilities of expression' by virtue of its internal fluctuations and contradictions. This discovery is found initially in the work of Wagner, for whom the difference between consonance and dissonance as referring to pleasure and pain, respectively, no longer holds, since dissonance in itself bears a range of contradictory feelings. However, insofar as there is now only dissonance, as it has become freed from its relation to consonance, it 'essentially ceases to function expressively at all'. As a result, it becomes harmonic material as it is 'wholly articulated and "polyphonic" in itself' and is thus able to be a constructive medium. This means that dissonance becomes its own form of dialectic, as is found in Schoenberg's early works where it is able to operate 'as the binding principle of harmonic selection'.[24] For even if it no longer falls into the same mode of harmonic development, its internal instability allows for the appearance of disparate tensions and inclinations. The point of distinction between dissonance and dialectics, which will become more important as Adorno develops his thinking of negative dialectics, is that dissonance is not primarily critical as it remains a mode of expression. However, in his later writings he will state that 'dissonance is the truth about harmony', which concisely captures his response to Hegel in that harmony is no longer a state in which truth can be found, for it has unfolded itself into a form that is more truthful [AT: 168/110]. It is thus that the aspect of responding to pain and suffering, and of realizing the singular and concrete elements of (musical) moments, remains central to the notion of negative dialectics. What becomes problematic is the necessity of finding space for this expression and of realizing its critical force. This is the tension that informs the relation of negative dialectics as such, which prohibits it from any positive statement or resolution. Dissonance radically suspends the fulfilment of dialectics, while still providing points of centrifugal rupture. Insofar as this remains a process in which internal contradictions work themselves out, it remains dialectical, but these contradictions are deeper and more intractable on account of their lack of a positive historical frame. There is no hope of resolution as there is no ground for hope at all, but this does not lead to nihilism, instead, the state of despair yields its own unpredictable results.

IV An Additional Factor

At the moment when Hegel is discussing the apparent obsolescence of art and the movements of art itself appear to be moving towards the absolute, this disparity is just beginning to emerge. The problem inherent in the so-called end of art thesis, which is concerned not so much with an end as a transformation in its role and status in the modern world, is that the loss of a universal ground and meaning for art in the secularization of enlightenment thinking is also the beginning of the absolutization of art as art. Art becomes a thing in itself, as it were, at the moment of its disappearance from the immediate milieu of life; art 'survives itself, it drives itself out', as Hegel remarked in 1828, and it thereby begins to appear as works of art, through which are also founded the role of galleries, museums, and concert halls, as well as the concomitant critics and historians of art.[25] From now on the appearance of art will be inextricable from its own uncertainty, its interrogation of its own existence, an interrogation that renders it both absolute and unfinished since this questioning can never be resolved as it only refers the work insistently back to itself. The praxis of the work thereby becomes intertwined with its theory as the very problem that the work poses to itself, and so this combined interrogation is also an examination of the work's relation to its material, social, and historical background. Art then becomes the name for this complex of experimentation or, rather, art understood as avant-garde, for it is only those artworks that explicitly address these questions and hold open their multiple reflections without seeking to diminish their seriousness or depth that remain true to this interrogation. Such a qualification is important for the way that it distinguishes the avant-garde work from those that suppress or deny the conceptual and historical problematic of art – the fact that it is always a question of and to itself – and instead seek to return to some kind of givenness of sense, a form of contextual immediacy that reassures the work and its experience. At the moment when art becomes a product and seems to die from its loss of transcendental value, it finds that in this exposure its doubt and insecurity becomes its praxis, the question that is its own origin and modality. In being thrust into history and into the world, art's reflexive absoluteness at the same time expels it from history and the world, leaving it in a perpetual hypothesis at the margins of existence. At the moment, then, when art seems to have become a thing of the past it enters a site both within and without time; practically ubiquitous and theoretically dislocated. Equally, the normative categories of aesthetic judgement become displaced through the dissonance in both its material and its temporal forms, as has been shown, since it is no longer the case that standards of beauty, for example, can be organized according to certain human and social norms of sensual embodiment in which consonance is seen as given. The Romantic and humanistic values of holistic meaningful engagement become suspended in the absence of any ground to subtend this holism; there is no natural security of form in the world, not just because its norms have become uprooted but also because sensuous holism is permanently altered by its theoretical self-interrogation. Abstraction and concreteness become notions that are as derivative of the manner of art's actualization through self-interrogation as are those of theory and praxis.[26]

In his persistent engagement with aesthetics Adorno was not attempting to aestheticize philosophy but was seeking a dialectics of the avant-garde, a thinking that would pursue the same complex of interrogation that marked the modernity of art, and thus also marked philosophy. In the avant-garde as it emerged in its post-Hegelian breadth, thinking finds itself engaged in a praxis that is its own interrogation, which is to say that it becomes an aesthetic theory, a theory that is materially, socially, and historically implicated in the world while remaining critically absolute and absolutely critical. This is a philosophy that is dialectically experimental. Alongside the way that the autonomy of philosophy is reasserted, even as it is undermined by reinforcing it with insights from sociology, psychoanalysis, and music, there is the historical impasse that it enters in being consigned to anachronism. Because of the aporetic ruptures that arise through its self-interrogation it is unable to develop or evolve; it cannot build on itself as it overturns its own grounds. Instead, a new form of temporality is found in its fragmentary interventions, one that is without development and yet is not static, a dissonant temporality that bears within itself both destruction and regeneration. This is not to associate Adorno with any one manifestation of the avant-garde as it was known in the twentieth century, but to indicate that the intrinsic limits within the form of the avant-garde as such, which lead to its collapse or subsumption, are those that also indicate its non-developmental history, its refusal of tradition. Hence there is no melancholic longing or Romantic valorization attached to this failure to establish itself on its own terms, but rather the awareness of the tasks inherent to a discontinuous history.

It is useful to turn to an example here:

> When Mr Keuner was asked what exactly was meant by "reversal of perspective", he related the following anecdote: Two brothers who were very attached to each other had a curious habit. They indicated the events of the day with a stone: a white stone for the happy moments, a black stone for moments of misfortune and displeasure. However, when evening came and they compared the contents of their jars, one found only white stones, the other only black stones. Intrigued by such consistency in the way of experiencing the same fate so differently, they agreed to take advice from a man renowned for the wisdom of his words. "You don't talk to each other enough", said the wise man. "Let each one justify the reasons for their choice, let them seek the causes for it". So they did from then on. As they quickly discovered, the first remained faithful to the white stones and the second to the black stones, but in both jars the number of stones had diminished. Instead of about thirty, there were hardly more than seven or eight. Only a short time had passed before the wise

man saw the two brothers return. Their features bore the mark of great sadness. "Not so long ago", said one, "my jar would fill up with pebbles the colour of night, despair permanently occupied me, I confess, I was only living through inertia. Now, I rarely place more than eight stones there, but what these eight signs of misery represent is so intolerable to me that I can no longer live in such a state". And the other: "As for me, I piled up white stones every day. Today, I only count seven or eight of them, but these fascinate me so much that I can never happen to evoke these happy moments without immediately wanting to relive them more intensely and, to be honest, eternally. This desire torments me". The wise man smiled as he listened to them. "Come on, everything is fine, things are taking shape. Persevere. One more word. On occasion, ask yourself the question: why does the game of the jar and the stones absorb you in this way?" When the two brothers met the wise man again, it was to declare: "We asked ourselves the question; but no answer. So, we posed it to the whole village. See the commotion that reigns there. In the evening, squatting in front of their houses, whole families discuss white stones and black stones. Only the chiefs and notables stand aside. Black or white, they say, mockingly, a stone is a stone, and all are equal". The old man did not hide his satisfaction. "The matter is proceeding as planned. Don't worry. Soon the question will no longer arise; it has become unimportant, and perhaps one day you will doubt that you asked it". Shortly thereafter, the old man's predictions were confirmed in the following way: a great joy had seized the people of the village; at dawn after a restless night, the sun lit up, stuck on the sharp stakes of a palisade, the freshly severed heads of the notables and chiefs.[27]

The significance of this story lies in two aspects: that of reversal, and that of the punchline whose form, as Adorno writes, is that of a hiatus, which, in opposition to the convention for pronouncing verdicts that would conclude a narrative, 'awakens the semblance of a reflective new beginning'. But this is only a semblance, for the appearance of the hiatus is a complex node of involution, neither moving on or back but stepping aside. It becomes a gesture of language itself, as Adorno finds especially in the writings of Kraus, for whom this gesture is one in which language steps back from its apodictic and expressive aspects to mimic the fact of language as a gesture [NL2: 384-85/54-55]. The punchline provides no closure but confounds reading with the introduction of a new movement, which in its interruption forces reading and thought into a momentary recoil. In this way the reversal that the tale unfolds is recapitulated in its form, compelling a revision of thinking, just as language is brought to the point of no longer simply being language as expression but of being language-like (*sprachähnlich*), an act that necessarily bears its own kind of sense.

One of the most characteristic moves of Adorno's thinking is to pose antinomies as chiasmic. Thus, nature and history, or freedom and necessity, are recast in forms that make possible the overcoming of their antinomies by virtue of their double articulation: nature realizes itself as history insofar as history realizes itself as nature. In this way, the static division that would seem to bring about an aporia is found to dissolve itself through its destabilization. There is no simple or linear transition from one state to the other but a complex contrapuntal reformulation in which there is neither assimilation nor cancellation. Both terms continue to exist without losing their distinctiveness, but through the chiasmus they become complexly interwoven as each is found to affect and be affected by the other. As such, the method of immanent critique is doubled as the contradictions of each side are unfolded and in doing so their duplicity undoes the possibility of a single path or goal for this unfolding development; each continues to unsettle the other in a way that cannot be reduced to the simple mediation or negation of the one by the other. However, the actual movement from antinomy to chiasmus remains unclear, and Adorno attempts to explain it through his discussion of what he calls the additional factor (*das Hinzutretende*), that extra something that arises to bypass or short circuit an antinomy. Faced by the aporia of deciding between freedom and necessity, for example, following one's own whims or abiding by the natural law, as Kant would frame it, the subject is torn by the equal weight of both pathways, their actual contradiction. Or, in other terms, in the division between the necessity and the impossibility of revolution the aporia remains unbreakable until the intervention of something extra, the additional factor that Adorno deliberately refuses to designate with a more formal or conceptual name. This factor arises as a jolt to the smooth causal chain of actions and events, and it does so by virtue of its commingling of the bodily and the mental [ND: 226/226-27].[28] Such a rupture is an action that appears to have arisen outside conscious planning but also to be fully invested with consciousness as it seems to be a direct act of will. Furthermore, it appears to be a mere material intrusion, an accident, but also to have the necessity of following from what is required of a situation. In this undecidability of the material and the volitional this factor becomes decisive, and in turn reveals a convergence of freedom and reason, of the conceptual and nonconceptual. Such acts seem to occur in situations of extremity, of desperation, when the necessity and freedom at issue are pushed to their most acute point of contradiction. But from this extreme contradiction an additional element appears, realizing a possibility that would have hitherto remained an impossibility, for in its extremity the bodily realizes itself as its other, as consciousness, just as the reverse is the case, and it is in the movement of this chiasmus that the aporia of its antinomy is breached. The cases that Adorno considers, the *experimenta crucis* of Kantian moral philosophy, are decisive or critical experiments, ones in which the empirical results can accord with only one theoretical interpretation, but in the additional factor there arises a cross-wiring in which the empirical takes on a theoretical value just as the theoretical finds itself appearing in the empirical.

Adorno's discussion of the additional factor occurs in his 1963 lectures on moral philosophy, which were delivered at the same time as he was writing *Negative Dialektik*, and in this initial appearance it is aligned with the problem of relating theory and practice.[29] Or, rather, there arises an additional factor in the disruption of this conventional division and the concomitant distinction between a Kantian ethics of conviction, which arises from the idealized situation of the will, and a Hegelian ethics of responsibility, which arises from the social framework of practice. The difficulty of discussing the additional factor lies in the fact that it is neither theoretical nor practical but exceeds and traverses both aspects, thereby indicating the insufficiency of such a distinction for any approach to morality. Nevertheless, this difficulty suggests the importance of the notion for moral philosophy, the task of which, as he goes on to state, is above all the production of consciousness. This production is complicated by the fact that the additional factor is neither theoretical nor practical but is related to that element of theory that resists its immediate translation into instrumental purposes and that, by virtue of this resistance, exhibits the practical element that theory bears within itself (its own gesture as theory). Adorno's initial attempt to define the additional factor is in terms of the spontaneous reaction to particular situations. It is as such that it exceeds theory and also refers to that aspect without which any valid practice would not be possible: a contingent material factor that is both a resistance to theory and practice and the means by which the one is found in the other, which is the basis of its moral status. The example that Adorno gives, an attempt by a German officer to kill Hitler in 1943, combines this sense of an act of resistance that is both irrational in its desperation and rational in its necessity, which places it beyond any simple division of acts as volitional or not; while the act was clearly one of free will it is also just as clearly one that has become entirely determined as necessary by the sociohistorical circumstances. Observation of these circumstances reveals that the action is both unavoidable and impossible, and by virtue of this impasse theory shows itself to be already involved in the resistance of practice; it is already taking up a non-theoretical stance whose desperation is the mark of its manifestation. Moral philosophy, as Adorno concludes this point, is itself contradictory, since it is not a question of merely discussing these issues in the abstract but of confronting their antinomies in such a way that consciousness itself emerges in and as the response to the problem, a response that is never only theoretical but is a form of action.

This model of historical change was taken up earlier in the analysis of musical material and the demands placed on the composer in relation to its conventions and possibilities. And, as was seen in the discussion of tact, the demands of the material allow for such a historical reformulation as musical material is never simply empty or given, and so composition is never simply free or constrained. It is because Adorno approaches philosophical issues of logic or morality by way of these aesthetic problems that he can realize the mode of chiasmus and find the key to his own sense of dialectics. The musical background to this renewed sense of dialectics is to be found in the temporality of its movement, as time is the ongoing experience that one is not what one was, which dialectics models, and it is this experience that music makes tangible and concrete. This complex notion of time implies both a sense of loss and of survival, and of the apparent but only possible notion of retrieval or realization, which is then enfolded and unfolded in Adorno's sense of dialectics. Music conveys the passage of this movement in logical and experiential forms and so makes available a sense of fulfilment that is not actual, an identity of identity and non-identity, as it were, that is never realizable – which is to say that it becomes a non-identity of identity and non-identity, which is the secular form of metaphysics that is marked by the name of natural-history. The latter point is then brought out in the non-identity of transience and persistence, which is to be found in the allegorical forms of ruins and decay, but also more formally in the notion of a suspended fall, otherwise seen in the use of a stuttered halt or aporetic series.

In an article on punctuation marks Adorno makes a similar estimation in regard to semicolons; as he notes, they combine a full stop, at which the voice would fall, and also a comma, which would cause the fall of the voice to be suspended. As a result, the semicolon is 'truly a dialectical image'. While this reading might seem to be no more than a witty aside, it should be recalled that musical notation ultimately arises from the cadences of the voice, which are recorded and regularized as they are transcribed onto the page, just as punctuation marks provide the measure of the reader's breath, the span of what is taken in. Thus, these marks do not merely provide a written account of vocal tones and rhythms, converting sound into a visual script, but mark the imbrication of thought and materiality, the topological translation of the multidimensional structuring of the finite and infinite into the two-dimensional plane of the marks on the page. So, for Adorno, it is history that 'has sedimented itself in punctuation marks, and it is this, far more than meaning or grammatical function that gazes out, petrified and with a slight shudder, from every one of them' [NL1: 107/92]. But the grammatical function is affected as well, for in its historical-syntactical disjunction a different mode of judgement is apparent. As Horkheimer noted in 1937, the classificatory judgements that are formed in relation to reality are indicative of their worldview:

> There are connections between the forms of judgement and the historical periods, about which a brief indication may be given. The categorical judgement is typical of pre-bourgeois society: this is the way it is, and people cannot do otherwise [*so ist es, der Mensch kann nichts daran ändern*]. The hypothetical or disjunctive forms of judgement belong especially to the bourgeois world: under certain circumstances this effect can take place; it is either this way or another [*entweder ist es so oder anders*]. Critical theory explains: it need not be so; people can change what is [*es muß nicht so sein, die Menschen können das Sein ändern*], the circumstances for this are now available.[30]

Horkheimer terms the last point an existential judgement, insofar as it affects the very modality of existence, and it is this change that Adorno is attempting to unfold in *Minima Moralia*, which is an attempt to explore the basis of contemporary social life by way of its seemingly marginal individual experiences, and in such a way that they become formally tangible so that we are able (potentially, critically) to perceive how they might be actualized otherwise.

As a result, to explore the status of the additional factor is to explore the relation between thought and gesture in terms of the contrast between the sociohistorical formation of gesture and its individual reflective reproduction. While this contrast has been addressed through Adorno's analysis of musical material, it is necessary to move into a different area to expose the full range of its aesthetic problems and possibilities and this means discussing the different sense of aesthetics that arises through sensuality. The presence of this thought in Adorno's work, or in critical theory more generally, seems marginal until the works of the Marquis de Sade are recalled. In just the same way that the argument in *Philosophie der neuen Musik* is structured by the interplay between the extremes of Schoenberg and Stravinsky, so too is the argument about the nature of reason developed by way of its most substantial historical extremes: Odysseus and Sade's Juliette. It is the latter argument that takes place in *Dialektik der*

Aufklärung, but the place of Sade's thought in this argument has often been missed, with considerable consequences for understanding the scope of critical theory itself and particularly the work of Horkheimer.

Horkheimer's response to Sade is twofold, reflecting the tension in Sade's own work between a desire for complete sexual liberation and the abstraction and rationalization involved in the systematic pursuit of this desire. In this way Sade exemplifies and extends a basic tension within the Enlightenment itself that persists into the project of modernity and can be captured in the question of whether sexual freedom is compatible with the idea of utopia, for the latter is fundamentally an idea, a rational extrapolation and reconstruction of society under certain terms. Sade's importance is to have shown this tension in its most naked and extreme form, which only indicates that it is most often concealed or denied. His ability to do so lies with the rather modest fact that his work is concerned throughout with the conditions of pleasure, but in exploring these conditions of possibility he also makes it clear that, as a result, thought cannot be considered in the absence of its relation to pleasure, and, conversely, that what is pleasurable is not without its cognitive dimensions. In saying as much the apparent division between materialism and idealism is shown to be spurious, and it is perhaps only by virtue of the extremes to which Sade pursues this inter-relation, both formally and thematically, that this point can be demonstrated. However, this fact also raises the question of its compatibility with society, for pleasure is intrinsically irrational in that it is opaque and uncontrollable, and yet its absence is unthinkable in any thought of utopia. It is perhaps thus that the interest in criminology and sexology becomes as central to the experience of modernity as that of urbanism or technology, as it is precisely the illusion of creating a logical discourse of crime and sexuality that exposes its centrality to the Enlightenment project and the impossibility of completing this discourse. Modernity is then the experience of the aporias of the Enlightenment, of living through the necessity and impossibility of realizing the inter-relation of thought and desire (the neoliberal project would then be the biopolitical capture of desire by reducing it to commercial and pharmacological terms). What Sade shows so emphatically is that this capture can only be an illusion, but breaking that illusion reveals a profound disintegration of the social.

Violence is not merely an unfortunate atavism, it cannot be suppressed or rationalized without causing a greater and more toxic violence, since it is not an accidental part of our existences. Violence is inescapable because it is part of desire, and desire is cruel because of its inherent egoism, all it wants is to satisfy itself and this drive cannot be managed or made harmless. In this sense Sade is perhaps the most honest writer and, as Horkheimer will suggest in the next chapter, there is perhaps a sense of 'morality' that arises from reading Sade, in that we are exposed to an extreme fact of humanity, not within a framework that can draw a lesson from this knowledge, however, except to bring about a realization that it is there. Perhaps, Horkheimer writes, the exposure to which Sade's works bring us is enough to strip away the mystery of desire, its ideological explanations, and show it in its banality and endlessness. It serves no purpose and accepts no attempts to safely contain it within rational frameworks. It is not surprising to find that *Les Cent Vingt Journées de Sodome* resurfaces in Germany in 1904, during the period when the first sexological research is developing (and only fourteen years after Krafft-Ebing defines the term 'sadism'), and that the very nature of this science is affected by that which it had discovered. Horkheimer's interest in Sade is thus not unusual given this background, and for a scholar equally interested in Marxist sociology and the possibilities of a sensuous materialism it becomes inevitable that Sade would become a crucial if minor part in the development of critical theory.

Part Two

Refractions of Aesthetics

3

Horkheimer, Sade, and Erotic Reason

Dialektik der Aufklärung is one of the most important works of critical theory of the late twentieth century, but it is also one of the most contentious and misunderstood. It was composed by Horkheimer and Adorno in the early 1940s and is made up of different elements that, initially, do not seem to be clearly coordinated. It begins with a theoretical chapter on the concept of enlightenment before leading into two excurses that seek to develop and apply the thinking of this first chapter, which are then followed by polemical analyses of contemporary cultural and political issues. It is, as the subtitle of the work makes clear, a series of philosophical fragments, and as such it has resisted the attempts of critics to assess the nature of the work as a whole. As a result, some parts of the work have received considerable attention, while others have been overlooked. For example, the first excursus, on Odysseus, which was written by Adorno, has been widely discussed, while the second, by Horkheimer, on Sade's *Juliette*, has largely been avoided by commentators. There are a number of reasons why this might be the case: it could be that this chapter is too ambitious (and perhaps less compelling), both theoretically and rhetorically, in its attempt to draw together an analysis of Kant, Sade, and Nietzsche, and this has deterred readers already challenged by the intense conceptual histories developed in the first two chapters. Or, alternatively, it may have to do with the different careers of Horkheimer and Adorno, in which the extensive later work of the latter has helped contextualize the place of *Dialektik der Aufklärung* in his thought, whereas the fact that Horkheimer's work (or perhaps Sade's) is not so well known, or so well regarded, has led to a feeling that this contribution is a minor and less significant aspect of the work. While these interpretations may have some validity, it is also the case that Horkheimer's chapter has an essential role to play in the development of the work. As the authors explain in the preface, the excurses have the specific task of explicating the theoretical theses of the first chapter, which sought to determine the constitutive intertwining of enlightenment and mythology in the history of European society. As a result, Adorno's excursus on Odysseus seeks to examine the origins of this conceptual knot, while the excursus on Sade is concerned with reading his works as 'the implacable consummation of enlightenment'. In this way the critique of enlightenment around which the work is oriented is not merely an historical analysis, which exposes the ways in which reason has sought to dominate nature and society, but is also 'intended to prepare a positive concept of it that liberates it from its entanglement in blind domination' [DA: 21–22/ xviii]. It is only thus that the work can develop a dialectic of enlightenment.[1]

As a result, Horkheimer's reading of Sade is intrinsic to the critical dialectic that the book unfolds and so its omission from the accounts of commentators becomes more problematic.[2] To rectify this lack I will first contextualize Horkheimer's account within the course of his writings in the late 1930s, which will provide the background necessary to understand his interest in the relation of sensuality and reason in the history of bourgeois thought, that is, in terms of the development of individualist and rational thinking. From this position it will be easier to understand why Horkheimer turned to Sade to provide an explication of enlightenment in its consummate form. However, it will also become apparent that problems emerge in Horkheimer's account that leave it undeveloped both as a critique and as a preparation for a liberated enlightenment. Some aspects of this problem are unique to the writing of *Dialektik der Aufklärung*, which leaves open the possibility that the suggestions that Horkheimer perceived in Sade's writings could be developed otherwise. In this way, the role of Sade's thought in the Enlightenment as such is given greater significance, one in which it is not merely an extreme example of unbridled reason but reveals the potential for an entirely reformulated understanding of reason on the basis of its erotic constitution and manifestation.

I Sadean Enlightenment

At the end of June 1936 Adorno wrote to Horkheimer to say the following, 'I am unable to leave London and return to Germany without having at least told you that your work on sadism, the study of which I have now completed, has seized and moved me to the core'. The work that Adorno was referring to was an essay by Horkheimer entitled 'Egoismus und Freiheitsbewegung' that had just been published in the *Zeitschrift für Sozialforschung*, and was possibly his most important essay from this period of his work. Horkheimer himself felt that this essay was one of his best, and it became a crucial touchstone for the work of Benjamin, Marcuse, Löwenthal, and others, as well as Adorno. However, what is intriguing about Adorno's comment is that Sade is barely mentioned in this essay; his name occurs just once, towards the very end of the essay, and only in parenthesis. What then made Adorno refer to this essay as Horkheimer's Sadismusarbeit? Moreover, the point is repeated as Adorno elaborates on his admiration: 'I know nothing of yours that has such a power of illumination and such a "spark" as the third chapter, especially the conclusion, the salvation of sadism and the abysmal interpretation of Aristotle; it is impossible for me to say more than that I agree with this work right to its heart'.[3]

Horkheimer's essay was a long historical study of the development of individualism that focused on the ambivalent role of self-interest. Emerging in its modern form with the Reformation and Renaissance, the notion of self-interest was critical to the development of capitalism and fascism, which formed the context of Horkheimer's thinking. The intriguing point that he raises, which forms the focus of the ambivalence that the study examines, is that while revolutionary movements have ostensibly worked towards the emancipation of humanity, they are also coupled with the most extreme egoism. Moreover, this egoism is unthinkable without its relation to pleasure and self-denial. In fact, it is the place of pleasure in the complex of self-interest and self-denial found in revolutionary movements that draws out the complex dialectic at the heart of Enlightenment thought. For while the revolutionary ambitions of the Enlightenment called for the liberation of humanity, in practice this was done on the basis of the denial of pleasure and the suppression of self-interest in favour of a national project of rejuvenation. But the revolutionary movement itself is, as we have come to see, riddled with self-interest and cruelty; liberation and happiness is not for the masses but only for the covert forces of bourgeois reactionaries. The masses instead find that their labour in the revolutionary movement is one of sacrifice and abnegation; freedom is not for them, or even for their descendants, but only greater obedience and coercion. Pleasure becomes a critical term in this framework as it refers to aspects of the human condition, bodily and sensual pleasures, which may have seemed to be part of the aims of emancipation but in practice have been disregarded as elements to be overcome by social education, either because they are elements of an inherently sinful bodily nature, or conversely, as aspects of a romanticized natural state that society no longer supports. Thus, in contrast to its putative aims, the rational ambitions of emancipation give way to cruelty and violence, not just in the form of an ascetic denial of the bodily, but also by privileging the virtues of cruelty and violence in the name of patriotism and progress. Rather than the revolution being geared to increasing freedom and happiness, the Enlightenment bears a suppression of these in favour of rationalized cruelty, as is exemplified by the guillotine, which is pursued in later times by the intensification of austerity and insecurity [EFB: 77/101–2]. The existence of these conditions then becomes a tacit demonstration of their justness: those who are miserable are so because they have failed to exert the required cruelty in relation to themselves and instead dwell in sloth and iniquity, indulging in bodily pleasures that only confirm their sinfulness. However, this is only the fate of the masses, the bourgeoisie who have channelled and harvested the results of the revolution find themselves rewarded by the triumph of self-interest, the pursuit of profit for its own sake, and the indulgence of pure egoism. But where, in the early phases of capitalist development, the pursuit of self-interest was mutually constrained, in the later phases of high capitalism and fascism the greater accumulation of political and economic control leads to greater indulgence and cruelty. As a result, social and bodily inequalities become strengthened and extended as pleasure and happiness are reduced to ever more alienated forms (sport and shopping and entertainment and other modes of prescribed hedonism) as a result of their denial and suppression.

As is apparent, Horkheimer's essay is very rich and draws together many of the points of the approach of critical theory, along with case studies of Savonarola, Luther, and Robespierre. But it is at the end of the essay that an additional aspect of the analysis emerges, which presents the most interesting suggestion. After discussing Freud and the essentialization of the death drive, which far from appearing innovative now seems to be another form of the Calvinist/Cartesian denial that has formed modern European notions of individuality, in that it demonizes the natural, indicating an inherent and mythologized compulsion of the body to destroy itself, a body that then needs to be controlled and educated. While Freud is right to say that violence and cruelty are not contingent aspects of humanity, this point needs to be understood in terms of the sociohistorical transformations that have exposed or suppressed their existence, rather than simply displacing them into the biological.[4] The role of egoism remains pervasive and problematic because the damage it causes is not merely part of bodily constitution but is variably concretized: 'In the present epoch egoism has become actually destructive, both the fettered and diverted egoism of the masses as well as the archaic egoistic principle of the economy, which still shows only its most brutal side. When the latter is overcome, the former can become productive in a new sense.' How this is to happen is an open question, Horkheimer admits, and neither Marx nor Freud can help.

> But there are signs in recent times that point in one and the same direction for a solution. In opposition to the prevailing spirit, some thinkers have neither veiled nor minimised nor accused egoism but professed to it in themselves. Not to the abstract and pitiful fiction as which it appears for some political economists and for Jeremy Bentham but to enjoyment, to the highest degree of happiness, which also includes the satisfaction of cruel impulses. They have not idealised any of the drives that were historically given to them as original but have denounced the distortion of the drives brought about by official ideology. These thinkers, since Aristippus and Epicurus, have essentially only been understood in modern history in terms of their opposition to prevailing morality. From which they have been defended and condemned. But there is a peculiar fact [*eine eigene Bewandtnis*] about these apologists of unrestricted egoism. In tracking down the scorned impulsive drives in themselves and raising them to consciousness without rejection or minimisation, these powers lost their demonic force.
>
> EFB: 86–87/108

Horkheimer does not at this point turn to Sade, although the resonance with his works is obvious, but to Nietzsche, for whom, as he notes in passing, Sade was a precursor. But Adorno's reading directs us to the stronger resonance that Sade's works play in this context, which is reflected in the extraordinary conclusion that Horkheimer draws, a conclusion that brings together the two points from the above citation that are the most contentious: the association of happiness with cruelty and the possibility that the force of this power can be exorcized.

On the surface it might seem that Horkheimer is trying to draw a moralistic conclusion, but the point is more acute, for it is rather a question of a liberation from ascetic morality that would lead to a transformation in human existence. However, this change does not involve learning from these violent excesses but something more profound. According to Aristotle's theory of drama, Horkheimer notes, the sight of suffering in tragedy causes pleasure, and in satisfying this drive the viewers are changed. Naturally, he adds, the application of this theory to the modern age is problematic since any suggestion of the instrumentalization of suffering is abhorrent. One does not create suffering in order to gain from it, and indeed nothing could be further from Sade's works. Instead, the combination of suffering with pleasure alone, without reason or aim, releases cruelty from any illusory justification or rationalization.⁵ Cruelty is not for anything, it serves no purpose, and its sheer enjoyment neutralizes its ideological use; it is simply part of the expression of self-interest in the same way as pleasure. It is just such a sense of catharsis and empathy that Horkheimer is indicating, insofar as cruelty is a pleasure that is received just as much as given, and just as little valued for itself. This sense of catharsis, he concludes, presupposes a changed humanity [EFB: 88/110]. In a way, violence ceases to exist from this perspective, for although it remains violent and cruel and inescapably so, it is no longer violence as taboo or as instrumental, it is, as Sade showed, banal. Whether it is possible to think through the ambivalence of this thought, which is, as Adorno pointed out, abyssal, is the challenge that Sade's writings bring before us, and rising to this challenge would inevitably imply a transformation in the form of human life.⁶

It is worth pointing out that with this thought Horkheimer not only moves away from Marx and Freud but also that the nature of the dialectic itself has changed, since this renewed sense of violence is one in which it is neither the mythologized rationality of warfare nor the rationalized mythology of original sin. For, in becoming banal, violence is no longer engaged in any form of enlightenment but is rather, as Horkheimer states, its precondition. The world that is revealed in Sade's libertine novels is both a vision of the world stripped of its justificatory illusions and a world reborn in being viewed anew. The vision may not in itself reveal anything, but insofar as it is a new vision it presents the world in its nakedness without becoming another passive rationalization. The key to Sade's works is that we cannot remain distant and unaffected by them, and the critique that they carry is entirely contrary to any justification. As Horkheimer would write six years later, 'the work of the Marquis de Sade exhibits "understanding without direction from another", that is, the bourgeois subject freed from tutelage' [DA: 109/68].⁷ The radical significance of Sade's works is to have demonstrated exactly what is meant by such maturity, what remains when all elements of ideological rationalizing are removed, and the subject is left exposed. Hence the challenge of reading Sade is the challenge of the Enlightenment itself, in all its implications: the challenge of learning to think and behave without recourse to spurious theological and political rationales, a challenge that, as Horkheimer goes on to show in his reading of *Juliette* in *Dialektik der Aufklärung*, is lived in modernity, insofar as the latter has made the aporias and contradictions of this emergence into maturity extremely concrete.

Kant's understanding of the moral law forms the basis of Horkheimer's counterargument in *Dialektik der Aufklärung*, and so it is helpful to give an example of how Kant formulates the implications of this thought, which is the imperative to act 'in such a way that the maxim of your will could always hold at the same time as a principle of a universal legislation'. While the content of the imperative is empty, its form requires for the limitation of one's actions based on their social implications, if those actions were to become a general rule. It is thus, in Horkheimer's terms, that self-interest is both actualized and restrained within the framework of the law. As Kant explains, in an example that is very appropriate to Sade's works:

> Suppose someone asserts of his lustful inclinations that, when the desired object and the opportunity are present, it is quite irresistible to him; ask him whether, if a gallows were erected in front of the house where he finds this opportunity and he would be hanged on it immediately after gratifying his lust, he would not then control his inclination. One need not conjecture very long what he would reply.[8]

Indeed, and one need not conjecture much as to the response of Sade's libertines, given that the threat of punishment does not have much of an inhibitory effect on their desires, but the implications of this divergence do not simply show Kant's censorious naïveté, for if we were to find a similar scenario in Sade's works the manner of its development would be very different. The abandon to which Sade's characters give themselves is not a return to 'primeval forms of behaviour upon which civilisation has placed a taboo' because, as Horkheimer writes, 'Juliette no longer actuates [these behaviours] as natural but as tabooed. She compensates for the value judgement against them, which was unfounded because all value judgements are unfounded, through their opposition. If she repeats primitive reactions in this way, they are no longer primitive but bestial. In psychological terms, Juliette [...] embodies neither an unsublimated nor a regressed libido but an intellectual joy in regression, *amor intellectualis diaboli*, the pleasure of defeating civilisation with its own weapons' [DA: 117–18/74]. That is, Sade's characters do not act out of a passive regression from the mores of civilisation to what might be called the merely animal, but rather from an active enjoyment of the transgression involved in this deviation (although the notion of transgression itself will be reformulated as the ground from which it deviates is rethought, as the next chapter will show). The response to the gallows that might ensue if it were to arise in Sade's works, and that Kant assumes would present a decisive disincentive, would not be one of a suicidal nihilism, or *Todestrieb*, but of the possibility for the enjoyment of its sensual extremes regardless of its seeming finality. There is a defiant rejection of remorse grounded in an excitement of reason that remains active despite everything.

The strength of Sade's thought of philosophy is that for as long as there is the libido, the intellect will be the subject and object of it. Kant's categorical imperative relies on the abstraction that it implies: the scenarios of the moral law and its application are only decisive for as long as one dismisses their corporeal specificity. Sade's response emphatically refuses to consider reason in abstraction from the body, but also, and just as importantly, it refuses to consider sensuous enjoyment in abstraction from thought, and it is with this renewed vision of the intimate imbrication of reason and materiality that the status of cruelty and suffering, or death and punishment, is rethought. This is not to revert to the common caricature of sadomasochistic behaviour, because rational enjoyment is one in which materiality is subject to thought, and vice versa, rather than there being an instrumental use of one side by the other. As a result, in replacing the value judgements of censored behaviour, the very subject position that they imply has been displaced. There is no moral subject in Sade's libertine works, not just because of their pursuit of immorality but because this pursuit, in its uninhibited critique of the basis of morality, also removes the notion of the subject as an autonomous individual dictating to themselves an adherence to the law. This subject position has been replaced by a persistent interrogation of the law and a sensual enjoyment of the fruits of this interrogation, come what may. Much like Kant, Sade promotes the activities of a reason that is apathetic, but for Kant this notion is a mark of the abstraction of moral feelings from sensible impressions, whereas for Sade it is the mark of a desire that is free from fear or remorse, instead of a complete indifference to sensory stimulation.[9]

However, for Horkheimer, the parallel with Kant's thought goes deeper, for despite its sensuous appearance the modality of libertine reason aspires to formality and, in becoming formal, reason loses its objectivity and necessity; it no longer has an aim but is a pure means, merely the arbitrary organizational structuring of pleasure. And this pleasure is just the feeling of a return to nature, in Horkheimer's words, not nature in itself (which only knows needs and the satisfaction of needs), and so the feeling of abandon to that which one has become alienated from is to an other that remains to that extent mythological. Hence the dialectic of enlightenment becomes reinstated, as reason finds itself becoming mythological in activating the archaic pleasure of sensual enjoyment just as myth becomes rational in organizing these pleasures into aimless and endless pursuits. In this way the dialectic is extended, but at the expense of thought. For thought, as that which has emerged in the overcoming of nature, is lost in this reversion to nature, which thereby appears as deranged from the point of view of society. Conversely, pleasure is made available in society only in controlled and limited forms as celebrations and holidays that are clearly distinct from everyday life. As such, he remains critical of Juliette for the superstition she holds in regard to pleasure, her belief in the excessive abandon to an other (although it should be noted that this belief is to some degree sublimated through its rational organization, in that it is not simply in relation to a mythologized alterity but to a nature transfigured through reason into sensuality) [DA: 128/82]. For Horkheimer, then, Juliette's pleasure remains subordinated to its relation to sacrilege, and its sublimation through reason only prefigures the compartmentalization that has become prevalent in modern life: the standardized and isolated moments of pleasure that are found as rewards for a life in which genuine happiness has been removed. Here the banality of Sade's vision becomes apparent in the insignificance of Juliette's passions and their empty recapitulation in the idle transgressions of organized life in modernity. Horkheimer has retreated from the point that he made at the end of 'Egoismus und Freiheitsbewegung', for in developing the dialectic of enlightenment in this way he has flattened the acuteness of its insights, as well as its radical implications, in favour of an acerbic critique of contemporary (American) society. And, in the crudeness with which this reconfigured dialectic transforms nature, the separation of sensuality from the full range of its affect renders it unavailable to the possibilities of an erotic thinking, which would, by contrast, not separate physical abandon from its mental transformations and would thereby yield more than just the repetition of sexual configurations. Thus, despite the shortfalls that he finds in the way that this dialectic is developed, both within the text and subsequently in society, its existence itself is (negatively) indicative of greater possibilities:

> Juliette's critique is conflicted like the Enlightenment itself. Insofar as the outrageous destruction of taboos, which was once linked with the bourgeois revolution, has not become a new justification of reality, it lives on, together with sublime love, as fidelity to the utopia brought near by the release of physical enjoyment for all.
>
> DA: 132–33/86

Nevertheless, I would argue that Sade's account goes further, both in the sense in which the thought of utopia is rendered very tenuous by the activation of physical pleasure, and in the way that it is through the reading of the text, rather than through Juliette's actions themselves, that this transformation is realized, a transformation that is not only one of emancipation.

Much of Horkheimer's account is coupled to a reading of Nietzsche, whose critique of morality is as strong as Sade's but operates at a different level and with different implications. As a result, the reading of Sade is turned towards a more Nietzschean rendering of the Sadean libertine as a form of Übermensch. It then becomes inevitable, from this point of view, with its concomitant loss of any role for social relations alongside the abandonment of sensual feelings, that the consequences of such a reading of Sade would lead to a picture in which the complete atomization of individuality exposes it to the domination of the fascist system.[10] But it is here that the significance of Sade's very peculiar way of rendering this transformation becomes apparent:

> Just as the deposed god returns as a more severe idol, so does the old bourgeois night-watchman state return in the violence of the fascist collective. Sade thought through to the end the state socialism whose first steps brought about the downfall of Saint-Just and Robespierre. If the bourgeoisie sent them, its most loyal politicians, to the guillotine, it banished its most outspoken writer to the hell of the Bibliothèque Nationale. For the *chronique scandaleuse* of Justine and Juliette – which, churned out as if on a production line, prefigured in the style of the eighteenth century the sensational literature of the nineteenth and the mass literature of the twentieth – is the Homeric epic after it has thrown off the last mythological shell: the history of thinking as an organ of domination. In now becoming frightened before itself in its own mirror, it opens up a view of what lies beyond it. It is not the harmonious social ideal that will also dawn for Sade in the future: "*gardez vos frontières et restez chez vous*", nor even the socialist utopia that is developed in the story of Zamé, it is the fact that Sade did not leave it to the opponents of the Enlightenment to be appalled by it that allows one to make his work a lever to save it.
>
> DA: 141/92[11]

As Horkheimer goes on to explain, writers like Sade have not tried to cover up the divisions inherent in the doctrine of the Enlightenment, nor have they attempted to justify the atrocities committed in its name. They have not sought to proclaim that reason is inherently moral or harmonious, instead they have shown in pitiless detail exactly what the supremacy of reason entails, which is also to show (negatively, dialectically) how it can be salvaged. Thus, this rescue does not proceed despite the ambivalence of reason, but through it. If the lack of grounds or goals for reason exposes it to the worst, then this is to say that it is through or in the worst that the nature of what is can be found, as unedifying as this may sound. Happiness is not the rule but the exception, it is cruelty and suffering that are constants in history. If there are no logical arguments against murder, no fundamental reasons, but only an assertion based in faith, then the recognition of this emptiness leads to a strange utopia, a world without illusion, which in turn, as Horkheimer concludes, reveals the utmost trust in humanity [DA: 143/93].[12]

II Ecstatic Expressions

Readers of Horkheimer have long been aware of a change of tone that takes place in his works during the late 1930s, in which his careful historical-materialist analyses of bourgeois culture give way to a more pessimistic account in which reason as such becomes culpable for the rise of fascist and capitalist state systems. This change is usually marked as being evident from the writing of two articles in 1941, 'Autoritärer Staat' and 'Vernunft und Selbstbehauptung', both of which anticipate his work with Adorno on *Dialektik der Aufklärung*, but the basis for this change, and thus its actual appearance, are not immediately obvious. This issue directly pertains to the understanding of Horkheimer's readings of Sade, and so its evidence needs to be carefully parsed for its significance to be made apparent. It is acknowledged that Horkheimer's work at this time was strongly influenced by the writings of Friedrich Pollock on state capitalism, which tended to diminish the role of historical economic analyses of power in favour of a more totalitarian political model, but it is also evident that Horkheimer was greatly affected by the historical pessimism of Benjamin's final theses on the concept of history, which formed the focus of the two articles he wrote in the early 1940s. This diagnosis broadly determines the subsequent (negative) reading of critical theory as being disengaged from the actuality of the political, with a concomitant loss of interest in the specificities of the worker's struggle and the economic conditions of social change, and thereby yielding to a pessimism over the emancipatory possibilities of the enlightenment, as reason itself is indicted over its relation to cruelty and oppression. The aporias of this diagnosis are obvious and have marked the lasting verdict of certain Marxist and Habermasian readings of Horkheimer's later works.[13] Some aspects of these readings are undeniably valid, as has been seen in the change in tone in his accounts of Sade, but the excursus on *Juliette* in *Dialektik der Aufklärung*, which Habermas avoids, also tacitly offers a different perspective on this transition.

While the account in 'Egoismus und Freiheitsbewegung', despite its brevity, is more suggestive than the later one in *Dialektik der Aufklärung*, the latter is not entirely one-sided, as there is a palpable tension between the pessimistic depiction of reason in the passages about Nietzsche and the more ambivalent notions expressed in the sections on Sade. Unfortunately, it does not seem that this tension is fully recognized by Horkheimer himself and so the possibility of developing the radical vision sketched out at the end of 'Egoismus und Freiheitsbewegung' is lost. The problem arises in the reading of rationality as unavoidably compromised by its coerciveness, which inevitably places the (self-)critique of reason on very uncertain grounds. Sade's response to this problem was by way of the ambivalence of sensuality, which reconfigures reason in terms of its concrete specificity so that cruelty is not disavowed or disguised but reformulated as part of its material actualization. As such, and admittedly in very challenging terms, the coercion is no longer fully manifest as coercion, but as a mutual sensual suffering or torment, a form of passion. The pain at issue here cannot be reduced or justified but is an aspect of the very pain of experience itself, of experience as that which goes beyond current bodily possibilities. The difficulty of this thought is self-evident, and it is important not to lessen it – as with any thought that seeks to recognize pain – as its difficulty comes from the attempt to consider pain without recourse to moralistic value judgements that seek to justify or dismiss its actuality. Sade's account of reason is one that is never rendered without reference to the manifold of its sensual expression, which makes it impossible to rationalize pain in any way. Reason reconsidered from this position entails a very different framework of thought, which does not desist from the demands of rationality (that is, it does not succumb to mere sensualism) but pursues them with a constant view to their sensual challenges and without the covert censorship of a reason devoid of actual physical consequences. This reading, if it is valid, seems to deviate from the Marxist account of materialist history that informs much of Horkheimer's early works, but it nevertheless retains a continuity with his regard for recognizing the importance of both suffering and pleasure as elements of any materialist critique of reason, enlightenment or not.

Conversely, the emphasis on the coercive force of reason, which is carried by relating Sade's works to those of Nietzsche, is found in Horkheimer's focus on the way that reason leads to an industrialized administration of sex and violence and a brutal subjugation and destruction of individuals, especially women. Although this destruction should not be overlooked, it should also be considered as a fantasy of dominance that is subordinate to the insatiability of desire, for it is scale and excess that are at issue, to the degree that desire cannot tolerate any limits, including those that distinguish it from suffering, but also those that subordinate it to instrumental reason insofar as desire is not for anything. Thus, the transformation in understanding the sensuality of thought, which was referred to (however allusively) in the essay on egoism, becomes missed the more the thesis of instrumental reason is held to dominate. This point is confirmed by the fact that the reading in *Dialektik der Aufklärung* also drops any discussion of Freud, in relation to which Sade's thinking of libidinal pain in the earlier essay was found to be profoundly innovative. The development of this alternative reading was unfortunately never taken up by Horkheimer, although elements of it can be found in the work of Adorno, albeit suggestively.[14] However, the challenge of the thought that he appears to have found is also that it cannot be fully developed from within philosophy and, as noted, may only be apparent through the *reading* of Sade's works. As a result, the role of aesthetics in the unfolding of critical theory is not merely incidental but intrinsic to its very form and possibility, and it is as such that the ambivalence in the notion of critical theory itself can be actualized. The scope for critical theory to become a general theory of social critique and emancipation is thereby limited, but its possibility of becoming a means for rethinking the relation of thought and materiality in terms of the actual specificity of the body is uncovered. The question of utopia around which critical theory develops is inflected by the very means that would appear intrinsic to it, sexuality, into an ambivalence whose aporia can never be reduced. It is not by avoiding this ambivalence that the question of the relation of sexuality and utopia can be approached but by seeking to respond to it in its depth, and it is through mimesis, which Adorno, rather than Horkheimer, pursues, that this possibility seems to arise.

The notion of sensuality that is brought out in Sade's works may deviate from Marx's ideas in many ways, but it also conveys a similar understanding of thought as sensibly mediated and as participating in a sociohistorical network of material expression and transformation. In this way there can be seen to be a reflexivity to Sade's thought in which ideas are taken up and manipulated and variably expressed; whether these are individual ideas of sensibility or more philosophical ideas about nature or morality, they are expressed as experiments both in and through Sade's works. And importantly, not only does this experience bring into play the unexpressed possibilities of sensibility but also reproduces them in a form that is actively differentiated. There is a kind of conceptual labour to these acts of imagination both as they are embodied in the text and as they are represented and discussed through the writing. Hence the form of reason itself is sensibly and imaginatively transformed in the act of reading these works. The engagement that is impossible to avoid in Sade's works is one in which our conceptual structures become transfigured, as has been seen in the rethinking of the apparently antithetical relation of pain and pleasure. Ideas, whether personal or social, are never just conceptual or abstract but are activated and modified through sociohistorical networks of variable concretization and pervasiveness. The significance of Sade's works lies in their sense of contamination, the fact that thinking becomes involved in the text in reflexive and material ways that enable its radical critique to take shape; a critique of reason by itself in which it cannot not take an interest insofar as it is sensibly engaged. It is in this way that the Sade chapter in *Dialektik der Aufklärung* explores the extremes of enlightenment reason just as the Odysseus chapter focuses on its origins; both are attempts to engage a rhetorical exposure of reason by showing how it cannot be separated from its material and historical background. As we have seen, Juliette is not only a figure of instrumental reason driven to excess but also a model of the actualization of reason in its extremes of sensibility, the two aspects are ordinarily opposed but are here found together and in doing so they reveal both the mythological collapse of reason into ideology and the sensible emergence of reason through a reformulation of the erotic. There is an excess in the writing of this excursus that almost seems to derive from Sade, and while it refers more directly to Horkheimer's earlier investigations of materialist history and the structural self-reproduction of society, it also bears reference to Adorno's understanding of the interpretation of musical material in the way that aesthetic experience bears its own cognitive forms that can be variably reconfigured.[15] Both aspects should be understood if we are to approach the text of *Dialektik der Aufklärung*, as is demonstrated by its readings of Homer and Sade: the mirror before which reason takes fright is one in which its exaggerations reveal the possibilities of going beyond itself, and it does so not by defusing or sublating its inner contradictions but by experiencing them *as* contradictions without resolution.

In the mimetic aspect of experience this contradiction is lived as an approximation of the mode of appearance of another alongside one's own appearance, not becoming the same but *like* the other, which thereby allows for a reflexive sensibility that does not dissolve its contradictions. And it is in sexuality and aesthetic experience that this mimetic capacity appears most fully, the basic characterization of which is expressed in an earlier passage from *Dialektik der Aufklärung*:

The cry of terror with which the unfamiliar is experienced becomes its name. It fixes the transcendence of the unknown in relation to the known and thus of the shudder [*Schauder*] as holiness. The doubling of nature into appearance and essence, effect and force, which first makes myth possible no less than science, comes from human fear, the expression of which becomes its explanation.

DA: 37/10

Except that, in the case of Sade, this cry is also that of orgasm, the word that irrupts at the point of ecstasy and is most often one of blasphemy, which is not to revert to the problematic of sacrilege but its opposite: it is the mark of the emergence of transcendence from bodily experience as the language and thought of the beyond, which goes by the name of the forbidden. Adorno later discusses this notion in referring to the experience of artworks as a shudder, a bodily awareness and trembling approximation of unfamiliarity, the shiver of a sense of objectivity as such.[16] Horkheimer can then begin his reading of Sade by showing how the Kantian account of thought implies that experience is a combination of real action and suffering, insofar as the contact of the subject with (second) nature involves the contestation of conceptual structures [DA: 105/64]. In emerging, the cry is not just the expression of transcendence but is the form in which the known and the unknown are combined: 'that which transcends the radius of experience [is] that of things that is more than their previously known existence' [DA: 37/10]. The ejaculation of language bears this unfamiliarity into words, but as that which remains unreconciled, unassimilated, which thereby allows for the reflexive awareness of sensible disparity without reducing it to the known.

To some degree this effect is carried by Sade's works as a whole, in that they almost appear as an extended cry of ecstasy, but it is more emphatically apparent in the discourses that irrupt from the orgies, which are not only radical conceptual challenges (if not challenges to the form of rationality as such) but also, necessarily, triggers for further sensual excess.[17] It is as such that the discourses remain anomalous and indigestible, as if they were material expulsions of thought that thereby transform it. However, this effect needs to be understood more carefully, which means examining Sade's most reflexive passage on the relation of thought and the sensible imagination:

> Go a whole fortnight without lusty occupations, divert yourself, amuse yourself with other things; but up to the last day do not let yourself even admit any libertine ideas. When this period is over retire alone to your bed in calmness, silence, and the deepest darkness; lying there, recall everything that you have

banished during this interval and deliver yourself indolently and with nonchalance to that gentle pollution by which no one knows how to arouse yourself or others as you do. Next, give your imagination the freedom to present aberrations of different sorts by degrees; cover all of them in detail, pass through them in review one by one; convince yourself that all the world is yours ... that you have the right to change, mutilate, destroy, shatter all beings as you see fit; you have nothing to fear; choose whatever pleases you but without exception, suppress nothing; without regard to anyone; without captive bonds or restraining checks; let your imagination take on all the cost of the ordeal and above all don't rush your gestures; your hand should take orders from your head and not your temperament. Without noticing it, from the various scenes that have passed before you, one will claim you more energetically than the others and with such a force that you cannot divert it or replace it by another; the idea acquired by the means I indicate will dominate you, captivate you, delirium will take over your senses; and believing yourself already at work you will discharge like a Messalina. Once this is done, relight your candles, and write out the type of perversion that came to inflame you, forgetting none of the circumstances that could aggravate its details; go to sleep on them, reread your notes the following morning and in restarting your operation add everything your imagination, a bit tired of an idea that has already cost you some come, can suggest that is capable of increasing its arousal. Now form a body to this idea and, in putting the final touches to it, once again add all the episodes that prompt your mind; then execute it and you will find that this is the perversion that suits you best and that you will carry out with the greatest delight. My secret, I know, is a bit villainous but it is certain; and I would not recommend it to you if I had not tested it successfully.[18]

The manner in which thought relates to the body through the sensible imagination indicates that representations in Sade's understanding are neither immaterial nor concentric, in that they do not consolidate and reinforce the subject by assimilating the unknown to the known, but rather the reverse: the sensibility by which thought is extended is intrinsically perverse and eccentric, it allows for the deviation of the known through the unknown, the material extravagance of thinking. Writing not only becomes the means for this extravagance but is also a mimetic demonstration of bodily ejaculation as it has just been formulated. The place and status of the subject becomes diminished or dislocated to the degree that this imaginary excess takes place, and in which, significantly, the villainous or criminal aspect also remains indeterminate.

It is worth going through Sade's account carefully for what it reveals of the mechanisms of the sensible or productive imagination. Firstly, we are told, it is necessary for there to be a period of privation in order to amplify, we assume, the force of desire but also its range by confirming the lack or negativity that is its inception. Then the imagination has to be given room to express itself by itself and so sensory stimulation is reduced by retreating into silence and darkness, in which there is only the sense of touch and its mental accompaniments. This stage involves a complex inter-linking of memory, sensation, and imagination, each of which stimulates the others to ever greater levels of excitement, emphasized not just by the privation that has preceded it but also by the breaking of the denial that grounded this privation, so that at each stage there is both repletion and transgression, satisfaction and dissatisfaction. Thus, the sensory lack is instated as a prohibition that inevitably entails its breaching, so that the imagination is given ever greater rein to submit to this excession because of the persistence of this sensory lack. At this point, the reflexive element arises in and as the form of ordering these fantasies and their sensations, so that they develop into a schema of escalation that enables the move from lesser to greater excitement. As a result, the mind finds that it can assert its absolute mastery in which thought knows no limits and nothing is beyond its scope, and in this way everything then passes before it to be used by the imagination. It is from this position that self-stimulation assumes the capacity of encompassing any possibilities, no matter how perverse or cruel. But, as can be seen, the close inter-linking of reason, imagination, and sensation leads into the most extreme bodily excitement. So, this is not a case of mere self-mastery in the Kantian sense but of subordinating reason to the senses and their fantastic representations such that it is resurgent in a new form, as ecstasy, in which subject, object, and thought are displaced into extravagance. At this point the form of the excitement becomes apparent, and in being drawn from memory, imagination, and sensation it emerges as a novel form that claims the self. This new form asserts an unequivocal force that thinking can only submit to, for through its development it is not entirely of thought even as it asserts itself with the force of an idea of reason. However, this is only the first part of the ascesis, for as the initial ecstasy is written down and re-examined, it is rationally and materially reformulated by being enlarged and extended through further imaginative escalations. This quasi-scientific process of repeated experimentation and refinement would appear endless, but, as Sade writes, there comes a point when it is possible to form a body to it, almost as if it were some kind of alchemical homunculus, as the very image of the idea of desire. And, in a final note, this image becomes the unique sign of one's own perversion (a notion that will be discussed in the next chapter), the one that is the form of one's own excess, as if it were one's own singular possibilities, which replaces the persona of the self with an extravagance that is unique to it, an extravagance that is villainous (*un peu scélérat*) as it is intrinsically bound to transgression, to the breaking of bonds and rules.

This passage in *Juliette* has often been discussed and it is important to realize that it operates as a key to Sade's own method, which in being made explicit thereby invites the reader into a similar relation to their own imagination, an imagination made concrete and rational as Sade's enlightenment ambitions have required, but that is also contagious in its villainy.[19] For the transgressive nature of this ecstasy is such that it cannot be limited to the subject but is communicated to others like a disease. Such a reason is not confined to the assertion and confirmation of the subject but rather exists to communicate itself without regard to the subject, it is excessive as such, and as a result cannot be limited to the instrumental, self-interested form that Horkheimer emphasizes in *Dialektik der Aufklärung*. The latter is merely an aspect of the unrestrained nature of reason, but one that limits it to the reinforcement of the subject position, whereas for Sade reason becomes absolute by way of its imbrication with materiality and the imagination, which places it beyond any subjective value judgements: for it, there is only extravagance, which communicates itself. And because this excess of reason is not for anything it is simply destabilizing, a fact that cannot be recognized by seeking to determine this lack but only through the mimesis of its material expression, as is found in sexuality or aesthetics.

It is perhaps in this regard that we can understand the following incident: In September 1937 Adorno married Gretel Karplus, whom he had known for about fifteen years. Horkheimer was Adorno's best man and, a year after the egoism essay to which Adorno had responded to so strongly, he gave the groom a copy of Sade's *Juliette* as a wedding gift.

4

Klossowski, Perversity, Criminality

Klossowski's reading of Sade developed through the 1930s in a series of articles and lectures, several of which were collected in his 1947 volume, *Sade mon prochain*. This book was the first serious discussion of Sade as a writer and thinker that did not seek to condemn or valorize his works. However, for as much as it was innovative, it was also heavily criticized for its theological approach, particularly by Bataille, Blanchot, and the Surrealist, Henri Pastoureau. In effect, Klossowski had constructed a form of inverted theology out of Sade's writings, where transgression itself became sanctified, almost as if it were a kind of extreme Gnosticism. In part because of these criticisms, but also because of the changing circumstances of his own writings, Klossowski's thought was transformed in the following years as he abandoned this theological reading for one closer to a Nietzschean understanding, but one very different from Horkheimer's reading. This revision took up two key aspects that are implied by the loss of a theological ground: a concern with the basis of linguistic relation and with the bodily nature of desire. Consequently, his later reading of Sade turned to a closer analysis of how transgression is possible, given the grammatical and physical basis of its form, and in 1967 he reissued *Sade mon prochain* in a very different form, dropping some essays, rewriting others, and contributing a new introductory piece, 'Le Philosophe scélérat', which would radically reformulate his reading.

Klossowski's concern with the possibility of transgression is explored by way of the idea of perversity. In perversity the very basis of an act, its gesture, is rendered doubtful by exposing the latent deviation that it carries, a form of counter-act that reveals a complex dissolution of relation. If we consider an act as simple as a caress, and then the manner in which this is distorted as it becomes a blow, or perhaps something stranger and more extravagant, then the unity and identity of the act has become perverted. Moreover, this perversion resides in the way that the act is repeated such that it becomes autonomous; it is not for anything other than its own repetition and so bears a compulsion that, despite its repetition, remains incommunicable and enigmatic. While the perverse act seems to rely on the norm from which it deviates, which would make its transgressive qualities dependent on that norm, the enigma of its autonomy is such that it makes both the norm and its violation problematic. The perversity of the counter-act is not just that it deviates from the apparent aim of the gesture but that in doing so it draws out and suspends both the relation of the act and its violation in terms of its physical and grammatical form, thereby manifesting an indissoluble tension that will become central to the revised understanding of transgression. This tension recurs in Klossowski's discussions of Nietzsche as he seeks to explicate the possibility of a social form that would arise from the ubiquity of such transgression, a social relation without relation, as it were, which leads to an interest in secret societies. Contrary to initial expectations that perversity may endanger the possibility of social emancipation, it instead seems that this sense of transgression is integral to a social relation that is not alienated, coercive, or reified, which has considerable consequences for the ethical basis of society.

I Criminal Philosophy

Despite the excessive content of his libertine works, Sade is not exactly a pervert in that there is no suppression or denial in relation to his desires, equally, while he may revel in the transgressive nature of his fantasies, he is just as determined to show that these are not just fantasies, or even transgressive, since they follow from the excessive and autonomous force of nature itself. His perversion instead lies at the heart of the Enlightenment project, and while this may appear to be an attempt to control and dominate through excess, it is just as much a domination by excess. The status of the work thus becomes integral to this perversity, for it is in the work that perversity fully realizes itself and in a way that, as Horkheimer began to intimate, is closer to Kant than it is to Freud.[1] Consequently, for Klossowski, the significance of Sade's writings comes from the fact that they develop a notion of perversion that goes far beyond a desire to shock or titillate by operating on and through the logical and discursive modes of thought. This radical perversion arises because the basis of the act is itself found to be ineradicably deviant, which then affects the possibility of the thought or relation that would seek to ground itself in it. For if an act can no longer be unitary or complete in its definition due to the unavoidable presence of a deviating desire, then the possibility of construing a logical or physical relation on the basis of such an act is also rendered doubtful. The relation and identity of the act is not thereby lost but rather made perverse: obscure and eccentric to rational norms. As a result, there arises a perversion of thought out of the thought of perversion, which allows Klossowski to speak of the figure of the criminal philosopher (*philosophe scélérat*) in Sade's works, a figure that has become transformed by that which it enacts.[2] In this figure the force of desire takes shape as thought, which then leads to a refiguring of thought, not to dissolve or negate it but to reveal its own displaced impulses. Thus, Sade's writing out of his thought in his libertine works constitutes a philosophical transformation in itself, which in its subsequent distribution bears social implications. It is not so much the content of Sade's writings that is important, but the mode of their development in relation to the norms of rational thought. As Klossowski explains, insofar as language has a generic structure that enables communication, by which it propagates norms as it reproduces itself, the reproduction of subjectivity through language occurs alongside a reproduction of rational norms by way of a reciprocal constitution. What Sade brings to this model is the disruption brought about by the passions, which establish a 'counter-generality' of singular cases of perversion that, 'in the existing normative generality, are defined by an absence of logical structure' [SMP: 19/14]. Principle in the latter is the breakdown of the law of identity or non-contradiction.

Sade is not looking to create a complete collapse of language or thought, but to displace it by way of a mode of expression that has remained latent in the normative model, a mode that Klossowski calls fully formed or unadulterated monstrosity (*monstruosité intégrale*), where the monstrous is that which persistently departs from all orders, norms, and rules. Thus, fully formed monstrosity is one that does not limit itself to the sphere of the passions, as the excessive content of Sade's erotic writings would seem to imply, but instead completes itself in a perversion of thought and its norms. This last point is significant as it enables Sade to move from the simple reactionary form of atheism, for example, which is merely a dependent negation of monotheism, to a more complete atheism that is able to extend the lack of norms made evident in the discovery of the absence of divinity into a thorough remodelling of language and thought. In doing so, rationalism's lack of fundamental reason is exposed to it such that, in seeking to apply itself, it comes to contradict itself and thus exposes the counter-generality of its perversity in the absence of rational normativity. Atheism as 'a decision of autonomous reason' thereby unravels itself and its (lack of) grounds, so that *complete atheism will be the end of anthropomorphic reason*' [SMP: 21/16]. This transformation leads to the monstrosities that Sade has revealed but also, as Klossowski adds, to the other, more positive aspect of a 'polymorphous sensibility', with the caveat that the one aspect cannot be achieved without the other.

Although it does not come across, Klossowski's argument in this essay is fairly straightforward, for he is concerned with working out the implications of the thought of complete atheism in the direction suggested by Nietzsche when he wrote that 'we have not got rid of god [*wir werden Gott nicht los*] because we still have faith in grammar'.[3] Complete atheism requires a re-examination of language, and once the grounding norms of theology have been removed, the position and predication of the subject will be put in question. This is a question of what language will reveal in place of the subject, when it is no longer that around which predication is structured, and hence what predication itself will become. This experience of the dethroning of the subject is part of what Klossowski understands as complete monstrosity, but to develop this thought it is necessary to understand the evacuation of subjective experience in terms of the acts and gestures that bring it about, and particularly, the perverse gesture that leads subjectivity into multiple estrangements.

The problem that Sade faces is twofold: on the one hand, he is put in a situation where he is not able to pursue his fantasies concretely but is only able to write about them, and on the other hand, there is the problem just alluded to that simply writing about atheism is not sufficient to extricate it from the norms inherent in language that maintain its onto-theological structure. Sade's response ingeniously manages to draw these two issues together, since he combats the problem of atheist language by combining a direct critique with a sustained distortion of language through the extensive and rational pursuit of perversion. That is, the more that perversion is pursued as a rational structure of its own, the more these rational norms are themselves submitted to perversion. In doing so he finds a way to continue to enact his fantasies by way of literature, which means, as Klossowski writes, that he has put in question the very decision that seemed to sanction his writing, by making it apparent that he has not compromised or limited himself by seemingly writing instead of enacting his perversions. This, precisely, is the import of Sade's criminal philosophy as 'it traces a sinister question mark over the division of thinking and writing, and particularly of thinking and describing an act *instead* of committing it' [SMP: 18/13].

As a result, in writing out his passions, Sade brings them into contact with reason through their appearance in language, that is, his writing is not merely descriptive of these passions but conveys their formal deviation, which brings them into contested relation with thought: 'in interpreting the aberrant act as a coincidence of sensuous nature and reason, Sade at the same time humiliates reason with the sensuous and the 'rational' sensuous with a perverse reason' [SMP: 22/17]. With this double-sided sense of perversity is found the extension of the dialectic that Horkheimer saw but did not quite grasp, for perversion is an expression of itself as well as a perverse counterpoint to 'natural' reason. That is, perversity cannot be decided as either natural or historical, rational or mythological, since it oscillates between the two by way of its ambivalent actualization. It is this more profound elusiveness in relation to reason that renders it perverse, as it is always in deviation from that which purports to be in relation with it, such that this relation itself becomes distorted. Consequently, this view leads to a rethinking of the idea that perversion is dependent on the law for its existence, with the apparent corollary that the aim of perversion to universalize itself would lead to its dissolution, for without the law there would be no possibility of perversion. While perversion can occupy this derivative position, as Klossowski makes clear, it also bears the possibility of being absolute as it only desires to propagate, so the apparent dependence on norms and rules is merely an image, insofar as norms are instead generated by perversion as it curtails itself. The tension between the two readings of perversion as absolute or relative, universal or dependent, is left unresolved in Sade's writings and it is only with Klossowski's later works that the lack of decision in relation to this issue takes on a more coherent form.

This discovery takes place through an inversion analogous to that which was found in Nietzsche's fable about the 'true world', for if perversion is dependent on norms to the same degree that the reverse is the case, then both perversion and norm are derivative constructs.[4] Underneath both lie sheer impulses, which are actualized in their ambivalence (as that which are active and reactive) so that in their actualization they interpret and censor themselves, through expression and limitation, which leads to a thought of perversion occurring both with and without norms. Following Sade, the challenge for Klossowski is to find a way to draw out this perversity in language, while avoiding a simplistic counterpoint between the universality of discourse and the singularity of sense. Thus, the attempt to respond to this challenge must pass through the norms of discourse in such a way as to make thought itself perverse: in finding that perversion bears its own reason, not only is the separation of rationality and the sensuous lost but so is the apparent distinction upon which reason grounds itself. In this way the reason of perversion leads to a perversion of reason, which is to lead thought beyond itself, beyond the sphere of norms into the excess of what is always otherwise, so that this outside recurs within thought. As he concludes, the significance of Sade's form of writing is that, through it, this outside reproduces itself in language as its own thought of excess, as an anomalous force or gesture [SMP: 53/42].

To understand the advent of this force it is helpful to turn to an account that Klossowski provides about the origin of the character of Roberte, who appeared in his 1953 novel *Roberte ce soir*. Although this account is peculiar, its very singularity grants it a concreteness that is more tangible than the wild excesses of Sade's libertine works, since it indicates the strange form in which the thought of the outside emerges and the challenges it raises for language and thought in trying to determine its perversity. Seated in his garden, Klossowski writes, he was thinking about the name 'Roberte' when he became fascinated by it and suddenly saw, as if in association with the name, an ungloved hand and the shifting, unlocatable shadow (*pénombre insituable*) in which it seemed to arise. These two images in their unreality are not actually seen but seem to come together as an isolated gesture, and a gesture marked by an aberrant desire in the form of its name (as Sade's account of the imagination had described). Furthermore, Klossowski appears merely to have received these images and only acted to draw them together as name and image, as if they bore their own force that sought to actualize itself: 'it was not me who designated that which I understood as "shadow" but thought, outside of me, which was looking at itself in the terms "shadow", "skin", "glove", etc.'. These are extraordinary lines, but their apparent mysticism is merely the surface for a difficult problem, that of the origin and status of thoughts, especially those thoughts that do not occur as fully communicable due to their sensuous idiosyncrasy. What is at issue is the relation between the singularity of the sign and the universality of its communicative basis, between the norms of its presentation and the perversion of these norms, and for Klossowski this relation cannot be decided in favour of one side or the other, as perversity is precisely that which holds to this juxtaposition as its form, which in turn constitutes its non-equivalence to itself, its non-identity. In addition, the image *occurs to him*, that is, it happens without his agency or decision and thus occupies a strange penumbra of exteriority as if it were not really his, or not really a thought, but an image that is concrete yet subjective, and objective yet abstract. In receiving such an image, thought may act to draw its elements together, but in doing so it is also drawn outwards by these elements in their persistent aberrance. Hence thought encounters the outside as that which is both outside and the outside as it is thought, such that the two aspects of this penumbra cannot be grounded in either its provenance or its determination. This experience is central to Klossowski's later critical and fictional writings, and exposes the *insituable* uncertainty that is passed over in any such encounter, as he phrases it (recalling but also deepening Montaigne's sceptical query): 'is thought making use of me, while I believe I am using a faculty?'[5] The ambivalent form of this experience contributes to its intractability, but its banality also indicates how these gestural ruptures of thought are not unusual but part of the suppressed desires of everyday experience. Thus, the perversions that Sade focused on are just a more extreme version of that which is ubiquitous to thought and language as the gestures defining and undermining its norms and generality. But from whence come such gestures, and what are their status, and how can they occur in language without betraying this anomaly?

Such an image can be given more focus in the notion of an *idée fixe*, which for the pervert is the singular form of the gesture around which their behaviour is oriented, so that the 'pervert's existence becomes the constant waiting for *the moment in which this gesture can be carried out*' [SMP: 29/23]. This singular gesture defines their existence and yet cannot be communicated and is over in a moment. As a result, the form of this gesture is not fully objective or subjective; it is both real and an image, an idea that is not of the individual and manifests an impulse that runs counter to those of life and its imperatives, since it is not for anything other than its own actualization (as if it were the perverse condition of Adorno's notion of the additional factor). As such, it expropriates the form of existence of the individual subject and, in seeking to respond to it, language is drawn into this expropriation even as it seeks to interpret its singular gesture. In the character of the pervert, this perversity is actualized as that which seeks its expression in general, which renders it dangerous by implicating the perversion of reason latent in language and thought, its unending emptiness and aimlessness, which the perverse idea manifests: 'Sade invents a type of pervert who speaks from his singular gesture *in the name of generality*' [SMP: 34/26]. It can be seen that there is a correlation here with the commodity-form, but Klossowski's innovation is to show how Sade realized a very different form of relation in the actualization of absolute or complete perversion. For, in their speech, the pervert may betray the singularity of their concrete idea, but in doing so they also render its perversity contagious. The language of the pervert does not seek generality to legitimate itself but to create complicity, so that it can extend itself, which is reflected in language's own betrayal of sense [SMP: 35/27].

Sade's vision operates at a more profound level than Marx's in terms of its effects on the body of thought and language and its expropriations thereof, although the broader sociohistorical effects of that expropriation remain to be worked out. The degree to which the Société des amis du crime in *Juliette* differs from the plutocratic corporations of contemporary capitalism I have discussed elsewhere, but the distinctions lie with the presence of control: the pervert seeks to repeat the gesture that defines them and to communicate this gesture, however unsatisfactorily; while neoliberal oligarchies are concerned with establishing the permanence of their mechanisms of rapacity.[6] Sadean relations are oriented towards an expropriation and contagion that leads to a rupturing of singularity, a transformation in which the norms of social and conceptual relations are replaced by the universality of prostitution and a fully formed monstrosity, which is marked in microcosm by the repetition of the perverse gesture in its undecidability. Klossowski offers an example of the effects of this undecidability in the disavowed gesture of an interlocutor who, on encountering the pervert, is repulsed by them and seeks to deny their behaviour and gives evidence of a contradiction in their own behaviour through this combined repulsion and denial. Thus, there is a critical element to the Sadean society, in its attention to the contradictions and unobserved betrayals of language and behaviour [SMP: 36/28]. However, this critique requires a methodology so that it can be pursued thoroughly, as it is only by way of such a praxis that the repeated actions can be understood in terms of what is expropriated and what is expropriating, as well as through the interplay of transgression and regression that occurs with each iteration of the act (as was seen in the last chapter). Such repetition is in itself senseless, since it is based merely in an empty but concrete reiteration, but this repetition allows for the thought of expropriation to be suspended without deciding its form [SMP: 42/32].

Here lies the importance of the sheer excess of Sade's writing, which conveys this suspended ecstasy of thought in the way that the repeated presentation of perversity leads thinking into an encounter with what cannot be presented in language, what arises as a form of non-language within language, or what Klossowski termed fully formed monstrosity: an unadulterated distortion of rational norms. Thus, the perversity of Sade's text lies not in its representations but in the excess by which it contests these norms, its lack of measure (and it makes sense that the gesture of excess *par excellence* in Sade's writings is that of sodomy, for in its repeated violation of social norms and biological imperatives it shows itself to be endlessly aberrant). And so, the absence of any formal or thematic constraints in Sade's libertine writings becomes significant because it carries thought into an experience of excess as its own sensible idea, or act. However, as excess, it necessarily fails to appear fully, so its appearance in language only confirms what has not (yet) taken place, but through the experience of this repeated act of rupture thought is drawn into a momentary awareness (within language) of the act in its exteriority to language. As is made clear in the last pages of *Juliette*, there is both an imperative to say everything and an aporia at this point, since it is only possible to indicate the sensible excess by way of its gesture; it can only be marked as an excess *in* its excess, by which it continues to propagate itself. Hence, in this situation, the exteriority of the act takes on the role of that which continually seeks entry into language, despite its censorship and limitation, and 'the *less the act is perpetrated*, the *more it knocks* on the door' [SMP: 53/41]. As a result, the situation necessarily becomes inverted, for in inviting the outside within, thought finds itself exteriorized, as it is displaced into a landscape in which the act and its images expose themselves not as themselves but only as further experiences of estrangement [SMP: 54/42]. For as thought seeks to designate this field of expropriation, its own position unravels through the failure of this designation. Thought is no longer outside the act but pervaded by it in its concrete dissembling even as it attempts to designate it.

Surprisingly enough, Klossowski's account partly coincides with that of Hegel, for whom the significance of the gesture is that it is already subject to perversion (*verkehrtheit*) by way of its actualization, which leads to it suggesting both more and less than its apparent intention [PG: 173/187, 179/194]. There are then two different levels of reading the gesture: in terms of its relation to contingency or to intention, and the significance of the perverse gesture is the way that the two are confused. Or, rather, there is an unstable oscillation between the two levels insofar as perversity is that which renders their distinction undecidable, since its gesture does not actualize a pre-existing intention; instead, the actualization is the intention in its singularity and its variability. Klossowski sees such a relation between gesture and language when he speaks of its solecism or contradiction, which he finds expressed in the image of a half-open hand – that is either opening or closing and so is intrinsically ambivalent, creating a logical or syntactical form that cannot be read insofar as its relation undecidably occurs in both directions; its movement cannot be determined as either approximation or withdrawal, for example, as its gesture is both itself and not itself. Such contradictory gestures make their linguistic appearance evident while also undermining it, as there is an emergence of abstraction in their indication of form at the same time that the possibility of securing this abstract form is undercut. A relation is indicated that is obscured in the same movement, so that the gesture is revealed as not equivalent to itself.[7] The gesture is found to bear a sense, but without reference, it is not clear who or what it is for, and so it is referentially isolated, except in terms of its own non-identical exemplarity.

Hence, as a gesture, it exists by way of the alteration and perversion that takes place in its objectification, without this leaving it entirely arbitrary. As a result, it can be singular despite its intransitivity, as it becomes determined through its repetition. Thus, the perverse gesture is one that seeks to remain singular despite these contingencies, which produces a constant pressure of dissatisfaction that becomes the pervert's obsession. Objective reality becomes subordinate to the search for moments in which the gesture can appear, which requires an arrangement of actuality according to the needs of desire, a desire that is itself unclear and uncertain before such arrangements arise. The act is neither subjective nor objective but only determines these poles in its appearance, and only for the duration of its appearance. It thereby happens each time anew, despite the constitutive role of repetition, for although it exists through time this is not because it persists but because it happens each time as if it were without precedent or succedent.

Klossowski finds in the contingency of the perverse gesture an ever-present ambivalence and betrayal, a necessary loss of identity. Perversity becomes the unique sign of this actuality, its absolute relation, in which there is no internal or external, and thus no expression, but instead what he calls a conspiracy, a movement of betrayals of sense that remains clandestine. In this way, the perverse gesture comes to resemble an aporia in which its ever-repeated sign is both superlative and empty, and it is thus that it repeats itself and thus that it is also a betrayal. For the return to itself of the gesture in its self-predication is both an affirmation and a displacement and, critically, an affirmation through displacement. In doing so, it remains clandestine and yet forms a movement of betrayal in its ever-repeated singularity. This idea recurs in Klossowski's interest in the role and nature of secret societies, which occurs on two different levels: firstly, and most obviously, it is addressed by way of the works of Fourier and Sade, and their ideas about a utopian libertine republic; and secondly, in the more discreet mode of the gestures and perverse abstractions enacted through society as it currently exists.[8] From this position, the form of the secret society emerges as the possibility of another mode of relation.

II Speculative Addendum: Negative Labour

In Georg Simmel's understanding, developed in an article from 1906, the significance of the secret society comes from the fact that secrecy and lying are far from being flawed or antithetical aspects of social relations but are as intrinsic to it as honesty and transparency. He gives as examples of this necessity the sphere of private relations, whose secrecy is amplified in the clandestine organization.[9] The presence of non-disclosure in these relations is not grounded in a sense of exclusion but is there to protect the intimacy of the relation. The secret society gives space for this relation to arise, from which also arises the need for a form of initiation as is found in religious, criminal, and political organizations, but that is no more than an extension of the induction into such a space that occurs in love. While these groups may come together to pursue a goal of some sort their primary aim is the association itself and the relation it unfolds. As a result, the members do not relate to each other as they are but only through the (hidden) relations of the group; their identity within the group differs from what it is outside it.

The non-relation with society is echoed in the negative relation that occurs within the group, as its movement away from the norm is replicated as part of its existence, such that it may remain secret in some way even from its members. There is then an antagonism between the secret and the society, as the secret can only be maintained through its sharing, which allows for its continued existence beyond that of the individuals who may bear it. And so, inherent to the secret is its betrayal, in relation to which it is in a constant tension, and this tension is increased by the society in which it is shared. Thus, the group exists in a state of exception, a blind spot formed by a mutual repulsion by and from society, and thereby follows its own rules and norms through a consensual abdication from the law, which is marked by the use of merely formal rules, parodying or perverting the very sense of the law. Consequently, there can be no programme or manifesto for such groups that does not betray itself, as they do not seek to manifest themselves, and it seems that Klossowski is interested in pursuing the idea of their generalization and what would take place if their secrecy and secession were immanent to society. Such an idea is intrinsically perverse, both in theory and in practice, but its necessity lies in the suppressed relation between society and this perversion, alongside its concomitant potential, which is exposed as an idea that cannot be pursued so much as endured in its negativity. It can be seen that this situation marks that of political and artistic avant-gardes, but it is also found in the artwork itself.

There is a sense of prefiguration in the secret society in that it seeks to establish by its existence that which it is pursuing; it attempts to prefigure its own actualization and through this attempt it maintains itself. Its secrecy thereby comes in part from the concealment of its arbitrary foundation, which gives rise to a requirement for trust. It is this requirement that is problematic, for although the secret is that in which the group is grounded, it is itself grounded in nothing but its own act, which thus gives rise to suspicion and doubt about the basis of its existence. A secret cannot be maintained in stasis; it has to be continually upheld and reaffirmed, which leads to its extension and exaggeration since it has no existence outside this undisclosed self-affirmation. Hence the status of the secret society can never be taken for granted, which might distinguish it from associations that ground themselves more explicitly, but this is only a distinction in time; the longer the association survives the more its foundation is assumed, its secret can no longer be betrayed as it is now taken to be a fact; its grounding has not revealed itself but has simply become established, so that such an association is no longer a secret society. Conversely, the secret society forms a kind of anti-tradition that arises from its inability to establish itself explicitly and leads only to secession and differentiation, for what occurs is not held together by any continuity.

Thus, the law of the secret society is one of betrayal, and this is not an accident or flaw but is the repetition of its intrinsic self-repulsion or non-relation, the *lex atomi*, or clinamen as Lucretius called it. While this might lead to the baroque proliferation of sects and factions, or to the self-destruction of criminal associations, it should not be seen merely as the triumph of self-serving individualism for it is rather the secret that is being recapitulated and the relation it unfolds. This secret is the germ of society, as that which both generates and dissociates it, and as such it is a burden that cannot be borne; its demands are too excessive, as it exposes a relation that cannot be maintained, quite precisely, but that can only be reinitiated. The optimistic sentiments expressed by Plato and Cicero (that justice is superior to injustice because even among thieves there is a necessity for trust) break down here, as it is apparent that they both view criminality as a form of work, that is, in terms of the society that the criminals have deviated from, for they are concerned with the criminals' productivity should they fail to trust each other.[10] But if the society of thieves is not one of positive works, then there is no need for their constructive coordination; these are not mini- or proto-corporations but networks of fragmentation and negative labour.

If, as Hegel writes, the criminal denies the possibility of right to their victim, then this exposes a disparity in that they claim such a right for themselves.[11] In Sade's libertine writings, the criminal asserts the right of violation in general, which is to say that it applies to themselves as well as to others. The will of the libertine asserts itself in claiming a freedom that includes the freedom to lose that freedom in becoming the victim of another, which is extended in Klossowski's works as the pervert subordinates themselves to the demands of their desire in which there is a loss of identity and any kind of propriety. The pervert thus appears to will their own loss of freedom, but, as Sade found, this inversion holds another interpretation, in which the will affirms its own loss as a freedom to lose oneself through one's material desires. There is no lack of objective determination in this thought, but there is a lack of determination of the self as identical. The will, in affirming its appearance through desire, loses itself as an affirmation of the self. What is of interest is the way that the experience of this loss, which Bataille and Blanchot would call sovereignty, is reformulated in the acts of the libertine or pervert from an aesthetic emptying and estrangement into one that also bears a social and political import. When the will affirms itself in an act that involves the loss of will, and the loss of the will as one's own, then this affirmation becomes an act of displacement in which the self is dissolved into this double-sided image of desire through the force of its self-effacement and violation. The mystical elements of this loss are then counterbalanced with the material aspects of its determination in acts of art or sexuality, which is the basis for Klossowski's understanding of the revolutionary possibilities of perversion. In this way, the acts of the criminal lead to a situation in which the incommensurability of criminal and victim is displaced by a conspiracy of loss, that is, a shared dissolution of what is one's own.

The occurrence of this thought in the writings of Klossowski and Sade is such that it is not limited to them, as its extremity testifies to the possibility of another form of social relation that is both clandestine and pervasive. It is necessary to reconsider perversity from a perspective in which relations to propriety are not foundational, a perspective in which it is oriented towards exposing disavowed possibilities. Such would be the import of Klossowski's thought of perversity as a gesture or act that, in betraying itself, leads to unacknowledged possibilities of relation, ones in which incommensurabilities of exchange are not acts of violation or exploitation but modalities of revolution in that they expose new forms of relation. Naturally, considerable caution is needed in this thought, but what it makes possible is an understanding of how the pervert occupies the same socio-political space as the revolutionary in that they both explore proscribed realities and make concrete the nature in which social possibilities are controlled and maintained. This sense is what is at work in the perverse gesture as a unique sign in a conspiracy of betrayals. The latter then becomes a logical form or mode, or perhaps it would be better to say that it is a mode of deformation without origin or aim, which is the basis of its integral violation of form as such.

It is thus that Hegel will state that crime 'constitutes a *negatively infinite judgement* in its complete sense', that is, a judgement of relation as one of complete incommensurability. In the positive infinite judgement (a rose is a rose) there is merely identity, whereas in the negative infinite judgement (a rose is not an elephant) there is only difference. These judgements are infinite as there is no limit to their relation, either as proximity or distance and so, to that extent, they do not really function as judgements.[12] That is, they express a relation and also deny it, as they take the form of a judgement while also undermining that form by showing that there is no relation being expressed. As Hegel remarks, the possibility of such infinite negative judgements is noted but rarely discussed as they are deemed to be merely absurd and anomalous, since their results are strictly meaningless. However, the logical peculiarities at work here become substantial when it is found that the form of the negative infinite judgement takes place in criminal acts. As noted above, the criminal act is one in which a complete incommensurability is present, as the criminal asserts a claim while denying even the possibility for such a claim by the victim (a theft is not just of a particular item but also a negation of the right to own): '*crime* is the *infinite judgement* that negates not merely the *particular* right, but the universal sphere as well, negates *right as right*'.[13] The victim is thus exposed to utter difference in that they have been completely stripped of any rights of their own and thus any parity with the criminal. As a result, when Hegel notes that 'crime can be considered as an objective example of the negative infinite judgement', this statement places pressure on both its aspects: the status of crime and judgement in this (negative infinite) relation. This point is only made more problematic when he goes on to say in the same remark that death is also a negative infinite judgement, in that body and soul fall apart completely, just as was the case with the experience of absolute fear endured by the bondsman.[14]

Consequently, the transition into the concrete makes the negative infinite judgement into a problem that is no longer merely absurd but of actual and indeed, critical, significance, and in actualizing itself the judgement takes on a profoundly unsettling form, revealing its violation of the norms of non-speculative identity, and undermining the nature of right as universal, just as Klossowski had suggested about Sade's perversions. It is just such a violation of norms that constitutes the offensive nature of crime, and it is logical that the discussion of crime in the *Rechtsphilosophie* should follow the account of property and contracts, as their analysis reveals that there is no necessary grounding for the respect of these forms, as the right to property can always be violated in its actuality. Hence the concrete necessarily implies the rupture of the property relation, which is only to acknowledge the degree to which logic as such is beholden to the concrete and the contingent for its integral determination. While criminality is only a form of negative act, or semblance, as Hegel would say, it is nevertheless through it that right comes to be recognized as such, which means that it becomes impossible to imagine a world without crime.

Crime is not to be understood as a side-effect, counterpoint, flaw, or default, rather, crime is an essential constitutive element of our legal, political, and economic systems. It is supported and nurtured, not just for negative reasons (as a mode and justification of penal control), but for positive reasons as well, insofar as it bears a motive force for social change, albeit one that is largely oligarchical, which enables society to maintain itself, as well as acting as a means of perpetuating class divisions for the benefit of capital. This kind of analysis has been explored by theorists following the insights of Evgeny Pashukanis and Georg Rusche that the legal form is a function of the commodity-form, which is to say that legal relations derive from and are expressions of the forms of commodity-exchange, which means that they derive from property relations, and that definitions of criminality and punishment arise out of the social relations historically current and particularly in reference to the control and exploitation of the labour market.[15] Crime displays the negative infinite judgement of society as a whole; that rights are for some but not for all, which would be an absolute inversion of Hegel's thought. It plunges society into an absolute fear that is an exposure to complete difference. It is not the crimes of the single individual that cause fear, as much as those of the forces of government (in poverty people suffer under an 'infinite criminal judgement' as the very possibility of their rights have been removed, which leaves them subject to crime in all forms).[16]

Just as hoarding is a form of negative expenditure, and unemployment is a form of negative work, with both being intrinsic to the maintenance of capital as a system, crime is a form of negative labour. Something of the significance of this situation can be found in Marx's tale about the origins of capital accumulation, where beggars, robbers, and vagabonds arise as a result of the expropriation of land and property and are then criminalized.[17] It is thus that these figures need to be considered as forms of negative labour, as the negative of labour and the labour of the negative, as well as the way that labour as the shared reality of *Sittlichkeit* is inverted in criminality into a reality that is not shared. The criminal is of course to some degree no more than a petty capitalist, so the reality of their negative labour is just that of the products of exploitation and expropriation, and as such they demonstrate the division of the ethical. But this is not all there is to negative labour, which develops its own inversions of the exchanges and uses to which it is put. This logic is speculative and infinite in that it perceives the possibility inherent in a situation where an impossibility is outlined; it begins from this perspective of incommensurability and seeks to bring it into actuality, as is the case with the work of aesthetics.

5

Beside Herself with Desire: Musil

I The Completion of Love

Near the beginning of his 1958–59 lectures on aesthetics, Adorno makes the following statement:

> I believe only someone who has realised – and I would almost think: in their childhood – that when one says "this evening is melancholy", that it is not a mood of the observer but that, of course in a constellation with the observer, the evening itself is melancholy – that someone who has not had this decisive experience, to a certain extent this "freedom to the object", the experience of self-oblivion towards the object, however, does not know what a work of art is at all.
>
> AS: 46/26[1]

As simple as this statement is, its boldness is only matched by its obscurity, and yet Adorno is clearly committed to its implications. Unravelling it is not straightforward, and it will be necessary to proceed via a literary account that offers greater detail on this idea of an objective mood. In doing so it will become apparent how the interaction with the object conveys this intrinsically aesthetic experience, and what this then implies about the nature of experience itself. As a result, perversity will be revealed as intrinsic to aesthetic experience insofar as it is part of the way that the latter is recapitulated, which further confirms what is at stake in perversion itself.

Musil's short story, 'Die Vollendung der Liebe', was completed in 1910 after a very intensive period of composition and was published the following year. It is one of Musil's densest pieces of writing and the difficulty he had in composing it related to the fact that he was not only trying to show but also to bring about an experience of what he would later call the 'other state' (*anderen Zustand*).[2] In outline, the story is straightforward, but as the opening scene demonstrates it is profoundly rich in detail. A couple sit in a room in their house talking about an impending journey and about a book they have both been reading. It is evening and the atmosphere of the scene bears a muted sensuality in which the relation between the two is characterized in terms of a gentle but divergent tension, so that the scene develops by way of the sensations emerging out of this tension. That is, there is a definite sense in which feelings arise from their milieu, both personal and impersonal, and as such carry a force that is marked on the one hand by their shared attention to a particular but uncertain object (the book) and on the other hand by a vague apprehension concerning a specific journey. Everything seems to take place within this space of divergence, and along lines of conveyance that are linked even as they are divergent. Furthermore, as their discussion of the book proceeds, the indeterminacy of their feelings arises from a null point that seems both to attract and repel their interest, creating an uncertain compulsion. The focus of this discussion is a figure from the book, G., and the problem of ascertaining how much his character is conscious and knowable. Musil's account is significant because he finds an approach that is distinct from psychoanalysis or phenomenology, and the literary rendition of what is at issue manages to convey the sense and turmoil of these feelings in a way that is no less forceful than it is fluid.[3] The description seems no longer to be subjective or even figurative, for the space is one where both the materiality and ideality of the feelings can be grasped by the reader such that their sensuality can be thought (and where this thought is both noun and verb). The discussion of G. is key to this approach, for he is not only a criminal – like Moosbrugger in *Der Mann ohne Eigenschaften* – and thus a figure of transgression and intensity, but also because the singularity of his character focuses something of the other state that these powerful and yet apparently indeterminate feelings seem to expose. Hence the material manifestation of sense in this scene introduces a form of aesthetic experience in its reading that is as grounded as it is strange.

While any attempt to paraphrase or describe the story will fall very short of its density, the point Adorno made about the peculiarity of referring to a melancholy evening provides a way of approaching this density, which in turn reveals how the objectivity of a situation can arise through but also in place of a subject.[4] The couple sit facing each other and their conversation is somewhat languid, giving the air of comfort and distraction. She is leaving soon to visit someone, and he cannot come along as he has work to do, or, as he says in a slightly unusual way, 'I must try to bring this to an end now quickly' [VL: 156/2]. Placing this statement at the beginning of the story is clearly pointed, especially as it is concerned with the completion of an act or feeling. But the initial focus is on the divergence of their thoughts, an inevitable and yet not unpleasant difference, and the momentum that arises out of this tension. For not only is there an attempt at completion but this occurs with a sense of increasing compulsion or desire, which will mark its fulfilment with an additional feeling of urgency or repletion. The blinds are drawn in their apartment, and they are drinking tea, and as she pours the tea her arm forms an angle with the gaze that she directs at her husband, a momentary but rigid angle.

> Certainly an angle, as one could see; but another, almost physical one could only be felt by the two people inside it, to whom it seemed as if it stretched between them like a strut made of the hardest metal and held them firmly in their places and yet bound them, despite the fact that they were so far apart, to a unity that could almost be felt with the senses ... it leaned on the pits of their stomachs and they felt the pressure there ... it raised them stiffly on the armrests of their seats, with unmoved faces and fixed gazes, and yet where it met them they felt a tender emotion, something very light, as if their hearts were fluttering into one another like two swarms of small butterflies ....
>
> The whole room clung to this thin, barely real and yet so perceptible feeling, as if on a gently trembling axis, and then to the two people upon whom it was leaning: the objects around held their breath, the light on the wall froze to golden tips ... everything was silent and waited and was there because of them ... the time that runs like an endless glittering thread through the world seemed to go right through this room and seemed to go right through these people and suddenly seemed to stop and get stiff, very stiff and still and glittering ... and the objects moved a little closer together. It was that standing still and then soft sinking, as if surfaces were suddenly arranged and a crystal was formed ... around these two people through whom its centre ran and who suddenly, through this holding of breath and arching and leaning around them, as if looking through thousands of reflective surfaces, looked at each other again as if they were seeing each other for the first time....
>
> VL: 156–57/3–4 (ellipses in original)

The architecture is very defined and yet oddly elusive. We sense the relation between the two figures, and that with the material objects around them, as well as the intensity of their mutual refractions such that the dual image of a crystal and a swarm of butterflies can coincide. A centripetal and centrifugal force is sketched out that is somehow stable despite its inner and outer tensions. (It is not necessary to stress the comparison, as their accounts have very different concerns, but it is worth noting how Musil's narrative dissipates the sensuality that was found in Klossowski's thought, not to render its atmosphere weaker but to make it more pervasive. Where Klossowski was focused on the nature and effects of the perverse gesture, this notion seems to have become expanded to the entire milieu in Musil's version.)

This point is borne out by what comes next, for after discovering each other again they seem to become lost in their shared thoughts. The preceding conversation about the impending journey is not revisited and instead they return to a topic to which they have apparently often been drawn, that of the peculiarities of the character of G. However, this is also a form of indirection, since in talking about G. they are only taking up another route to reflect upon themselves. G. is a criminal, he takes advantage of women and children and seems to find some kind of erotic stimulation in doing so, but the question of his motivation remains unclear, and thus of his culpability. As she asks: 'Do you believe that he means to do wrong?' [VL: 157/4] The fact that G. seems to enjoy what he does suggests that he does not think he is doing wrong, which implies that, as appalling as his acts are, they are for him a way of finding pleasure, and so this kind of pleasure would seem to occupy a space that is distinct from what is ordinarily considered right and pleasurable. The sense of what G. is doing then becomes extraordinary and fascinating, with the borderline between his eroticism and criminality rendered almost non-existent and, as a result, the couple keep coming back to him in their thoughts. The husband suggests that perhaps one should not ask questions about G.'s intentions, that such feelings are possibly beyond what can be discussed. Neither agreeing nor disagreeing with this thought she says that she believes he means to do good, although it is not clear what she is basing this belief on, other than a kind of empathy. G. is no longer merely a fictional character but a concrete extension of her own feelings, with the profound uncertainty of not knowing how much this extension derives from herself or from what she has read. The encounter she has had with G. in reading the novel has given rise to a new feeling, which has emerged just as her feelings in relation to her husband emerge within the situation of their home, as an obscurely sensual deviation. She seeks to put this feeling into words:

'...he hurts his victims badly, he must know that he is demoralising them, disturbing their sensuality and drawing them into a motion that will never again be able to find rest in any goal...and yet, it is as if you saw him smiling...very soft and pale in the face, very sad and yet determined, full of tenderness ... with a smile full of tenderness that hovers over him and his victim ... like a rainy day over the country, the sky sends it, it is incomprehensible, in his sadness lies all apology, in the feeling that accompanies his destruction ... Isn't every mind something lonely and alone? ...'

VL: 158/5 (ellipses in original)

There almost seems to be a form of religious Romanticism here: the inscrutable and tragic figure who brings destruction and a strange justice insofar as his acts are as incomprehensible as the weather. But it is also the case that her description seems to lose its bearing, since the merging of these feelings with what seems to surpass them suggests a breaching of the pathetic fallacy. It is not the case that the weather is being personified through G.'s acts, or even vice versa, but that both G. and the rainy sky seem to refer to an incomprehensibility that is beyond both. The tenderness and melancholy are neither fully human nor inhuman, and it is perhaps in this excess that they find a state that is singularly alone. Moreover, it is in its sensuality that this excess appears to be grounded, a sensuality that is condemned to be perpetually unsatisfied.

Musil confirms this sense of subtle transformation in the following lines in writing that the couple, led into silence by these meditations, 'thought together about that third, unknown person, about this one of the many third persons, as if they walked together through a landscape' [VL: 158/5]. It is not just G. who is at stake in these meditations but the very notion of a third, which as the reference to the landscape indicates is not just a third person, but the idea of a third, of that which arises out of the interaction of others and is not reducible to them. Such an idea is abstract in its removal and concrete in its sensual existence, and yet it remains peculiar, estranged, by virtue of its lack of clear provenance or purpose. Hence this is not just the third that arises from reading or conversation but that which comes from the divergence of sensuality and thought, which subtends the former engagements and leads them to deviate into uncertain landscapes, as she is beginning to experience under the influence of G. The quasi-mystical sense of this third is further extended in its incomprehensible violence, as it acts in ways that cannot be grasped, for in its abstraction there lies a mysterious distance or emptiness that fascinates, a sub-Nietzschean form of transgression that Musil offers as a problem and as a critique. While the critique of this fascination is brought out more fully in relation to Moosbrugger in *Der Mann ohne Eigenschaften*, Musil already recognizes the problematic condition of this state in his early account. As a result, it is not simply to be dismissed as ersatz mysticism, for desire unfolds in a way that appears inhuman in its excess but also unavoidable in its bodily imperative. The woman in 'Die Vollendung der Liebe' appears to confront this problem by exploring the demands of her sensuality while seeking to remain within its concrete emotional ambits. Part of the force of this problem is captured in the notion of completion (*Vollendung*), which attempts to encompass the fulfilment of that which seem unfulfillable, and the excess that comes with this sense of fulfilment; at what point and in what way is completion to be recognized if it surpasses itself?

It is the singularity of this sense that seems to bear out its excess, however, in this excess, desire brings a sense of dissociation, 'sometimes all things are suddenly doubled as they stand there, fully and clearly, as one knows them, and then again, pale, twilit, and frightened, as if they were already being looked at secretly and distantly by the other' [VL: 159/7–8]. Such an image was used to describe G. in his distance from those whose suffering he brings about, and it is part of the estrangement that is intrinsic to desire that it transforms those that it subjects to its force, which thus makes the idea of completion unreachable and yet also provides it with a form of reflexivity, its own sensuous thought. In this way, the distance seems to provide its own answer as its dissonance is not suppressed but reflected, or refracted, and so the couple find a response to the disturbance that has arisen between them by staring out into the night, just as they had imagined G. doing in contemplating his victims from afar, and in looking out of their windows at night they of course see nothing more than themselves staring back, but differently, doubled. The feelings within which they had existed now seem estranged, extending out from the angles and bonds that had arranged themselves around them to the far corners of the night sky.

The first part of the story ends here and is taken up again with the woman's journey. She is now given a name and a background, but these are mere notes before returning to the experience of her feelings, which finds an almost Sadean form, for 'with a strength of passion she committed and suffered acts to the point of humiliation and yet never lost a consciousness that everything that she did had not, at root, disturbed her and essentially had nothing to do with her' [VL: 160/10]. Furthermore, this feeling of distance has the effect of leading her into a certain kind of space, as it makes her feel 'like a guest who enters a strange house only once and, thoughtlessly and a little bored, abandons herself to everything [*allem überläßt*] she encounters there' [VL: 161/11]. As has been seen, the space of the house is centrifugal and centripetal, involving both separation and intimacy, and thereby operating as an analogue of the mind, of its abandon and reflection. But in finding herself in the place of a guest, Claudine discovers that she has retained the liberty of distance, which arises not only from thought but through the reflection of a hidden sensuality. This notion of sensuality remains just beyond the reach of perception, either because it is too slight, like a memory, sound, or thread of intangible experience, or because it is too broad, like the feeling of sickness, or of the crowds, or the movement of the train, which both repel and attract her as a kind of subliminal sublime, suggesting the possibility of giving herself up to it, of losing responsibility for one's actions. The disturbance brought about by this pervasive but elusive sense becomes ever more powerful and tantalizing. Objects that would have ordinarily appeared innocuous are now felt to be bearers of some form of resonance, everything becomes potent, and the borders of her body are found to be permeable. In entering the movement of the crowd or the train, she finds that its movements enter her, just as her sense of entering a strange house became one of abandonment to its strangeness. But throughout it all she remains aware of the impulse to submerge herself, and of the reservation or inhibition that seems coupled to this impulse almost as its metric. The experiences of modernity described here, the crowds and the trains, are thus rendered into a form of modern sublime that is profoundly sensual and also critical, insofar as the feelings aroused by these experiences are precisely those that have been suppressed in the rationalization of modern life. Musil does not refer to the sublime, any more than he refers to any psychic or social economy, but the sense of what Claudine undergoes is captured in this way because of its combined repulsion and attraction and its breaching of the subject-object relation. In its place is found a perversion that is no longer a perversion from a previously established norm, but mere divergence, deviation, which bears away the fields of thought and sense at once. Thoughts and objects become confused, inside and outside are no longer delineated, what she sees outside the windows of the moving train comes to resemble the feelings that surface in her mind, so that it is not clear from which side they derive or where lies the sense of their concreteness. She formulates her feelings in terms of what she sees, and vice versa, which means that the world and her feelings come to merge without being fully united as there is still a force of distancing or estrangement within them as they diverge from each other and themselves.

Thus, infidelity is not opposed to fidelity, but extends it into a different kind of relation, a yearning. 'And she noticed that it came from a distant place, where her love was no longer just something between them alone but hung, in pale roots, uncertainly in the world' [VL: 165/18]. A feeling like a suspended rootlessness has expelled the couple from any sense of bearing love between them and instead it is found only in and as a 'painful expanse'. Their happiness has become 'something loose, supple, and obscurely sensitive', which leads to 'an almost sickly longing for the most extreme tension' [VL: 164/17]. The opening out found in this sensitivity appears to exacerbate itself, to yield to ever greater extremes, in which it finds a doubling or tension within itself even in its abandon. As a result, when Claudine encounters a man on the train he is at once irrelevant and an irritating stimulant and she responds to him as such, as what she had earlier called the contingency of mere factuality (*Tatsächlichkeit*). However, in this disruption there is a perverse pleasure, the pleasure of going out of oneself, of countering oneself, which derives from its extension, as when 'one hits someone weak out of tenderness, a child, a woman, and then wants, alone in the dark, to be the garment around their pains' [VL: 168/24]. Such had been the impact of the character of G., who exemplified this enigmatic self-transgression: the pleasure of going against oneself that comes from allowing oneself to be affected, touched, by reality, as had been suggested earlier when he was described as wandering through the house of his feelings until he came to press his face against the window in contemplating his victims, where this act of touching upon the outside imparts its own complex disturbance of abandon and distancing that takes shape as reflection [VL: 158/6]. Fidelity yields (to) infidelity, just as relinquishment to the sensual bears its own eccentric thought.

And so, in the intimate surroundings of the snow and the night and the warmth, she begins to become aroused, a feeling that arises as an impression of a dense but inconspicuous reality into which she sinks with a sense of inevitability. For in it the sense of her present is replaced by an overlapping of the reappearance of the past and the urgency of the future, which marks this presence with a sense of fate. Such an understanding of time may help explain the movement of the story itself with its slow development concealed within an intense and extravagant imagery. As commentators have noted, the difficulty of the narrative derives from its insistent allusiveness; concrete descriptions barely appear before they are consumed by a turmoil of vague intonations.[5] The text is constructed from its language of sensations, however eccentrically, rather than any events or characters, and these sensations bear their own inevitable course of changes and displacements. Language then becomes a moving field of obscurely intimate approximations in which the occasional object becomes both a spur and a distraction. In reading the work we are immersed in this field as it transforms objects into sensations and, conversely, as the imagery itself becomes the object or matter of the work. It is thus that sensuality takes place in language as an experience of the elusiveness of its consummation, for even as it expresses itself it becomes delayed and deferred by its own expression. The imagery does not progressively unfold as much as it seems to expand and contract and thereby find its rhythm.

> And yet she obscurely grasped that it was not this stranger who lured her, but only this standing and waiting, a fine-toothed, wild, self-sacrificing [*preisgegebene*] bliss of being herself, human, cracked open like a wound in her awakening among the lifeless things. And while she felt her heart beating, as if she were carrying an animal in her breast – disturbed, lost somewhere in her – her body lifted itself oddly in its silent swaying and closed around it like a large, strange, nodding flower, through which the strained intoxication of a mysterious union [*Vereinigung*] suddenly shuddered in invisible expanses
>
> VL: 173/32

The body of the sensuous takes shape as its own singular form, within and in contrast to that which surrounds it, just as her feelings do in the language of the work, and in doing so it bears itself out as a tensely open waiting, a pressure building without clarity or direction.

In her meditations there arises, vaguely and ominously, a memory of debasement that seems no longer to be a memory but to be a portent or temptation to which she can find no resistance, and significantly no language, and so her thoughts are cast adrift on its formlessness. Lost to herself she begins to imagine that if she had been unfaithful to her husband before she knew him, then it was also the case that she loved him before she knew him [VL: 175/35]. The equivalence of love and infidelity is thereby marked and leads to a disruption of temporal and semantic order, of the logic of relations, which becomes concrete in the distance from herself in which she has found herself, meaning that she is not only disoriented but also displaced in and from herself. A dislocation that takes place across space and time through the emergence of the sensual. This is not to suggest mere confusion but a more complex disturbance of thinking and the self that arises from and bears itself away on the force of desire. An abandon that is not limited to one order of sense but makes possible a thought of fidelity that does not exclude infidelity through an incomprehensible coexistence of yes and no. And with the imbrication of past and future, there is a sense of incipient completion to her love that nevertheless remains at a distance, which leads, as she says, to a peculiar air of pastness (*Vergangenheit*) over everything [VL: 175/36]. Intrinsic to this sense of completeness is thus its corruption, its passing away and disintegration, since this is not a whole that is constructed from unity and coherence but from the consuming force of desire, which bears out its whole from within.

At the institute, where she meets her daughter's tutors, she encounters the same heavy and impassive objects that had surrounded her in her hotel rooms, and in response to them she finds the same tension of repulsion and attraction, a desire that arises (almost in a Hegelian manner) out of the distance from that which it comes up against, so that this distance is converted into a desire that does not lack distance. That is, the objects in their imposing appearance compel and resist her and this force, as it turns upon itself, bears the distance and constituent density of that from which it derives. In subordinating herself to the objects she is thereby subordinating herself to the force of her desire, which has become just as opaque for her as these objects. Hence in her desire she experiences this distancing as both overpowering and alienating, dominating and yet somehow removed from her, a tension that makes it doubly engaging:

> something secretly moved inside her and shook her softly; not an individual feeling but some ground in which they all rest – as when you sometimes walk through apartments that disgust you, but gradually you get an idea of how people can be happy there, and suddenly there comes a moment when it embraces you as if you were one of them, you want to jump back and yet feel frozen, the world is closed in on all sides and stands calmly around this centre . . .
>
> VL: 177/40–41 (ellipsis in original)

Desire becomes an experience *of* abstraction (in both its subjective and objective aspects) that remains material and so allows for a feeling of concreteness as such, which the language itself conveys in its slow circling of sense. This link to an objectivity that has become one's own, as Adorno had noted, is also inflected as a link to the past, which is as inevitable and arbitrary as any other object. Desire comes to bear a movement of its own that is both spatial and temporal, a kind of sensible estrangement that constitutes existence as that which is continually separating from itself. But this separation sets up a tension, for in it there is both consistency and indifference, since the betrayals of this perpetual faithlessness become more regular and insignificant, leading to a perverse solitude in relation to the ever-changing world. Thus, infidelity comes to be a perverse form of fidelity, but a fidelity to oneself and one's relation to the world.

It is worth remarking on the uniqueness of this text, for as noted it seeks neither to analyse, in psychoanalytic terms, nor to describe, in phenomenological terms. Although Musil studied under Carl Stumpf for a PhD on Ernst Mach just before writing *Vereinigungen*, his approach does not adhere to the proto-gestalt psychology introduced by Stumpf. Instead, the slow and meandering examination of female desire is intended not just to explore its vicissitudes but to convey them to the reader. As such, he is not following the movements of Claudine's consciousness as much as the way that her feelings are triggered or ruptured by the things around her. This leads to a staggered development, as it is the interactions of the material and sensual that are in focus rather more than the movement of consciousness itself. It is possible to go further, for in the persistent use of a vocabulary of analogy, Musil seeks to develop a language that is not spatio-temporal but transitional, that is, it attempts to sketch the movements by which spatiality and temporality pass into or disrupt each other and that his language is demonstrating more than just tracking. Alongside its ambiguities and allusions, through which images are raised only by way of their intimation, the repeated use of ellipsis suggests an approach to content that (initially, at least) avoids or resists its consummation. By exposing and then suspending such determinations, the writing extends the distance and tension inherent in the movement of desire, not to engage in a mere play of deferral but to find that in which this movement insists and also what it bears as its own thought and sense, its own dimensions and relations. In this way, it might be said that Musil's account is closer to Schoenberg's *Erwartung*, or the paintings of Egon Schiele, than it is to literary works like Mann's *Tod in Venedig* or Rilke's *Malte Laurids Brigge*, which also date from this time. In developing this approach Musil was not interested in making judgements or diagnoses but in finding the language in which the movement of feelings could express itself. That is, feelings do not simply take shape in language but in a stronger sense express themselves through it, as he stated in a letter to his editor: 'The comparisons, images, and style are not dictated by the author but are the psychic constituents of the person whose emotional range is transcribed [*umschreibt*] in them.'[6] This creates a different kind of psychological novel, one that is provoked but also hampered by its attempt to allow these feelings to emerge in all their detail and fluidity.

In a sense, and in a move that recalls Adorno's aesthetics, Musil is pursuing a reversal of the trajectory by which feelings derive from mimesis, to show the ground of changeability that is consolidated and organized into emotions. This ground operates between subject and object and before these categories fully arise, which can explain the difficulty of putting its movements into words, as it is 'an independent, incomprehensible world of feeling, which only arbitrarily, accidentally, and silently, fleetingly, connects itself with everyday reason, like those deep, soft darknesses that for no reason sometimes move across a shadowless, rigid sky' [VL: 182/49]. Again, there is a return to the sky as an image of impassivity and distance that nevertheless seems perturbed by those things that are estranged from it. The uncertainty of these feelings is the basis of their strangeness as they lack a foundation either in reason or in fact, instead, they remain obscure and fleeting and a constant source of disruption. What is found in cases like those of G. or Claudine is the effect of this reversal, where the sky can no longer remain distant from that which disturbs it, and as this disturbance cannot be fully isolated or determined it persists, bringing its own sense of informal parsing of the world with all its ambivalence and sensitivity. In this state Claudine finds herself closer to animals or objects and, as a result, these things begin to resonate oddly, appearing no longer at a distance but somehow out of place – crude, ugly, disgusting – for they, like her, are not part of the regular order of things anymore. Instead, there is a field of uncertainty in which things open up or move, as if inside and outside were confused: 'Holes opened up before her feelings, as if – since that last security in her had begun to stare dreamily at itself – something had loosened in the otherwise imperceptible embedding of things in her sensation, and instead of a concatenated ringing of impressions, the world around her became like an infinite noise through these interruptions' [VL: 184/52]. The calm perceptual relation between subject and object has turned on itself and somehow released itself, replacing the systematicity of sense with something more like a dissonance without borders. Desire tears her away from herself, out of herself. This feeling is not the harmonious oceanic experience apparently felt in religious moments, but something of greater wildness and abandon, a swirling mass out of which fragments of sound and sense appear and disappear. In this way, and against the vector of consistency with which they would attempt to draw themselves together, thought and language reveal that which subtends their nominal order. The idea that language can be a bulwark against this disorder, a counter to both noise and silence, is then lost, for language becomes that in which both noise and silence express themselves. It is thus that a reversibility comes to affect the thought of faithfulness that had held her back, just as it is found that faithlessness is reversed into its other in her bodily relation to objects. Almost as if her feelings were oscillating (with desire) in the way that Hegel described the negation of negation involved in the resonance of materiality.

Amidst these ideas there are more conventional notions of a separation between conscious and bodily intentions, and of a longing for unity with the other, but these only appear as attempts to formulate the uncertainty that assails her, to contain it within readily available concepts, which all too quickly give way to a more profound and unsettling feeling that is at one point called the *Sterbenssehnsucht* of her love, a mortal longing, or yearning for death, which is its culmination as both its closure and its release, love realizing itself in its own death, so that the latter becomes the perfection of love, just as fidelity is actualized as infidelity [VL: 186/57]. This radically alienating thought separates her from herself, her past, and her husband, and also from the clumsy clichés that the Ministerialrat uses to seduce her.[7] He is no more important than the other objects that surround her and only appears within her feelings as a source of reflection or provocation. This alienation serves to counter the isolating, individualizing alienation of everyday life (as Adorno suggested) in which all things swim in their own circles, undisturbed and undisturbing. The ruptures of her existence have shown that its purported necessity is no more than a habit based on contingency; that the bonds that tie her to herself, her past, and her husband, could have been otherwise or not at all, which means that within her love there lies a force of meaninglessness below the apparent order. Where previously such a thought would have frightened her, now she sees that in bearing out its insignificance to its end there is a kind of union, like that of a 'love gliding between two mirrors' with nothing beyond [VL: 188/60]. So, and perhaps because of this discovery of the empty and accidental nature of her life, she finds intimacy in a state of abandon, on the old carpet in her room, and in her almost elemental pleasure she remains beside herself, both distinct and together, as if accompanying her abandonment. But the councillor is not there, the act of infidelity is itself unfaithful; even though he appears to have been nearby, the act is only consummated in the sense of the loss that ensues, the feeling of impermanence and unimportance with which desire completes itself.[8] 'A pain that was like a space, a dissolved, floating, and yet gently rising space, as if connected to a mild darkness' [VL: 190/63]. The space of abandonment seems to close in on itself without being limited, so that desire does not achieve a point of actual culmination but instead endures its own end as its ending, which informs the dissolution of its terms in thought and language that the text has demonstrated, since the apparent opposites of closure and excess no longer define her. The subsequent and final scenes, in which the infidelity actually occurs, are not important anymore as everything seems to have already taken place and the councillor retreats to being no more than the object he was earlier. The urge to give in to him has no resonance and so it happens like all other meaningless things happen. Her desire is beyond the point of tearing her apart just as it is beyond the movement of expansion and contraction, instead, there is only suspension and contingency, and the emptiness into which they pass.

Twenty-five years after completing 'Die Vollendung der Liebe' Musil wrote some notes for a preface to a projected re-edition of *Vereinigungen*. In these notes he made the following statement about his style in these early stories: 'The decision was formed to choose 'the path of the greatest burden' / the path of the smallest steps / the path of the most gradual, most imperceptible transition. / This has a moral value: the demonstration of the moral spectrum with continuous transitions from something to its opposite'.[9] This quasi-dialectical procedure would seem to fulfil itself in the narrative in the move by which it carries on after its apparent culmination, and in which Claudine lives on beyond her own climax, surviving her own end, to find in the last lines of the story, and yet still very far away, an image of her love. It is worth looking at this passage more closely, as it bears an explicitly conclusive flourish that is nevertheless profoundly uncertain: 'And then she felt with a shudder how, in spite of everything, her body filled with lust. But it was as if she were thinking of something that she had once felt in the spring: the way one can be there for everyone and yet only for one. And far away, the way children say of god, he is great, she had an idea of her love' [VL: 194/70]. This is not a straightforward image of a woman giving in to passion, however ambivalently. Instead, there is a consciousness of this submergence that keeps her at a distance from what she undergoes, which enables her to reflect on the dissolution at the same time as she endures it. It is in and as this differentiation, or through it, or from it, that she comes to apprehend the distant image of her love, an image that persists insofar as it remains distant, and remains the image of her own persistence after the end, remains *unfaithful to the end*. The mention of god is surprising in its familiarity and seems almost parodic in its suddenness. This name has not appeared elsewhere in the narrative, so its appearance in the last sentence cannot be taken casually, but its appearance is merely that of a vague analogy. If Claudine has an idea of her love in the same way that children talk about god, then it is very real and yet indeterminate, which means that it is not, as an idea or image (*Vorstellung*), given any greater definition but remains merely the sense of the distance that occurs to her in her passion.

II Perverse Works

Sensuality is not just its own form of aesthetic experience as it provides an analogue of the aesthetic experience of artworks, except that it is not just an analogue. Instead, it is the condition and prototype of such an experience insofar as it is a form of mimetic recapitulation, and tacitly, reflexively, a recapitulation of its own experience. From such a perspective it is possible to understand the perversity and endlessness of sensuality, and also its image-like quality, for in sensuality it is the notion of identity itself that is perverted. For Adorno, this experience is integral to aesthetics in general in that the experience that is aesthetics is one in which subject and object are transformed, both in themselves and in their relation. Thus, the works of Sade, Klossowski, and Musil are not only demonstrative of the extension of aesthetic experience but are also indicative of the mode and status of the experience of artworks as such.

Sensuality, like the avant-garde artwork, is not socially useful as it partakes in acts that are non-procreative (it does not sustain the reproduction of society), which is the basis by which perversion in general becomes morally reprehensible. Insofar as procreation is not just a moral issue but a national duty, both in fulfilling the life of the nation and preserving the structure of the family, perversion becomes a political challenge. It is thus that it leads to medical and legal programmes of control, wherein the private sphere of personal satisfaction becomes a challenge with pathological or criminal connotations. Underlying these issues, much as is found in the avant-garde artwork, lies the problematic status of the 'nature' that is unveiled, which is found not to be a harmonious and beatific nature that can be controlled but one riven with tension. Perverse sensuality is a sphere in which this anomalous nature, in relation with its sociohistorical determinants, becomes exposed. In doing so, it contests the basis of its medico-legal categorization by refusing the identification of such perversity with the person's apparently underlying 'nature'. Just as with the artwork, such sensuality does not derive from an essence, and so does not partake of normality or abnormality, but rather responds to the combination of its materials and its context to pursue the extremes of sensuality that emerge from it.

At a key moment in Claudine's ordeal, just after she has realized the implications of how the councillor views her, she is struck by a thought: 'For a moment something in her shuddered and warned her, the word sodomy occurred to her, shall I commit sodomy . . .?!' [VL: 180/45 (ellipsis in original)] The strength of this word comes from the fact that it refers not just to anal sex but, in historical terms, to a wide range of non-procreative acts, like bestiality, masturbation, oral sex, and coitus interruptus (and even sex between a Christian and a non-Christian, or sex in which the woman is on top), all of which are condemned because they were (believed to be) incapable of leading to reproduction. These points are probably not all present in Claudine's thought, but they indicate the potent sense of social disruption that the word bears and the force with which her sensual experience is seizing her, since it is concerned not just with infidelity but with a perverse sexual encounter – it is the idea of 'sodomy' that occurs to her, not 'adultery'. Moreover, as scientific interest in sexual 'perversions' grew during the nineteenth century, the argument about their status changed from one in which they caused mental or moral disorder to one in which they were caused by mental or moral disorder, and so the individual became pathologized on the basis of their sexual *identity*, insofar as they were now deemed to *be* a pervert, that is, someone suffering from abnormal perversions of the mind or of morality. The scope of perversity then became defined and prosecuted as a danger to public health.[10] As Adorno notes, this essentialization arises out of a very significant lineage of thought, for where in Protestant and Kantian morality there is a turning away from a morality based in what one *does* to one based in what one *is*, this apparent removal from the natural world only reinstates its ideology more profoundly, 'by establishing its so-called essence [*Sosein*] against the individual act and against the individual work of the individual person, this anti-naturalistic moral philosophy turns back, at its highest point, into a kind of natural doctrine, into a kind of natural morality, which amounts to saying that if someone is noble, namely of noble nature, so to speak, everything is allowed to them, while "inferior" people should not be allowed anything' [LGF: 356–57/256]. Nature receives a covert re-endorsement based upon a perceived natural morality, which then allows for the same ideological separation of normal and abnormal. 'Nature' is thereby recruited as the basis and justification for a historical judgement, whereas in the study of perversion and libertinism, as has been seen, nature is found to be refractory to such judgements. The importance of Sade's works in particular comes from his realization of the range and depth of effects that sensuality generates, and the way that this brings about an encounter between nature and history that is profoundly challenging to any social order. Contrary to the readings of nature as either beatific or satanic, which lead to its Romantic valorization or its moral suppression, Sade's nature is strictly amoral, and in acts of sensuality it is taken up to exhibit its potential and its autonomy, just as aesthetic material is taken up in artworks. However, just as is the case with artworks, such acts are necessarily always at risk of succumbing to the forces of commodification and instrumentalization, as is found in the fields of entertainment and advertising, for example, where they are made socially useful.

Nevertheless, sensuality is not the same as the experience of artworks, for the latter are intrinsically linked to the notion of disinterest, however much Adorno comes to criticize this notion. It is important to remember the nuance of his argument, which is to distance aesthetics from interest only on the basis of instrumental needs: 'Artistic experience is only autonomous where it discards enjoyable taste. The path to it leads through disinterestedness; the emancipation of art from the products of the kitchen or from pornography is irrevocable. But it does not come to rest in disinterestedness. Disinterestedness immanently reproduces, transforms, interest' [AT: 26/12–13]. Here lies the importance of the distance that is taken in and alongside the abandon of sensuality, for even though artistic autonomy can never separate itself from sensual interest, it nevertheless distances itself from merely culinary tastes, as a result: 'In significant works, the sensual, illuminated by its art, becomes spiritual, just as conversely, the abstract detail, however indifferent to appearance it may be, gains sensual brilliance from the spirit of the work. Sometimes articulated works of art, which have been fully developed through their differentiated formal language, play into what is sensually pleasing as a secondary role.' This emergent dialectic of interest transformed by disinterest then takes on the form that is distinctive of modern works of art: 'Dissonance, the signature of all modernity, even in its optical equivalents, grants this alluring sensual inlet by transfiguring it into its antithesis, pain: the original aesthetic phenomenon of ambivalence' [AT: 29/15]. Pleasure comes together with pain in its own form of dialectic, or dissonance, as a pain that is pleasurable alongside a pleasure that is painful, as is found in many aesthetic experiences or acts of sensuality, as Claudine has discovered.[11] Although, just as is found with the status of autonomy, such dissonance can fall into a reified amelioration and indifference as a result of the taboo on the sensual, which is also a taboo on pain. So, while sensuality is distinct from the aesthetic experience of artworks, the dissonant nature of sensuality renders it in a form that is able to bear its own complex of interest and disinterest, or fidelity and infidelity. There is thus an important corollary to this combination, for in the shared and reciprocal estrangement of the sensual and the abstract, 'the immanent play of forces of the artwork converges with external reality' [AT: 30/15].

As a result, neither Musil nor Claudine manage to extricate themselves from the network of social, psychological, and historical forces that determine female sexuality, but the singularity of the story is that something emerges by way of a resistance to these forces. As has been seen, the relation of female sexuality to a reified sphere of bodily intuition or animal sensuality is both marked and undercut by Claudine's experience, which also distances it from a notion of humanistic naturalness. In place of these repressive or sentimental notions, a form of sensuality arises that is not mythologically given or pathologically contained but is rather material and intellectual, and it is thus that the sense of its dissolution can be felt, as both its critique and its experience. As a result, the idea that a completion of love would involve infidelity embodies, in very concrete terms, the idea of a radical praxis that does not merely submit to material pressures but undergoes them as that which is its own painful end. That is, these pressures are taken up as part of the experience of sensual desire and realize its force of estrangement and fulfilment. Sensuality does not become an alienation that returns to itself but counters the pervasive alienation of bodily and social experience by deepening it and thereby uncovering its critique as that which can be endured and made radical. And, necessarily, as Adorno pointed out, the experience of this play of forces converges with that of reality, which allows for the reformulation of subject and object and their inter-relations, which is the experience he had marked in speaking of the mood that arises out of a freedom to the object, the further implications of which will be taken up in the next and last chapter. As he noted in 1963: 'It is part of sexual utopia not to be oneself, to love not merely the beloved in themselves: negation of the ego principle. It shakes that invariant of bourgeois society in the broadest sense, which has always aimed at integration, the demand for identity. First it had to be produced, then it would have to be sublated [*aufzuheben*] again. What is merely identical with itself is without happiness.'[12]

6

Modernity and Utopia

I Absolutely Modern

The figures that have been examined in this study – the libertine, the pervert, and so on – may be extreme but their possibility is inherent in Adorno's thinking of aesthetics insofar as they arise from the dissolution and abandon that takes place in the engagement with aesthetic material. As such, they are intrinsic not just to the development of his dialectical thought but also directly affect its role and status. On the one hand, this understanding of aesthetics reconfigures the position of his thought in relation to the problematic of theory and praxis, and on the other hand it implies that his thinking of aesthetics is no longer simply a philosophy but is itself an aesthetic theory.[1] What is uncovered in the encounter with the demands of aesthetic material is its dissonance, which leads thinking beyond itself, into perversity and eccentricity, through which it is always deviating from itself. This excess is part of dialectical thinking but is brought out unavoidably in aesthetics such that dialectics itself is led to change through this estrangement. The nature of this change can be further understood by returning to the examination of aesthetic material.

If, as the current of modern aesthetics demands, we are to seek to respond to the material on its own terms without imposing preconceived notions on it, then we are met with a problem, for in allowing the material to express itself it is found that this can only occur by way of our investment. That is, it is through our interest in the work that it expresses itself. The converse case is found in aleatory works, where the randomness of the work leaves it empty and inexpressive, or open to a myriad of arbitrary personal interpretations. There is no purity to the material that can be revealed by way of practices that seek not to intervene in it. Instead, the work can only reveal itself by way of its mediation and alienation, by which it negatively indicates what it might be, and thus provides not only a critique but a model of society. Two results of this line of thought thereby arise: firstly, that the crisis of meaning that Adorno presents – that materiality cannot come to express itself on its own and yet it is no longer acceptable to impose meanings on it from without – this crisis within the aesthetic object is 'also the crisis of the state of the world itself' [AS: 119/73]. Secondly, due to our mediated place in the world and the alienation presented by the work of art, 'the alienation of the world can only be reproduced in the work of art', where the emphasis is equally on the work of art and its reproduction of alienation [AS: 127/78]. Hence the construction of the work is equally an abandonment to it, and it is solely in this way that we should understand the term language when we speak of the language of artworks; that our use of it is equally our use by it as Kraus and, later, Paulhan made clear [QF: 538/319].[2] And so, because meaning is not given or natural, the dialectic of sense is such that it can only arise on the basis of its working through, which is just as much a working out of the subject, and in doing so it enables the material and its construction to come into themselves, to find their own form of ground.

Adorno says quite plainly that 'substantiality no longer has the power to carry art as something objectively binding'. That is, the apparently objective basis of art is no longer given: in regard to its place in the world and its concrete appearance, art lacks necessity, and this means that 'there is no longer an art movement today, and it is very difficult to imagine an art movement that draws its strength from assuming such a meaningful aspect as positively given' [AS: 123/76]. Modernity is then the condition in which there is no possibility for such an objectively given art movement, instead, there is only fragmentation and disarray. This positioning is not itself remarkable; however, Adorno traces the issue back to earlier formations that seemed more grounded, but in which the transition was already apparent, and in saying as much the problematic of modernity becomes dilated or dislocated. As he notes in reference to Romanticism or Expressionism, there is a perpetual tension between the effort to construct meaning out of the material and that which seeks to bring the material to express its own meaning, and thus a tension in the nature of expression and construction as such. The surprising point comes with the next step in his argument, where he turns to Plato's *Phaedrus* in order to show how the entire history of aesthetics is contained in its analysis of beauty. This discussion appears to be Adorno's only extended reference to Plato, and it is unusual in its positive appreciation and its emphasis on the madness that marks the experience of the beautiful, which is manifested as an erotic delirium, for through this enthusiasm the concept 'becomes what it really is, namely the objectively valid idea' [AS: 143/89]. The Hegelian move by which the soul leaves the body to return in a more informed state, which then realizes the idea of beauty, is rethought on the basis of the rapture or abandon of love, which is necessary if the thinking of beauty is to surpass mere reasoning.

A further point is mentioned in Adorno's introduction to this account, which is that the *Phaedrus* is a particularly complex dialogue in formal terms because it does not develop in the orderly way that the other dialogues do, like the *Symposium*, for example. The consequence of this different structure is that the parts of the dialogue condition each other so that there is no progressive dialectical elucidation of the topics but a spatial codetermination, which is perhaps closer to what is found in Schoenberg's twelve-tone technique. As a result, enthusiasm comes to take on the role of actualization in the argument that would have been undertaken by its development. It does so by suspending the movement of the dialogue in bringing about a relation between the conditionality of existence and the unconditionality of aesthetic experience, which is to say that the dialogue appears to actualize its own rupture and transgression through the experience of beauty, in the rapture of the fables that Socrates relates. But the situation is more complex, as Socrates explains, for in enthusiasm it is as though one had grown wings but was unable to fly, and so the sense of the unconditional is only felt as a kind of utopia alongside the pain of its distance (*Phaedrus*, 249d). While the individual faced by the beautiful is transported – as Socrates himself experiences in the presence of Phaedrus and that inspires (and is conveyed by) his fables – they are also made aware of their lack of movement, of their weakness and finitude, by which the sense of utopia is merely negatively presented. However, this means that the vision of the unconditional is accompanied by a reflexivity so that it is both interested and disinterested, enthused and aimless, grounded and released. Pain comes to be the term that discloses this doubled tension and thereby unveils the full scope of aesthetic pleasure:

> Pain, suffering, is to a certain extent the only form in which, in the face of the beautiful, we can even think, feel, or experience utopia as conditioned beings – because, as Plato says, we are not in control of it. If we were to see the beautiful in its primal image, then our whole life would be suspended; we can only experience it by longing, as it were, only in the form of the rupture that above all separates us from it, and therein is already laid out, further than an essentially dynamic moment in the experience of the beautiful, precisely this: that suffering, pain, and dissonance essentially belong to the beautiful and are not mere accidents.
>
> AS: 147–48/92

Intrinsic to Adorno's reading is the fact that beauty is not defined in itself but only through its conditions and effects, a form of negative circumscription that leaves its experience open and indeterminate while also making clear that it is of a different kind. Significantly, this reading means that the beautiful requires a subjective dimension, as it is found to occur through its effects, and yet it is not lacking in objectivity, as it actually occurs in and beyond its encounter. Hence, as Adorno concludes, this idea of beauty is dialectical, in that it takes place as mediated in itself, as 'something like a tension between subjective and objective moments' [AS: 151/94]. As such, the beautiful lies in a tenuous situation as it can succumb to the desire that animates it or remove itself entirely from this apprehension. The sublimation at issue, which only occurs in the absence of erotic satisfaction, is then at risk of falling into its subjective or objective moments.

Adorno is in part taking up Benjamin's notion of the constellation to show how the experience of the beautiful is formally prefigured. However, through its tension the form of the constellation is given greater material and constructivist moment. For in presenting itself by way of the constellation, the beautiful appears as sensual and as an idea, that is, as an intellectual image or feeling of abstraction, as can be felt in the shudder or goosebumps that accompanies the encounter with the beautiful (or sublime).[3] In this encounter the beautiful becomes an image of beauty itself, which is to say that it is, in Platonic terms, a form of mimesis, although Adorno reads this not as an imitation of the eternal idea of beauty, but simply as imitation. That is, the beautiful does not resemble some original image, but conveys the movement of similarity as such, the absolute quality of semblance, in which is also found its identification with what it is not, insofar as being like is not being the same but being different. Consequently, the feeling is one of likeness in itself as that which is resonant and yet remote, which confirms the unstable combination of pain and pleasure, attraction and repulsion, interest and disinterest that the beautiful manifests [AS: 161/100]. This anomalous sense of frustration is borne out in the fact that the feeling of utopia that the beautiful conveys cannot be made actually concrete, since its sense is precisely that of an image or semblance. So, it can either remain a work of art, and thereby relinquish its actualization, or it can actualize itself and thereby lose its sense of remaining unconditional. The frustration in this experience comes about because the moment of transition from one side of its dialectic to the other is elusive and uncontrollable. It then becomes apparent that the significance of Plato's account derives from the way that it finds the Kantian duplicity of the sublime in Hegel's description of beauty as the sensual appearance of the idea, and vice versa, and consequently exposes the tension inside and outside its dialectic (although Adorno admits that in this reading he is extending Plato's account beyond what is usually found in it). As such, the notion of the beautiful is characterized by the problem that its two aspects can neither be separated nor united, for each is mediated by the other: 'it is essential to the beautiful that the spiritual itself becomes sensual in it, that it appears, and that on the other hand the sensual itself, as the bearer of something spiritual, is at once spiritualized in its sensuality' [AS: 165/103]. Moreover, the tension of this dialectic is not released in the beautiful artwork but rather becomes its force field. The work of art possesses no essence or being that is somehow given in its appearance, instead, it presents itself in and as the contradiction between its reality and its form, which is both resolved and unresolved. It is this final contradiction that then takes place as the dissonance of the work: its appearance as that which is the image and the wreck of utopia, which is never stilled.

It is necessary to pause here because Adorno seems to be suggesting that the tension that he finds characteristic of the modern work of art can be detected in Plato's thought and, conversely, because this doubled tension is constitutive of the work, that what we understand by modern works of art will not be superseded or obscured by another seemingly later phase. Indeed, the description of the significant work of art seems to become coextensive with a form of modernism.[4] In addition, this coupling is also the form in which utopia takes place, such that it too becomes coextensive, in all its ambivalence, with a form of modernism. The category of modernism would then appear to be evacuated of any chronological, periodic sense, and instead made equivalent to the contradictory force field that takes place in and as the significant artwork. There are certainly advantages to removing the historical frame from the notion of modernism and finding it pervasive to artworks of all periods that sustain this sense of doubled tension, but it is also obvious that the term itself becomes unhelpful at this point. Despite the image of Adorno as a modernist, this was not a designation that he claimed or supported, for while its historical specificity may be useful in describing art movements of the nineteenth and twentieth centuries, with which he was mostly concerned, more critically, however, his focus was on the manner in which the dialectic of natural-history takes place in and as the work of art, which refers to the way that its temporal contours occur. 'Modernism' in this revised sense is apparent in his thinking as an aspect of the form that transpires in this dialectic as the mode of its natural-historical occurrence.

Describing Adorno, or his aesthetics, as modernist on the basis of his interest in Schoenberg or Beckett is clearly insufficient; he was not interested in their works because he or they were modernist but because of what they were seeking to do, something that he also finds in the works of Beethoven and Balzac. More helpfully, the form in which the term arises in his thinking is captured by Rimbaud's phrase 'il faut être absolutement moderne', which is more a statement of artistic necessity than a simple historical positioning. As Adorno says:

> the concept of the modern chronologically dates back long before the modern as a historico-philosophical category; however, this is not chronological but the Rimbaudian postulate of an art of the most progressive consciousness, in which the most advanced and differentiated procedures are saturated with the most advanced and differentiated experiences
>
> AT: 57/33

As such, Rimbaud's statement 'remains normative', and because 'art has its temporal core not in its material actuality but in its immanent formation' it is not tied to any particular material instance and so its norm remains as a persistent if unconscious rejection of what is not progressive, what is enervated by convention [AT: 286/192]. Importantly, the statement itself then becomes modern, by sustaining its own demand, and so Adorno can go on to say that it is not just an aesthetic principle but a categorical imperative for philosophy. As a result, it becomes removed from the tendency of history as such by taking its movements to an extreme.[5] The modern is thus distinguished from modernity or modernism in that it is, as Adorno writes, an intrinsic part of the work's development and it is also that part that bears the utopian in its contradictory tensions. Rimbaud's statement is a utopian declaration to the degree that it exists as an imperative, but only as an imperative; its force bears no guarantee of actualization. Indeed, and as was the case with the work of art, the existence of the imperative is a tacit recognition of the impossibility of its actualization, which nevertheless does not undermine its necessity. The statement formally enacts its own transgression, as it were, in the tension between its status as modern and its persistence as an imperative, which is to say that it is never merely formal.

> The new is the longing for the new, hardly the new itself, that is what everything new suffers from. What feels like utopia remains negative compared to the existing and yet belongs to it. Central among contemporary antinomies is that art must be and wants to be utopia, and all the more decisively, the more the real functional context obstructs utopia; but that, in order not to betray utopia in semblance and consolation, it must not be utopia.
>
> AT: 55/32

The question of the utopian aspect of the work is harder to define, for although Adorno speaks of the importance of the sensual elements of the work, the necessity of keeping a distance from their mere consumption or enjoyment requires an understanding of the way they sublate themselves without entirely disappearing. In understanding a work, one is drawn in by its sensual elements only to find that these are changed through their integration into the work as a whole, which brings them to express more than themselves, to express the sense or universality that the whole now makes apparent, but 'the more adequate the sensual experience of artworks, and the more perfectly one perceives a work of art sensually, the more one also distances oneself from the merely sensual element of artworks' [AS: 184/115]. As he notes, this model of aesthetic experience aligns itself with the thought that one 'throws away, in order to gain', but this notion, although often remarked in Adorno's works, seems to fall too closely into a form of Hegelian or theological sacrificial redemption, which risks losing sight of the complexity that has been uncovered. Instead, and following the reading of Plato, the model that arises in this understanding of sensuality is more like that of the abandon of lovers, such that the relation to the work of art is precisely that of giving oneself up to its movements, not in order to gain, but to be transported. It is this sense of completion or perfection that Musil sought, and that indicates the utopian aspect of the experience, which is not simply to be transported generally but is 'the inner spiritual co-enactment of what the work of art actually decides from itself as a sensual appearance' [AS: 189/118]. And what the work decides arises from and as the tensed combination of its material demands and its formal semblance, in both their natural-historical density and construction.

One of the most intriguing examples of this model comes from *Minima Moralia* and has often been discussed as an image of utopian longing. In examining the idea of a world released from oppression, the image of emancipation often inclines towards one of uninhibited pleasure, a notion that would seem close to what Sade's libertines enjoy. However, the world of libertinism is not simply one of sheer hedonism since it is combined with the coldness and perversity that allow its excesses to be pursued. Instead, their exploits are closer to an untrammelled experiment of the senses that seeks ever greater stimulation as their own demand. Thus, the image of emancipation is perhaps, as Adorno writes, more like a simple freedom from want and from the mercenary cycles of commodification that lead to ever more production and activity.

> Perhaps true society will grow weary of development and, out of freedom, leave possibilities unused instead of rushing towards strange stars under an insane coercion. For a humanity that no longer knows want [*Not*], something dawns of the delusional, futile nature of all the arrangements that up to then were taken to escape want, and that reproduced want with wealth. Enjoyment itself would be affected by it, just as its present schema cannot be separated from activity, planning, having one's will, subjugation. *Rien faire comme une bête*, lying on the water and gazing peacefully at the sky, "being, nothing else, without all further determination and fulfilment" could take the place of process, doing, fulfilling, and thus truly deliver on the promise of dialectical logic to flow into their origin. None of the abstract concepts come closer to fulfilled utopia than that of eternal peace. Onlookers of progress like Maupassant and [Carl] Sternheim have helped to give expression to this intention, as shyly as only its fragility permits.
>
> MM: 177/156–57

This passage is very dense and unfolding its details reveals an image that is not quite as peaceful as it might suggest, which is unsurprising given that it is unlikely that Adorno would simply endorse the idleness of the suggestion to *rien faire comme une bête*. Firstly, it should be noted that the reference to eternal peace in the penultimate line is a recollection of Kant's discussion, which begins with the satirical point that such a notion is captured in the 'Dutch innkeeper's signboard picturing a graveyard'. Secondly, the internal citation refers to Hegel's *Wissenschaft der Logik*, not to the fragmentary opening line of the determination of being, but to an earlier point in the introduction, where Hegel discusses the sheer immediacy of pure being.[6] To align this absolute starting point with that of idleness is almost parodic, but it indicates something of the sheer indeterminacy of the situation, which can, as with the logic, develop into everything that follows and thereby redeem the basis of the logic as one that, in unfolding, returns to itself. Finally, the reference to Maupassant is confirmed by the title of this aphorism, 'Sur l'eau'.

This last reference requires some more analysis as Maupassant wrote two texts with this title, both of which belie the peaceful image of lazy days on the water. In the first, a short story that first appeared in 1876, a man going home on a river at night suddenly finds that his boat cannot move and he is overcome with a strange anxiety as he is enclosed in the fog. Only later, after a night of terrors and wondrous visions, does he discover that his anchor had snagged on the corpse of an old woman who had drowned herself. The second text, a collection of sketches of boat trips along the French Riviera that was published in 1888, seems more suggestive until the bitterness of Maupassant's perspective manifests itself. For while the boat is an isolated sanctum away from the wretchedness of the world, and the expanse of water upon which the narrator gazes is calming and fascinating, there is at the edge of this expanse the spectre of land, with its endless stupidity, selfishness, and corruption. Clearly, the image of lying around on the water with nothing to do, like an animal, is far from harmonious, as it is torn between the space onto which it opens and the finitude that grounds it, while the situation itself is, as Adorno notes, fragile and uncertain. Indeed if, as Gerhard Schweppenhäuser suggests, we recall Odysseus's encounter with the sirens, then the first story, with its deadly submarine figure, appears even more resonant, for rather than sailing on regardless of the sirens' spell, the boatman is first terrified by the strange immobility that has trapped him and then, lying drunk on the floor of the boat and staring at the night sky, he is given a chance to wonder at its beauty without recognizing the material burden that anchors his perspective. The later text extends this tension to a degree that renders it all-encompassing, and as a result it becomes less tangible but more inescapable, for now the siren song is that of the land itself, and human society, which forever draws the narrator back.[7]

Enjoyment itself would become affected by this changed view of utopia; not to find it in mere culinary hedonism or obsessive consumerism, but to rethink it entirely from the sober vision of a finite transcendence that Maupassant has revealed. The thoughts of Kant and Hegel are also combined in this notion, with the tension between peace and death, and being and indeterminacy. The dialectical torsion that arises from the compression of each of these motifs constricts this passage in Adorno's text such that it is only in its careful unfolding, or co-enactment (*Mitvollziehens*), that it can find (and thereby lose) itself in its interpretation. What is initially presented as a straightforward image is reversed and complicated with each new phrase, so that it is no longer simply an image but, as he had earlier written, an exact imagination, which derives from a 'rigorous self-surrender to the material' [AS: 190/118]. In abandoning oneself to it, the form of the idea has arisen from the material, through its own demands but by way of our intervention. And it is only in this way that the passage can provide an idea of emancipation; not in the simple image of lazing on the river like an animal, but as that which is caught in the field of forces between death and the absolute that arises out of this image. In this way there is no mere redemption of the sensual in favour of the broader spiritual meaning of the piece, for what has been found continues to refer to its sense within the context of its concerns, a sense that to this degree remains materially indeterminate insofar as it cannot be precisely located.

However, this account has an important corollary, as has been noted, which is that it only leads to an image of utopia, not to an actual reorganization of the world. This is a problem that all aesthetics confronts in the form of its semblance, its illusory end to alienation, no matter how radical it may purport to be, but the counterpoint to this image-quality must also be grasped: that non-aesthetic life is also pervaded by this image-quality in the form of ideology, which directly affects experience. Thus, the artwork is engaged, as Adorno wrote, in trying to bring about a rearrangement of these schemata of experience, to remove their apparent immediacy and givenness by formally challenging their modes of development and reproduction. The semblance that then arises in thinking through the work does so as a moment of release, just as the boatman was struck by a wondrous vision of a moonlit valley amidst the fogbanks. This moment is not lost by the subsequent discovery (of the corpse, or its 'meaning'), just as the latter is not extrinsic to it; instead, the two aspects exist alongside each other in their never resolved dissonance, and it is this sense in all its concreteness and abstraction that the work provides. As a result, in terms of the intrinsic abstraction that the work conveys, its sense is thought, such that its experience is both sensual and reflective. In fact, Adorno goes even further: 'The sensual moment of art is perhaps itself [...] the very highest moment that is possible for art, in the sense in which sensual fulfilment is that which comes closest to what is called metaphysical experience; just as one can also rightly note the deepest sympathies between utopia and materialism' [AS: 228/143].

Hence what is thought in such (utopian) experiences is negativity, the experience of what there is alongside what is not, an experience of the object as that which is not entirely there, and as such is both fallible and indicative of something else, even if this alterity is not determinate.[8] Even though this experience cannot be entirely converted into cognitive terms, without it there would be no sense of change at all, and it is thus that negativity becomes a source of possibility. This would seem to be a very muted form of metaphysics, if that is what it is, however its significance does not come from its abstract formulations but from its actual occurrences, which is where thought gives way to the concrete. It is in the concrete occasions of this negativity that its dimensions become tangible and conceivable, so that, as Adorno later states, if we are to think of utopia at all, then it is as 'the colour of the concrete', which is its mode of formulation [LGF: 352/253; cf. ND: 66/57]. In this phrase it is necessary to hear the notion of timbre (*Klangfarbe*), the particular kind of sound formation that is unique to a material form, which indicates that utopia is not the concrete but that which arises from it and gives it its sense. And thinking through the concrete to its abstraction is what gives it its thought.

In turn, this redirection of thought indicates its aesthetic grounding, which is to emphasize the primacy of the object as that through which thinking takes place. Such a redirection implies that both the form and the content of thought are reconsidered on this basis, which is to say that it is perhaps by way of the minor but concrete models in *Minima Moralia*, for example, that its insights are developed with the most resonance. As has been seen with 'Sur l'eau', the construction of this piece and its bearing are oriented towards the mundane, not just the image of idleness but the sombre realization of its conditions. The minor key in which Adorno is working is reflected in the form of the works themselves, as is found in *Minima Moralia, Parva Aesthetica, Moments musicaux, Noten zur Literatur, Stichworte, Prismen*, and others. These titles are not signs of false modesty but mark the status of the work in relation to thought (which repositions the status of the major philosophical works, *Negative Dialektik, Ästhetische Theorie, Philosophie der neuen Musik*, in terms of their focus on the concrete). It is possible to gain an understanding of what is underway here by recalling the revision of Kant's thoughts of the sublime that Adorno develops. For, rather than the vision of the overwhelming size or power of nature granting an equal insight into the freedom and nobility of human thought, the sublime sense in Adorno's aesthetics is to be found in the dissonance it develops, the sense of resistance and interference, which is both a recognition of the kinship with nature and an awareness of the distance that such a kinship is stretched across, which only makes it fragile and ambivalent. The key to the sublime is not geared to the assumption of the human spirit but to its subtle disturbance, which is nevertheless profound and ineradicable. What it provides is exactly that shudder of thinking that is both sensual and cognitive, which arises when the 'patient contemplation of works of art sets them in motion' [AT: 124/79].

This motion is objective and reveals the instability of the work, its metaphysical negativity, as he had termed it, which then comes to affect the subject and occurs as the shudder of thought, its reflective but fascinated recoil. The shudder is the intimate awareness of uncertainty, a state in which something unknown is apparent that is directly and unequivocally affecting (and is the necessary reflection of desire in its yearning and negativity). It is not primarily painful or pleasurable but is rather a vital quickening, or alarm, to which thought must respond if only to register it, to mark it with a cross or a question mark or an exclamation. These marks punctuate thought as points of concrete intrusion and cannot simply be regularized or assimilated:

> Being struck by significant works does not treat them as a trigger for one's own, otherwise repressed, emotions. It belongs to the moment in which the recipient forgets himself and disappears into the work: that of shock [*Erschütterung*]. He loses the ground under his feet; the possibility of truth, which embodied in the aesthetic image, becomes incarnate for him [...] The experience [*Erfahrung*] of art as that of its truth or untruth is more than a subjective experience [*Erlebnis*]: it is a breakthrough of objectivity into subjective consciousness. It is mediated by it where the subjective reaction is most intense.
>
> AT: 363/244-45

Hence the range that aesthetics takes for Adorno, which involves the most intense reaction that is not just a reaction to the work but a mediation by it. As the use of *Erschütterung* indicates, this reaction is akin to a vibratory shock, a shaking resonance with and through the object by which *Erfahrung* is distinguished from *Erlebnis* insofar as experience is mediated by objectivity. As a result, this mediation is also of objectivity in its experience, so that its formation is in part determined by the subject, which means that this 'constitutive relation of the subject to objectivity in aesthetic behaviour marries eros and knowledge' [AT: 490/331]. This is the only occasion in *Ästhetische Theorie* where Adorno mentions eros, and it comes at the end of his discussion of the theories that seek to determine the origin of art. As such, it provides an important modulation of his thinking, which had largely considered the shudder in terms of a frightening encounter and thus of potentially primal origin. However, in associating it with the notion of eros, he approaches the idea that sensuality is the sphere of subjective and objective formation and deformation. Thus, this sphere is not without a relation to language and thought, to the knowledge that arises in these encounters precisely by virtue of their intimacy with the object. And, importantly: 'These moments are not pleasurable, rather the happiness lies in that one has them' [AS: 197/123].

At the beginning of this study aesthetics was said to be critical for the development of Adorno's understanding of dialectics. It is now apparent that it goes further than this by changing the form of dialectics itself, so that it is no longer possible for it to take shape in a systematic philosophy; aesthetics has displaced Adorno's thought into the concrete, through which is found both its strengths and its weaknesses. In addition, by effectively subordinating dialectics to aesthetics, Adorno's thinking appears to have become aporetic in that it not only finds but loses itself in the concrete; it reaches a point beyond which it seems unable to proceed philosophically. However, in this position it is also on the brink of its own natural-historical horizon, with its concomitant avant-garde demands, which places it in a very different situation in terms of its status as thought.

II The Challenge

In early 1963 Adorno gave a talk on Swiss radio about a piece of literature that he particularly 'loved', a section from Balzac's *Illusions perdues* [NL2: 363/36]. Adorno's fondness for Balzac has been noted, but this talk went a lot further than a simple endorsement, partly due to the oddness of the material that he selected and partly for the way that he chose to discuss it. As such, this brief discussion will help bring my enquiry to an end as it ably demonstrates the problems faced in seeking to approach a work of art, and how the work becomes resituated by way of this critique. In doing so, Adorno will be able to address the apparent weakness in his thinking about its relation to praxis through the way the situation of the artwork makes this relation concrete.

The main character of Balzac's novel, Lucien, finds work in Paris as a journalist. His break comes with a review that he writes of a popular melodrama. Balzac does not simply describe this review but includes it within the novel, and it is this piece that Adorno has selected. This passage interests Adorno because of its ambivalence, for through it Balzac is able to provide an insight into the venality of contemporary journalism as well as the personal and artistic truths that occur alongside this venality. Significantly, the review is then a work within a work (that of the novel) as well as a work that is concerned with its relation to another work (the play). But this is not all, Lucien writes the review for personal reasons because he wants to prove himself and make his name, but also because he is in love with an actress in the drama. Consequently, alongside its role as a review, his writing is a performance for himself, for her, and for his friends and so presents a complicated comingling of interest and disinterest. The review thereby stages quite concisely a number of issues relating to the question of how we are to approach the work of art, and what the role and possibilities of critique may involve. However, it is also a work in itself, and so through its relation to the play and its place within the novel it appears as a reflexive microcosm of the work as a whole, such that it is both a dependent and independent work.

This positioning may recall the novella within Goethe's *Wahlverwandtschaften*, but Balzac's work is striking in its modernity, since the review is a product and critique of journalism and the burgeoning capitalist world of mercantile culture. As such, it presents the compromised autonomy of the work in very stark terms, which have not lapsed in their significance, but it also shows how this compromised position is conditioned by the intense personal and artistic needs that Lucien brings to it and that he is unable to disentangle from it. Equally, Adorno's own relation to the text may come from the recognition that, in some ways, it offers a mirror image of aspects of his own work in that it is working through the same issues of recapitulation and critique, but falls on the other side of the compromise, which only indicates the delicacy of the critical situation and its perpetual risk of losing itself. This risk is not in itself problematic; rather its presence indicates the non-givenness of autonomy, which is a necessary aspect of its work, for if there were no risk then the artwork would lack a rationale: it only exists because it might not exist, because it could be otherwise or not at all. It is this point of (in)dependence that begins to show how the work of the critic can resemble that of the work itself, which in turn shows how the *thought* of the work becomes the thought *of the work*, in its own concreteness. Confirming this point, Adorno opens his short discussion by referring to the fact that this extract 'is an autonomous piece of prose, and yet it is not' [NL2: 358/32]. It is evident that this essayistic mode of thinking and writing is what is in operation in *Minima Moralia* and in many of his works on music and literature, a mode that, as he insists, is also a model: a form of thinking into the world by way of the problematized relation of autonomy and reflexivity that the work bears. These brief pieces are constitutively incomplete insofar as they are essays of thinking and, in this way, they provoke further remodulation through their interventions.

Lucien arrives in Paris with the intention of making his name as a poet but soon abandons this idea when he discovers the lack of opportunities. One night he visits the theatre and sees the actress with whom he falls in love, Coralie, and later writes the review that Adorno will discuss. This transition in Lucien's career is made quite clear as, upon entering a café to dine with a friend who wants to nurture his literary writing, Lucien turns aside to eat with a journalist who then takes him on a tour of the publishing underworld. Balzac arranges this sequence very carefully so that although each step of the process occurs out of Lucien's free will, it also happens in the face of increasing pressures that make his choice inevitable. In this way, the decision over his fate is undecidable, for while his naïveté and ambition might predispose him to this path, and while his poverty and his encounter with journalism might make his choice likely, everything still hangs in the balance. He is initially appalled by the corruption of the press, but as its seductive pressures emerge, he gradually submits, and following one suggestion after another he is led to the point of agreeing, which is when he sees Coralie. Everything has been coordinated so that his response is both determined and spontaneous, which culminates in the review that formally realizes his decision, and in which his desire to prove himself as a writer merges with his infatuation for Coralie. The piece is written quickly, almost casually, as a result of a challenge from his friends, and the gamble pays off since Lucien is rewarded, albeit temporarily, with money and fame:

> Lucien stumbles into the betrayal of his ideals and soon, although unwillingly, of his former friends as well. But the seduction itself is so plausible, the world that opens up to the young man is so phantasmagorical and corrupt, according to Balzac's will, that the concept of betrayal melts away in it, as great moral concepts often do in the infinitely gliding events of life. Even if it goes against Balzac's express intention, Lucien gains as much right as undiminished sensual fulfilment from the spirit. The latter [spirit] always carries something postponing and consoling with it, while people in the counter-rational present have a claim to happiness, without which all reason would only be unreason: this moment speaks for Lucien. The interweaving of his fate into a society to which he knows he is alien, his own splendour and his own misery, all of this is gathered as in a burning mirror in the feuilleton that Balzac dictates to his pen, as if he shared the writer's wish "to prove himself in front of such remarkable people". In the microcosm of the essay, the heartbeat of the novel and its hero is counted from second to second.
>
> NL2: 358–59/32–33

It is thus essential that Balzac actually introduce the feuilleton; it cannot just be described but must make its presence felt as its role is not merely reflexive but demonstrative in relation to events. In this way, Balzac is also taking up the challenge that Lucien sets himself, as if it imposed itself on all who heard it: to show oneself for what one could be, to go beyond what is and to essay what might be, to 'prove intellectual talents concretely in its product' [NL2: 359/33].

This demonstration necessarily means that the work will escape its author (both Lucien and Balzac) and that they will have to bear out the consequences of this evasion and excess. In giving Lucien a destiny that is both concrete and unpredictable, Balzac is also making this true for himself in writing the novel, as his dedication to the work leads to such a form of actualization. To explicate the necessity of this approach, Adorno returns to an idea that Schoenberg developed, that of the obligations of a work, which arise within the first few notes of a composition as a form of tension that the subsequent work is committed to pursuing, so that the work as a whole unfolds from this initial contradiction (say, Lucien's idealism and his vanity) in such a way that the satisfaction of one of its obligations only yields another. While these tensions are not reconciled in themselves, their combination across the work as a whole is such that they come into a kind of dynamic balance, which Schoenberg referred to as homeostasis [AS: 259–60/162–63]. It can be seen how pertinent this idea is to the broader outline of *La Comédie humaine*, but in the discussion at hand Adorno focuses on the nature of this initial obligation as one in which Balzac bears out a form of morality in the work: to 'say nothing that would not be reported [*berichtet*]', which means that, by way of this consistency to its own demands, 'spirit itself becomes narrative [*Erzählung*]' [NL2: 359/33]. On the one hand this point has a resonance with the Sadean imperative to say everything, not to omit or curtail any aspect of its conditions, no matter what their implications, but on the other hand, and within the framework of the epic narrative, it reflects the necessity of writing to actualize the contents of the work so that its tensions are unfolded into a secular, concrete *histoire*. Thus, the contents of the play are not of material consequence in themselves but only insofar as they are taken up within the review (and the novel) and reveal, alongside the unfolding of their natural-historical moment, the contested intentions of Lucien's work in writing it.

The strength of this point can be better grasped when it is placed in the context of Hegel's thinking of history, where the double sidedness of history as that of events and their account is realized in concrete terms as the tradition with which the state founds itself, such that there is no establishment of a state without its history, and no history outside that of the state that it confirms; the two are mutually dependent and constitutive. This model is partly repeated in Lukács's later reading of Balzac, as was shown earlier, but in a more simplistic manner, whereas for Adorno, the significance of this episode from *Illusions perdues* is that it does the opposite of confirming the narrative of the state. While this incident arises out of the initial contradictions of the work, it leads only to a shadow of the whole that is punctuated by moments of excess, as is marked in the review. Balzac's account necessarily records the background of Lucien's experience, but it also displaces it by the rupture that is formally realized in the review, which only negatively confirms the actuality of the whole insofar as it is ruptured by Lucien's enthusiasm that reconfigures it according to his desire, just as the *Phaedrus* is punctured by Socrates' desire. In doing so, the initial antagonism in Lucien's character, between his idealism and his vanity, is not resolved but rather reposed, and it is as such that it is realized in the review, with all its own contradictions. The review thereby comes to reflect the relation of subjectivity and objectivity in their ruptures.

Because he wants to show himself as a writer, Lucien is keen to demonstrate his talents through the review, but because he is writing as a journalist his job is to promote the play. This tension is hardly unusual for reviews and was very evident in Balzac's time as a symptom of the petty corruption of the press. However, it is also the case that no critique that is to be substantial can ignore the personal responses of the critic, which will amount to a form of promotion of the work if those responses are warm. In which case, what is the status of the critique? If Lucien writes approvingly of the play, is he serving his artistic ideals or his monetary needs and, as a result, is the work determined autonomously or heteronomously? Our approach to an artwork cannot occur outside its emotional affect, as Adorno has shown throughout his aesthetics, even as these affects are subject to distortion and ambivalence in their actualization. But Balzac's importance is to have shown that this compromise in the position of the reviewer is integral to that of the writer and artist as well. The work itself provokes this ambivalence, however tacitly, and is in turn affected by its results. Hence it is not just in terms of a fidelity to Lucien's position that this compromise is made manifest in the review but also in terms of the approach to the work as such, so that Lucien's review makes vividly apparent what is evident in any work, which is its lack of purity, its impassioned contingency. In an unexpected turn this means that Hegel's oft-derided affection for the soprano Anna Milder-Hauptmann should be reconsidered, as Adorno explains: 'No one would fully understand what an opera is if they had not, as a youth, fallen in love with the coloratura soprano during the performance; in the intermediate realm of eros and disinterested work, the images crystallize whose quintessence is art' [NL2: 360/33–34]. Balzac's feuilleton preserves this moment in both its innocence and its impurity, such that its compromises and contradictions are presented without attempting to rationalize them, which is to say that it appears as a work in itself by honestly declaring its dishonesty, the semblance of its semblance.

While the strength of Lucien's review undermines the notion of a disinterested judgement of artworks, it does not displace this into subjective relativism.

Instead, the objectivity of the artwork is substantiated by its erotic provocation, by its inability not to appeal to the senses, by which it shows that it is not indifferent in its existence but has such a provocation, which marks its relation between the conditional and the unconditional. So, in realizing this provocation, the work is brought to reveal itself in its more than existent status, its unexplicated demands and tensions, which are potentially recapitulated, or co-executed, in the work of the critic. It is thus that the review is more than just a review, more than just a response to the play and a demonstration of Lucien's talents, but something else altogether. The position of the feuilleton in the novel then becomes uncertain as it is both part of the work and a work in itself, a reflection of the work (and as such exterior to it) and that which is in continuity with it. As a result, the work becomes aware of itself as semblance, just as, conversely, Lucien loses himself in the same world of semblance. The centrifugal lines of estrangement between artist and work appear inescapable, as if they were bound to each other in their mutual alienation. And so, despite these compromises, the review becomes objectively decisive, albeit obscurely, for in its contingency it will 'become symbolic without symbolizing at all'. In an intriguing formulation Adorno states that in this way 'semblance is raised above itself [*über sich erhoben*]', so that it becomes a form of sublimation, not referring to any meaning in particular but simply referring, as the discussion of imitation had earlier suggested [NL2: 362/35–36]. Such a development has implications for the so-called realism of the novel, in the tradition of which Balzac is often placed, for in this sense of realism there is an aspect in which the novel overreaches itself. In Adorno's words, the apparently self-evident distinction between realism and illusion is displaced by a work that takes on the form of reflection, which sublates these aspects into a new form. In the review, this form is one in which what is not real is made real (not just the play but its truth, in all its compromised ambivalence), which presents a glimpse of what is not, what is otherwise. That is, it does not merely indicate but concretizes what is not, such that it can be felt, and in so doing it not only overreaches itself but involves what is not in its appearance without assimilating it. There is then a gesture implicit in the work, as Adorno concludes, in which everything is won and everything is lost, a utopian ambivalence that cannot be resolved [NL2: 363/36]. With this point he seems to have reconfigured the notion of 'losing, in order to gain' so that there is no causal relation between its parts, instead, there is merely the fact of everything being won and lost. This is a notable change of emphasis that Adorno seems not to have recognized, but it removes the idea of utopia from any kind of sacrificial logic of redemption. And, in stating the facticity of ambivalence without seeking to lessen its sharpness through a logic that would seek to give direction to it, the decisive impact of its undecidability is increased. Thus, the gambit of the work is one in which it is not possible to state its outcome unequivocally and, as a result, everything remains at stake in it even as it occurs as decisive and irreversible. This is the tension of its appearance that the critic or artist is called to recapitulate, which is the intention, if such can be said, of its objective aesthetics.

Consequently, the relation to the work does not fall into either a decision or its abdication but rather a reflexive abandon. There is no decision to relinquish, nor a relinquishment of decision, but the decision of relinquishing, as it were, which comprises its awareness. In a sense, the moment of decision is an illusion, or semblance, as Balzac's account shows, as it has already taken place and yet it remains unfulfilled, which is how it is restaged in the review. This divergence is captured by Adorno's use of the phrase 'freedom towards the object', which he adapts from Hegel, however, in doing so he has subtly altered the mode and direction of its dialectic. As was seen in the last chapter, the freedom to the object is one in which the subject loses themselves in the movement of objectivity, which reformulates them as subject of the object. There is no longer an estrangement that returns to itself and culminates in an absolute self-realization, for the dialectic only unfolds through a pursuit of the logic of its materials. Kracauer was very critical of this tendency in Adorno's thinking and at one of their last face-to-face meetings he complained of the dizzying effect that it created. However, he then claimed that the lack of systematic aims in Adorno's rendering of dialectics stripped it of content and objectivity, leaving it entirely formal, which is the basis of the vertiginous feeling that emerges [BW: 514/350].[9] Although it is clear that Adorno's thought is far from lacking content or objectivity, the effect of giddiness is not out of place, but it is a result of the pursuit of thought without the security of a firm ground or outline, which not only has implications for the form of thought but also for its mode of developing. Vertigo becomes the way that the undecidability of its decision is felt, the way in which its inherent ambivalence becomes a force field that both concentrates and unfolds this disorientation.

The problem that Adorno has come up against here, that of the status of his thought in the face of the concreteness in which it develops itself, is to be worked out in terms of the negativity of its dialectics. That is, the status of his thought is marked by the negativity from which, through which, and towards which it is oriented. This is not to say that his thinking fails to be philosophical insofar as it takes place by way of these models of concrete negativity, but that its status is continually being affected by way of its emergence and critique through these models. Oddly, considering the image of Adorno that has often circulated since the 1950s, as a thinker of elitist, formalist, and aestheticist obscurity, it is more to the point that his thinking occurs pervasively through the concreteness of the negative.[10] From this perspective, his thinking takes place without the positive aims or systematic outlines of Hegel's dialectics but nevertheless, in its negativity, is always in reference to them. It is as such that its negativity is concrete in both its bases and its direction, and by working through this negativity thought finds itself in the force field just described, in that the persistent negation of the negation of the artwork, its alienation from and of alienation, is both determinate and endless as it can only be reproduced in the artwork, as he had earlier stated. The weakness that this thought has in terms of its lack of systematization is countered by its interrogation of this notion, that is, the way that this thought develops in its negativity provides it with a consistent counterpoint through which it is able to find a kind of coherence. Thus, the form of this thought arises by way of the objectivity of its models, in the negation of their negation (or alienation of their alienation), which does not turn to positivity but takes shape as a concrete resonance, or dissonance, that is then experienced as vertigo. By virtue of its objectivity, this thought is less of a theory and more of a praxis, and yet by virtue of its negativity, it is the thought of this praxis. As Adorno writes, negative dialectics is 'the critical and self-critical consciousness of such a change in the idea of a philosophical system that disappears but releases its powers as it disappears' [VND: 62/38]. These powers are those of the negativity in things that generates systematic thinking (despite the absence of a system in which to ground and orient it) insofar as this negativity bears a universality that merely indicates that things are more than they are. Hence the utopian critique carried by negative dialectics is that it 'not only specifies this moment but also the reality that is affected by it' [VND: 37/20].

By opening itself up to what is not known, and remaining open, philosophy opens itself to the fullness of experience, its lack of positivity, which is also to open itself to infinity. This opening is part of the notion of freedom towards the object, since 'the more philosophy really surrenders itself to its object, the less it misuses objects with which it is concerned as objects of demonstration for that finite system of coordinates that it usually maintains' [VND: 121/81]. Aesthetics is not just the object of this thinking but its mode: the problems of what philosophy should focus on and how, and what its status will be as a result, are conveyed in the way that aesthetics involves a release to the object in its negativity, which is to open thought to the experience of that which is not posited. Insofar as this experience is brought to reflection, philosophy finds the unfolding of its vocation in aesthetics as much as the reverse is the case, and so the apparent separation of the two approaches is redrawn, not to erase it, but to find its imbrication. Adorno refers to this combination as intellectual experience (*geistige Erfahrung*), in the full Hegelian understanding of these terms, which is, despite its simplicity in principle, very difficult in practice, as Kracauer found, for it depends on no prior judgement or position but relies entirely on its development through its experiences, and as such remains closer to an aesthetics than a philosophy. Except that the role of this thought is two-fold: on the one hand, 'the contents of such experience are not examples for categories, but they become relevant because the *new* arises in them', while on the other hand, there 'is the unwarranted, vague, obscure expectation that every singular and particular that comes to it ultimately represents that whole in itself that keeps slipping away from it [...] of course, more in the sense of a pre-established disharmony' [VND: 123–24/82–83]. Thus is found the mutual lining of modernity and utopia and their resulting discourses, as has been seen. It is no accident that Adorno turns to a discussion of artworks to demonstrate his critical analysis of philosophy since, as he says, aesthetic experience 'in a certain sense must be prototypical for knowledge, for the philosophical knowledge of actuality' [VND: 126/84]. However, he clarifies this relation by stating that philosophy should not simply adopt the methods or results of aesthetics, rather 'philosophy has to sublate [*aufzuheben*] this aesthetic moment in the obligation [*Verbindlichkeit*] of its insights into actuality' [VND: 136/92].

While doing so will mean that philosophy will transform aesthetics by preserving it within its conceptual knowledge, this will only occur if it is first able to respond to the moments of its bonds with actuality. Thus, it is only possible to view a work of art as a work of art if its demands are followed through in the same way that the artist seeks to respond to the obligations that arise in the opening movements of the work. It is a question of 'how far you are ready to actualize in yourself, as a viewer, the process that is present in the work of art in a congealed form as potential' [AS: 295/186]. This impulse arises out of the demands of the work but also indicates that the work cannot be approached solely by way of intuition, or passive contemplation. In this way Adorno is marking out the necessity of a conceptual approach to the artwork, just as he had in response to the informality of modern music, which is to say that his approach is not dependent solely on the visual, textual, or aural form of the work but on its demands upon thinking as well, by which the work can be actualized anew. But this approach, while necessary to respond to the thought of the work, comes up against a problem when it is found that the thought of the work is not itself conceptual, or at least does not permit of a conceptual synthesis and so of a synthesis that bears a judgement. Instead, the work presents itself as a gesture that simply says, 'it is so', rather than any kind of statement that would say, in a predicative manner, 'that it is so'. Thus, in thinking through the work, thought encounters a limit in which it thinks the work in its sheer facticity, without ground or purpose, but also, in the perverse impurity of the gesture, as that which bears out its own necessity and development, which is what its shudder indicates and what its dissonance holds open. In turn, this means that although the work does not support a conceptual judgement, this lack does not imply the absence of conceptual engagement, quite the opposite, for its lack is provocative or suggestive and thus the basis for actual innovation. Hence the simple appearance of the work does not mean we can simply apprehend it, because for 'as long as we surrender to these stimuli, without exerting the same effort of the concept or the work of synthesis that is inherent in the thing itself, we are missing the work of art itself' [AS: 300/188]. Instead, to experience an artwork is to know it, in the full range of its senses, by which Adorno means 'the immanent knowledge [*Erkenntnis*] of the thing itself: that you surrender yourself entirely to those syntheses, actively-passively enact [*vollziehen*] those syntheses, which are to a certain extent prefigured by the relations of the individual sensual aspects of the artwork, but that only become living when you retrace [*nachvollziehen*] them yourself' [AS: 301/189]. Such a relation to the work is as far from intellectual purism as it is from intuitive purism and, indeed, the border between thought and sensuality becomes ever harder to determine as our knowledge of the work extends. The thinking that then emerges from this experience takes shape through the mutual determination that is underway in the notion of aesthetic theory.

Insofar as the structures of thought are provoked by the work in a way that is not oriented towards an act of positivity, thought becomes estranged from itself, or at least from the aims and means with which it is ordinarily associated. As such, in coming up against the work, thought encounters that which is unfamiliar, that which does not unfold in an expected manner and instead leads into novel pathways. This encounter is thus both an aporia and a breakthrough since it appears as a denial of the conventional as well as an opening onto what is not conventional. The combination of these aspects is central to its resistance, both its resistance to us and our resistance to it, which is the form of its centrifugal (natural-historical) force and is marked in the imperative that Adorno suggested in his discussion of *musique informelle*: to make that of which we do not know what it is. The enigma of the work is precisely that it presents itself divergently as aporia and breakthrough, and it is only by way of this divergence that thought can proceed, but in doing so its own movement occurs through rupture and uncertainty. The relation of art to praxis is then provocatively marked with this question mark. While this mode would render art unusable for fascism, as Benjamin stated, it only does so because it renders art unusable as such because it makes its contradictory status concrete and unsurpassable. Adorno is clear about the implications of this thought and refers to the relation between artworks and praxis as one not of direct illumination but one that is faded or dimmed (*abgeblendete*), as if to avoid dazzling, with the risk of blindness being possible for either side [AS: 318/200]. There is only the suggestion of a relation, which thereby preserves its ambivalence and openness, that is, the relation is itself suggestive (for actuality) insofar as it is only suggested. As a result, and following what he had said in relation to *musique informelle*, thought, like art itself, 'can only become practical if it is not restricted in advance by the practice to which it is intended to be directly applicable' [VND: 84/54].

Lucien's review makes this point quite evident, insofar as it fails to be a review in any conventional sense, and yet succeeds in going beyond this convention to show what needs to be said according to its circumstances. He is bored by the play, that is clear, and so provides nothing in the way of a review – people come and go on stage in a confused and farcical manner, that is all – but then something happens: 'At the end of the act, someone asked me how the play was going, I told them: She has red stockings with green clocks [*coins*], a foot as big as that, in patent leather shoes, and the most beautiful legs in Andalusia!' Not only is the form of the review subverted by making its selling point very obvious, but this point is then reversed by making it genuine; Lucien has taken the flawed illusions of the play quite literally. The sight of Coralie's legs occurs as an additional factor, a sensuous explosion, launching the review into an entirely different space of affect and possibilities, as he goes on to write: 'Ah! this Alcade's daughter, she makes your heart leap into your mouth, she gives you terrible desires, you want to jump onto the stage and offer her your cottage and your heart, or thirty thousand francs a year and your pen'.[11] This is no longer simply a review but an actual intervention and, as this line emphasizes, even someone as humble as a poor provincial poet is able to respond to such an astonishing appearance, for he has his pen. And, of course, the review is itself the product of his pen as both a love letter and a demonstration of his literary skills; it is his mode of praxis, no less effective than jumping on stage and offering her money and property. The somatic moment in this thought is irreducible even as it is anomalous, and it is as such that it is re-enacted by Lucien (and Balzac) in form of the review, thereby instating its truth in its sensual concreteness and excess, while unfolding its historical account as that which has occurred and yet still awaits its actualization insofar as its desires are only phrased as desires. The results of this move, in all their contradictions, are proved by the subsequent episodes in the book as this moment is decisive for Lucien's career, or rather the rupture of its undecidability is irreversible. For the personal subversion of the form of the review cannot survive its commercial distribution, which remains latent in its praxis; the movement that assures his success is also that which will lead to his downfall as it cannot be secured against its own subversion by market interests. At this moment, as Adorno wrote, everything is won and everything is lost, and there is no way to ameliorate or avoid this ambivalence, and it is this that the review conveys and reflects through its dissonance, which exposes its move beyond itself.

Notes

Introduction: Dialectic of Aesthetics

1 Horkheimer and Adorno, 'Diskussion über Theorie und Praxis', in Horkheimer, *Gesammelte Schriften* 19, ed. Gunzelin Schmid Noerr (Frankfurt am Main: S. Fischer, 1996), 53; tr. Rodney Livingstone as 'Towards a New Manifesto?', *New Left Review* 65 (2010): 46.

2 The major studies in this area are by Joel Whitebook, *Perversion and Utopia: A Study in Psychoanalysis and Critical Theory* (Cambridge: MIT Press, 1995); Benjamin Fong, *Death and Mastery: Psychoanalytic Drive Theory and the Subject of Late Capitalism* (New York: Columbia University Press, 2016); and, Amy Allen, *Critique on the Couch: Why Critical Theory Needs Psychoanalysis* (New York: Columbia University Press, 2020). The only work to examine sensuality as a specific part of Adorno's thinking is Eva Geulen, '"No Happiness without Fetishism": *Minima Moralia* as *Ars Amandi*', in *Feminist Interpretations of Theodor Adorno*, ed. Renée Heberle (University Park: Pennsylvania State University Press, 2006), 97-112.

3 Klossowski's place in this survey is not gratuitous: in 1936 Benjamin and Adorno arranged for him to translate a selection of Horkheimer's essays, which was to be published by Gallimard under the title of *Essais de philosophie matérialiste*, and although the work was completed the volume, unfortunately, never appeared. The Institute then asked Klossowski to write an essay on Sade for the *Zeitschrift für Sozialforschung*, but this also never materialized (Benjamin had written positively about Klossowski's 1934 article on Sade in *Zeitschrift für Sozialforschung* 6 (1937): 174). See, Adorno and Benjamin, *The Complete Correspondence 1928-1940*, ed. Henri Lonitz, tr. Nicholas Walker (Cambridge: Polity, 1999), 188, 197; and, Horkheimer, *Gesammelte Schriften* 15 and 16, ed. Gunzelin Schmid Noerr (Frankfurt am Main: S. Fischer, 1995), letters from October 1936 to August 1937. Alongside discussions on the progress of the translation of his essays, Horkheimer briefly discussed with Adorno the first issues of *Acéphale*, the journal written by Klossowski, Bataille, and others. While they are very critical of this project, the first issue of *Acéphale* from 1936 contained another of Klossowski's early articles on Sade, 'Le Monstre', which would also later be included in *Sade mon prochain*. Consequently, it is apparent that Klossowski was as aware of Horkheimer's work as the reverse was the case, which is especially significant for their later readings of Sade. Michael Weingrad produces an extensive overview of the general interactions between the French and German

ventures in 'The College of Sociology and the Institute of Social Research', *New German Critique* 84 (2001): 129-61.

4   Jay Bernstein's Kantian reconstructions of Adorno's thought remain the most substantial readings available, however his attempts to extract a doctrine of Adornian ethics or aesthetics from the text of Adorno's works raises many problems. While his book on Adorno's ethics (*Adorno: Disenchantment and Ethics* [Cambridge: Cambridge University Press, 2001]) has been very influential in rescuing his ideas for philosophy, or at least for a certain philosophical reading, it only does so by denying any validity to the manner in which Adorno's ideas developed. This is not an incidental flaw as the mode and form of Adorno's thinking is intrinsic to its dialectical operation, so that it is never simply a doctrine of ideas but, as he insisted, a philosophy that also takes the form of an aesthetic theory such that it can break the impasse over the division of theory and practice. Bernstein's book on aesthetics (*Against Voluptuous Bodies: Late Modernism and the Meaning of Painting* [Stanford: Stanford University Press, 2006]), which deals with visual art rather than pursuing Adorno's own interests in music or literature, only confirms this division by considering modern art as a counter-impulse to instrumental reason that holds the promise of a (cognitive) reconciliation with nature. The lack of a dialectical reading of the inter-relation of nature and reason makes the division between the two insurmountable and so Bernstein is led to a merely formal defence of this reconciliation as an idea, despite his extensive treatments of materiality, which ultimately entails a position of Benjaminian mourning over its irretrievable loss. Both these works remain valuable, and provide very many stimulating readings, but their distance from Adorno's thought cannot be overlooked and their limitations are directly related to this distance.

5   See, especially, Rodolphe Gasché, 'The Theory of Natural Beauty and its Evil Star: Kant, Hegel, Adorno', *Research in Phenomenology* 32 (2002): 103-22; and, more broadly, Ayon Maharaj, *The Dialectics of Aesthetic Agency: Revaluating German Aesthetics from Kant to Adorno* (New York: Bloomsbury, 2013).

6   The issue of Adorno's relation to Hegel is of central importance and I will approach it indirectly, but pervasively, in this work. It is certainly true, as Robert Pippin has stated (see, 'Adorno, Aesthetic Negativity, and the Problem of Idealism', *Nonsite* 33 (2020), although the argument has often been made since the readings of Gillian Rose and Michael Theunissen), that Adorno's understanding of Hegel is sometimes tendential, and that the positioning of his thought in contradistinction to that of Hegel is thereby undermined, but this does not make his critique worthless. While his criticisms of the notions of system, concept, and identity in Hegel's thought fall short of grasping the speculative nature of these notions, the terms that arise in their place (like the non-identical) seem at risk of falling into a pathos of generalized indeterminacy. However, the aim of this work is to show that Adorno's rethinking of

these notions does not just take place theoretically but also practically, it does not come only from philosophy but also from his work in music – it should be emphasized that Adorno was an accomplished composer and musician as well as a theorist and critic of musical works in their creation, interpretation, and reproduction. In this way, the analysis of musical forms and musical material provides exactly the specific concrete content that his philosophical accounts sometimes lack, and thereby gives form to the notions of mimesis and recapitulation through which he attempts to rethink Hegel's terms in modernity. It is here that Adorno's significance lies, which is why it is important to see how his thoughts on music extend those of Hegel himself, but the corollary of this rethinking is a resituation of Adorno in relation to philosophy, in favour of what is perhaps better termed aesthetic critical theory.

7 As Martin Jay explains in 'Adorno and the Role of Sublimation in Artistic Creativity and Cultural Redemption', *New German Critique* 143 (2021): 63-84, Adorno's account of sublimation avoids treating it simply as a mechanism of affirmative culture, or a mode of sacrificial logic, by emphasizing the role of sublimated rage against suffering that takes place in the artwork and across history. While this is certainly a valuable reading it passes over the unfulfilled sensuality that is also expressed in sublimation.

8 The following books are the main studies of Adorno's aesthetics, but none of them include any substantial discussion of his musical writings: Lambert Zuidervaart, *Adorno's Aesthetic Theory: The Redemption of Illusion* (Cambridge: MIT Press, 1991); David Roberts, *Art and Enlightenment: Aesthetic Theory after Adorno* (Lincoln: University of Nebraska Press, 1991); J. M. Bernstein, *The Fate of Art: Aesthetic Alienation from Kant to Derrida and Adorno* (Cambridge: Polity, 1992); Tom Huhn and Lambert Zuidervaart, eds, *The Semblance of Subjectivity: Essays in Adorno's Aesthetic Theory* (Cambridge: MIT Press, 1997); Christoph Menke, *The Sovereignty of Art: Aesthetic Negativity in Adorno and Derrida*, tr. Neil Solomon (Cambridge: MIT Press, 1998); Bernstein et al., *Art and Aesthetics after Adorno* (Berkeley: University of California Press, 2010); Peter Uwe Hohendahl, *The Fleeting Promise of Art: Adorno's Aesthetic Theory Revisited* (Ithaca: Cornell University Press, 2013); Espen Hammer, *Adorno's Modernism: Art, Experience, and Catastrophe* (Cambridge: Cambridge University Press, 2015); Owen Hulatt, *Adorno's Theory of Philosophical and Aesthetic Truth* (New York: Columbia University Press, 2017); Samir Gandesha, ed. et al., *The "Aging" of Adorno's "Aesthetic Theory"* (Milano: Mimesis, 2021).

The most helpful works here are those by Zuidervaart, Bernstein (1992), and Hammer, all of which provide strong introductions but nevertheless come unstuck over the status of Adorno's thought in relation to modernism, which is viewed as too rigidly or too narrowly constitutive of his thought. Hammer's book is particularly vulnerable in this regard, as he seems to adopt a position that because the period of modernism has apparently passed, and because this was constitutive not just for Adorno's aesthetics but also for his philosophy more generally, then much of his aesthetics is outdated. This tacit historicism is not unusual in responses to Adorno and seems to derive from the nature of the demands he raises, for which the conditions are no longer held to be current, and so the demands are no longer held to be relevant. The premise of this formulation, however, is not necessarily given. Responses to Adorno's thought from art theory, especially Marxist-oriented aesthetics, are more sympathetic, which says much about the apparently dated quality of his thought, see especially, Peter Osborne, *Anywhere or Not at All: Philosophy of Contemporary Art* (London: Verso, 2013); James Hellings, *Adorno and Art: Aesthetic Theory contra Critical Theory* (London: Palgrave, 2014); and, John Roberts, *Revolutionary Time and the Avant-Garde* (London: Verso, 2015).

While the many works on Adorno and music are largely written by scholars from a musical background, they do not ignore his philosophical writings, making the division of labour very striking. See especially: Max Paddison, *Adorno's Aesthetics of Music* (Cambridge: Cambridge University Press, 1997); Michael Spitzer, *Music as Philosophy: Adorno and Beethoven's Late Style* (Bloomington: Indiana University Press, 2006); Andrew Bowie, *Music, Philosophy, and Modernity* (Cambridge: Cambridge University Press, 2007); Berthold Hoeckner, ed., *Apparitions: New Perspectives on Adorno and Twentieth Century Music* (London: Routledge, 2013); Gianmario Borio, ed., *Immediacy and The Mediations of Music: Critical Approaches after Theodor W. Adorno* (London: Routledge, 2022). And also studies by Daniel Chua, Murray Dineen, Michael Gallope, Lydia Goehr, Richard Leppert, Susan McCleary, Rose Rosengard Subotnik, and Alastair Williams.

9 Adorno, 'Amorbach', in *Ohne Leitbild. Parva Aesthetica*, in *Gesammelte Schriften* 10.1, ed. Rolf Tiedemann (Frankfurt am Main: Suhrkamp, 1977), 306.
10 Adorno's lecture, 'Vers une musique informelle', was delivered at the Internationale Ferienkurse für neue Musik as a critical reflection on the musical developments of the previous ten years. Of particular interest is the fact that he was drawn to respond to composers who had been influenced by his *Philosophie der neuen Musik*, and thus had to confront criticisms that arose from the implications of his own thinking in terms of the apparent radicalism of serial music in relation to that of the Second Viennese School. The transcript of the lecture can be found in *Kranichsteiner Vorlesungen* ed. Klaus Reichert and Michael Schwarz (Frankfurt am Main: Suhrkamp, 2014), 383-446; tr. Wieland Hoban as *The New Music: Kranichstein Lectures* (Cambridge: Polity, 2021), 233-72, which was then extensively revised for its appearance in *Quasi una fantasia*. Borio provides invaluable detail about the background of this talk in 'Die Positionen Adornos zur musikalischen

Avantgarde zwischen 1954 und 1966', in *Adorno in seinen musikalischen Schriften*, ed. Brunhilde Sonntag (Regensburg: G. Bosse, 1987), 163-80.

11 This concluding line does not appear in the lecture transcript. The sense of what Adorno is discussing here thereby differs from the metaphysical category of not-yet being that Ernst Bloch discussed, as well as from the looser definition of experimental music that Cage suggested in a lecture at Darmstadt in 1958, as one that involved actions, 'the outcome of which is not foreseen', see, *Silence: Lectures and Writings* (London: Calder and Boyars, 1968), 39 [however, cf. QF: 523/303].

Chapter One: Kracauer and the Dialectic of Natural-History

1 This discussion can be taken much further, as is evidenced by the increasing prominence of concreteness as a term of philosophical significance in the 1920s. Two publications in particular are representative of this trend, Herbert Marcuse's 'Über konkrete Philosophie' from 1929, and Jean Wahl's *Vers le concret* from 1932 (Marcuse, 'On Concrete Philosophy', tr. Matthew Erlin in *Heideggerian Marxism*, ed. Richard Wolin and John Abromeit [Lincoln: University of Nebraska Press, 2005], 34-52; Wahl, 'Preface to *Toward the Concrete*', tr. Leonard Lawlor in *Transcendence and the Concrete*, ed. Alan D. Schrift and Ian Alexander Moore [New York: Fordham University Press, 2017], 34-53). Both were drawn from the work of Heidegger, and both sought to develop the notion of the concrete in opposition to apparent Hegelian idealism. Marcuse attempted to read Heidegger by way of Lukács, and Wahl tried to rethink Heidegger's works from a Kierkegaardian perspective. Wahl's work was more successful and proved very influential to the future development of existentialism, despite the flawed reading of Hegel from which it was derived. Marcuse later became disillusioned with Heidegger and returned to the Marxist critique that underpinned the work of Lukács in order to reread Hegel, which would also become a very influential approach. It was primarily Lukács's use of the term concrete in his analysis of reification that supported Marcuse's reading, but this usage, while deriving from Marx's account of the commodity in *Das Kapital*, nevertheless simplifies Marxist thought by focusing on one aspect of the interplay of the abstract and the concrete in the commodity-form, in which 'concrete labour becomes the form of manifestation of its opposite, abstract human labour', see, *Capital: A Critique of Political Economy, Volume One*, tr. Ben Fowkes (Harmondsworth: Penguin, 1976), 150. As Louis Althusser would remark, in his 1969 preface to the French translation of Marx's work (*Lenin and Philosophy and Other*

Essays, tr. Ben Brewster [London: New Left Books, 1971], 76), the relation of abstract and concrete is much more complex:

> What makes abstraction scientific is precisely that it designates a concrete reality that certainly exists but that one cannot "touch with one's hands" or "see with one's eyes". Every abstract concept therefore provides knowledge of a reality whose existence it reveals: an abstract concept then means a formula that is apparently abstract but in reality is terribly concrete because of the object that it designates. This object is terribly concrete in that it is infinitely more concrete, more effective than the objects one can "touch with one's hands" or "see with one's eyes", and yet one cannot touch it with one's hands or see it with one's eyes.

2   Kracauer, 'Die Tat ohne Täter', in *Werke 5.2*, ed. Inka Mülder-Bach (Frankfurt am Main: Suhrkamp, 2011), 275-76. Richard Herbertz was professor of philosophy at the University of Bern from 1910-1948 and had been Benjamin's tutor for his dissertation on Romanticism. His work focused in a broadly Hegelian vein on the relation of the unconscious to experience, during the 1920s he became interested in criminal psychology and particularly questions of punishment and the effects of criminality on the wider public.

It may help to offer some background on the Angerstein case as it came shortly after the cases of Fritz Haarmann and Karl Denke, which were extraordinarily violent and provoked considerable fascination and horror. The Haarmann trial followed a similar pattern to the Angerstein one, with little attempt to understand the character of the murderer, despite his atrocious crimes, and with the psychological interpretations offered by Theodor Lessing being received as sceptically as Herbertz's comments on Angerstein. However, *Die Rote Fahne* had already begun to show the social and political background to Haarmann's crimes, just as the *Frankfurter Zeitung* attempted to do in relation to Denke. Both were seen to be representative of the latent violence and injustice of the times, which Lessing spelled out in his major study from 1925, *Haarmann. Die Geschichte eines Werwolfs*, to suggest that these crimes could lead to a wave of public hysteria. Aside from his reference to reification, Kracauer's reading is entirely in accord with these contemporary accounts in which social pressures lead to psychological tensions, which then explode into a reformulated social psychosis. Much has been written on this period, but it is worth consulting Maria Tatar, *Lustmord: Sexual Murder in Weimar Germany* (Princeton: Princeton University Press, 1997); and, on the historical background, Scott Spector, *Violent Sensations: Sex, Crime, and Utopia in Vienna and Berlin 1860-1914* (Chicago: University of Chicago Press, 2016); and especially Alfred Döblin, *Two Women and a Poisoning*, tr. Imogen Taylor (Melbourne: Text Publishing, 2021).

3 Kracauer's doctoral dissertation was published in 1915 and was a study of the development of forging techniques from the seventeenth to nineteenth centuries in reference to the ornamentation of iron gates in Berlin and the Mark of Brandenburg, a subject that not only anticipates his interest in surface phenomena but also gives evidence of the appearance of historical content in concrete forms. It is also of note that such iron gates are of course formal markers of points of access or the prohibition of access, which their ornamentation visibly consolidates. See Henrik Reeh, *Ornaments of the Metropolis: Siegfried Kracauer and Modern Urban Culture* (Cambridge: MIT Press, 2004), 63-72.

4 It is evidence of the importance of this notion that it will be central to Adorno's understanding of the way that form is sedimented content, as he later observes: 'ornamentations are in general rudiments or residues from necessities of older phases of production that are left over. The ornament is, so to speak, the scar that arose on a vase where it could not be produced at the potter's wheel without such an interruption' [AS: 241/151]. Adorno's concern with the status of such historical concretions is here apparent, as is the way that it will become legible in the artwork. The explicit association with Adolf Loos is made clear in a lecture from 1965, 'Funktionalismus heute', in *Ohne Leitbild*, 378.

5 The nascent Frankfurt Institute conducted its own research in this area, developing one of the first analyses of working-class attitudes by combining sociological and psychological techniques to examine the question of how party affiliations were related to attitudes to authority, with a view to understanding how far the working class would resist or welcome an authoritarian government. This research was conducted in 1929, at the same time as Kracauer's work, but was much more extensive, so extensive in fact that compiling and analysing the data from the questionnaires took some years, with the result that the work was not published until much later. See Erich Fromm, *The Working Class in Weimar Germany*, ed. Wolfgang Bons, tr. Barbara Weinberger (Leamington Spa: Berg, 1984).

6 In this regard see Hegel's letter to Pieter van Ghert from October 1810, *Briefe von und an Hegel, Bd I: 1785-1812*, ed. Johannes Hoffmeister (Hamburg: Felix Meiner, 1952), 330, where he mentioned a review of the *Phänomenologie* that had focused exclusively upon the content of the work, whereas, 'that on which the main emphasis in all philosophizing is to be laid, and now more than usual, is of course the method of necessary connections, of transitions from one form to the other'.

7 Overviews of this study can be found in David Frisby, 'Between the Spheres: Siegfried Kracauer and the Detective Novel', *Theory, Culture, and Society* 9.2 (1992): 1-22; Harry T. Craver, *Reluctant Skeptic: Siegfried Kracauer and the Crises of Weimar Culture* (New York: Berghahn Books, 2017), chapter three; and Michael Mack, 'Literature and Theory: Kracauer's Law, Benjamin's Allegory, and Chesterton's Innocence of Father Brown', *Orbis Litterarum* 54 (1999): 399-423, which compares

Kracauer's work to Benjamin's Trauerspiel study. Only one chapter from *Der Detektiv-Roman* was published, on the hotel lobby (Die Hotelhalle), which appeared in *Das Ornament der Masse* in 1963, dated 1922.

8 This reference has a definite grounding in Kracauer's thought insofar as his interest in Georg Simmel, with whom he would study, was triggered by reading his 1908 article 'Das Problem des Stiles', which arose in direct response to Loos's lecture, 'Ornament und Verbrechen'. See Jörg Später, *Kracauer: A Biography*, tr. Daniel Steuer (Cambridge: Polity, 2020), 25.

9 Horkheimer, 'Materialismus und Metaphysik', in *Gesammelte Schriften* 3, ed. Alfred Schmidt (Frankfurt am Main: S. Fischer, 1988), 87; tr. Matthew J. O'Connell as 'Materialism and Metaphysics' in *Critical Theory: Selected Essays* (New York: Seabury, 1972), 28. This article was first published in 1933.

10 Paddison provides a detailed analysis of the debate with Křenek in *Adorno's Aesthetics of Music*, 81-97.

11 In a discussion with Horkheimer in April 1939, Adorno made a strong case for thinking of their reformulation of Hegel's thought not in terms of an incomplete or open dialectic:

> The gentlemen who would speak of real rather than materialist dialectics, the Grisebachs and Tillichs, would embrace the concept of unfinished dialectics with open arms, not to mention that the later Rickert also came up with an open system. I would like to raise the question of whether our approach is actually "ontologically" different from Hegel's, namely whether the concept of fact already has a wholly different meaning for Hegel than it does for us, whether the elements of Hegel's philosophy are not already so preformed by the whole that with him the factual counterpart is under the spell of the principle of identity from the start. When we speak of the immediate, it is actually not identical. In the case of Hegel, it is only not identical insofar as the whole process is not already developed in the immediate. The whole difference from Hegel lies a layer deeper than the distinction between totality and incompleteness, namely whether everything that falls into the circle of thinking appears as just a thought or whether it is actually viewed as something that does not fall into it, but what, at the same time, can only be understood in relation to thought. It must not appear as if we are saying that Hegel's principle is wholly correct, only that an idea of the absolute, of the blind givenness of the infinite, plays into it, as if there were basically only a quantitative difference between him and us. Much more depends on the re-functioning, on the use of the Hegelian scheme for something else, than on the difference between the closed and the unfinished. Hegel is not merely to be critically "restricted", but it is necessary to confront his ontology in all

seriousness with another, namely the ironic one that there is no longer an ontology and that the concept of ontological ground itself must be suspended.
Horkheimer, *Gesammelte Schriften* 12, ed. Gunzelin Schmid Noerr (Frankfurt am Main: S. Fischer, 1985), 488.

These discussions, which mostly took place in January and February and then again in October and November 1939, in New York, were the first extended sessions in which Horkheimer and Adorno began to develop their thinking together and so laid the ground for *Dialektik der Aufklärung*.

12 Marcuse, 'A Note on Dialectic', preface to the paperback edition of *Reason and Revolution: Hegel and the Rise of Social Theory* (Boston: Beacon Press, 1960), xiv.

13 However, Lukács does retreat from these earlier insights in relation to his thinking of nature, as is found in *Geschichte und Klassenbewußtsein*, in *Georg Lukács Werke 2: Frühschriften II* (Neuwied: Luchterhand, 1968), 175 and 410; tr. Rodney Livingstone as *History and Class Consciousness* (London: Merlin Press, 1971), 24 and 234, where it is emphasized that the method of dialectics is limited 'to sociohistorical reality', and that nature is only experienced in terms of the sociohistorical processes of labour and science. In doing so, he rejects the Hegelian understanding of a dialectics of nature and also seemingly prohibits any sense of nature outside of what has been developed through second nature. It is possible that this is one of the reasons why Adorno prefers to focus on Lukács's earlier *Theorie des Romans*.

14 As Adorno explains in his seminar on Benjamin's Trauerspiel book in the summer of 1932: 'Ideas, in Benjamin's sense, are not eternal forms existing beyond time, rather they are only given *with* and *in* history. They do not "reveal" themselves in spatio-temporal constellations but are identical with them. They are not "ideas" in the actual sense, but rather definite structures of being that appear only on the basis of a definite constellation in a definite historical moment, which also dissolve with the dissolution of this constellation. They are therefore neither eternal nor, as in Plato, are they limited to a definite number. At any time and in any space, new constellations can arise and old ones die off'. See, 'Adornos Seminar vom Sommersemester 1932 über Benjamins *Ursprung des deutschen Trauerspiels*. Protokolle', *Frankfurter Adorno Blätter* 4 (1995): 69-70. These notes were made by Wilhelm Emrich.

15 This article, 'Naturgeschichte des Theaters', is made up of seven pieces that were mostly published in various journals in 1931-1933. See also the letter from Benjamin to Adorno from September 1932 in, Adorno and Benjamin, *The Complete Correspondence 1928-1940*, 15.

16 The 'Frankfurt discussions' to which Adorno refers were a series of debates he had with members of the faculty in Frankfurt, principally, Kurt Riezler, Paul Tillich, and Max Wertheimer, who had welcomed the existential focus of Heidegger's work and

in turn criticized Adorno's Habilitationsschrift. Unfortunately, very little documentary evidence of these talks has survived, but an attempt to reconstruct this dialogue appears in Mikko Immanen, *Toward a Concrete Philosophy: Heidegger and the Emergence of the Frankfurt School* (Ithaca: Cornell University Press, 2020). Of the many interesting points that this account raises, one of the most significant is the way that it demonstrates how the young Frankfurt School thinkers had already moved beyond the terms of the Heidegger-Cassirer debate of 1929 and were seeking to develop a body of thought that would respond to the challenges of Heidegger's and Lukács's works without falling into the problems of a generalized ontology of historicity or a secularized theology of class, and thus could respond to the specific issues of the contemporary world without undue optimism or pessimism.

17 I have discussed these works further in *Aesthetics of Negativity: Blanchot, Adorno, and Autonomy* (New York: Fordham University Press, 2016), 74-89, and, *Blanchot and the Outside of Literature* (New York: Bloomsbury, 2019), 111-17.

18 This point is recognized by Adorno in the note that he attached to the republication of *Kierkegaard* in 1966, where he admits that he 'knows and understands Hegel, and thereby Kierkegaard's controversy with him, better today and would no longer express metaphysical intentions in such an affirmative manner, the tone often sounds more solemn, more ideal, than is justifiable', *Kierkegaard*, 261. In one of the strongest readings of this work, Peter E. Gordon concludes that 'It is therefore crucial to note that Adorno's affiliation with Kierkegaard did not imply anything like a genuine affirmation of theology. While resisting Kierkegaard's leap of faith, Adorno nonetheless saw in this faith a species of negativity, although this theological negativity could never be transformed into a positive religion', see *Adorno and Existence* (Cambridge: Harvard University Press, 2016), 195.

19 Adorno, 'Thesen über die Sprache des Philosophen', in *Philosophische Frühschriften*, 366-67, 369; tr. Samir Gandesha and Michael K. Palamarek as 'Theses on the Language of the Philosopher', in *Adorno and the Need in Thinking*, ed. Donald Burke et al. (Toronto: University of Toronto Press, 2007), 35-36, 38.

20 It is clear that Adorno's response to Schoenberg is not without nuance, as the impact of Schoenberg's innovations was quickly lost for him as the twelve-tone technique became formalized. Nevertheless, he voices considerable reservations about this essay in a letter to Křenek from September 1932, where he particularly underlines his dissatisfaction with the clarification of the relation between material and expression [AK: 38-40]. Martin Hufner gives an extensive overview of Adorno's changing relation to Schoenberg's music in *Adorno und die Zwölftontechnik* (Regensburg: ConBrio, 1996).

21 Adorno makes this comment about Benjamin's essay on Goethe in a letter to Kracauer from May 1930, the same letter in which he robustly criticizes the foreword to the Trauerspiel study [BW: 208/140].

22 Horkheimer first developed this critique in an unpublished manuscript from 1928, which was based on his then current lectures, 'Zur Emanzipation der Philosophie von der Wissenschaft', but it was most fully elaborated in his polemic against logical positivism nine years later, 'Der neueste Angriff auf die Metaphysik'. The latter essay was a crucial step in the friendship of Adorno and Horkheimer, as their correspondence reveals, as it emerged out of the discussions they had had around Adorno's dissertation on Husserl in which they had first recognized their mutual interests.

23 Adorno's understanding of interpretation refers not just to text or to music but also to other arts, as his remarks on abstract painting from a contemporary lecture course on aesthetics indicate:

> The danger of mere decoration seems to be particularly obvious for internal painterly reasons and there is no broad, non-representational, immanent self-development of painting according to the analogy of music, where the decisive factor is probably that the painterly material and painterly representationality are not interpreted as natural phenomena qua lines and curves, as abstract painting intends, but only as historical. The problem of abstract painting seems to me to be posed in such a way that its fate depends on how far it is able to detach its lines from the play of nature and to fulfil them historically. Of course, one is in a dialectic here, because the apparently mathematical natural material of abstract painting is itself historically produced and can therefore perhaps only be interpreted as historical ciphers.

See, 'Aufzeichnungen zur Ästhetik-Vorlesung von 1931/32', *Frankfurter Adorno Blätter* 1 (1992): 75. This course, 'Probleme der Ästhetik', was the first that Adorno taught and its aim is spelled out quite clearly at the beginning, where he states that 'the seal of authenticity of all aesthetic problems is that they originate historically, and – anticipating – the layer of truth in a work of art is all the more guaranteed, the deeper its material content adheres to the historical material layer of its time' [38].

24 Susan Buck-Morss discusses this meeting in *The Origin of Negative Dialectics: Theodor W. Adorno, Walter Benjamin, and the Frankfurt Institute* (Hassocks: Harvester Press, 1977), 22-23. Her book is one of the first to show that 'Adorno's understanding of dialectical logic was influenced by his study of musical logic, and this fact accounts for much that was original in his theory' [15].

25 See, Max Pensky, *Melancholy Dialectics: Walter Benjamin and the Play of Mourning* (Amherst: University of Massachusetts Press, 1993), 147-50.

26 As a result, as he says a few years later: 'It is not the case, as relativism would have it, that truth is in history, rather history is in truth', see *Zur Metakritik der Erkenntnistheorie. Studien über Husserl und die phänomenologischen Antinomien*, ed.

Rolf Tiedemann (Frankfurt am Main: Suhrkamp, 1971), 141; tr. Willis Domingo as *Against Epistemology, a Metacritique: Studies in Husserl and the Phenomenological Antinomies* (Oxford: Blackwell, 1982), 135.

27 It is not clear where or when Heidegger may have made this statement about sociologists, as it does not appear to be found in any of his early publications or lectures. However, Adorno repeats the comment twice in his later works: first in a paper from 1954, 'Beitrag zur Ideologienlehre', in *Soziologische Schriften I*, ed. Rolf Tiedemann (Frankfurt am Main: Suhrkamp, 1972), 457, and then in his 1960 lecture course, *Philosophie und Soziologie*, ed. Dirk Braunstein (Frankfurt am Main: Suhrkamp, 2011), 16; tr. Nicholas Walker as *Philosophy and Sociology* (Cambridge: Polity, 2021), 6-7.

28 For Benjamin, the *ars inveniendi* was clearly distinguished from the practice of the imagination, in that the latter was a modern term drawing from a different understanding of thought, while the former was based in an idea of the genius as one who 'could confidently switch between patterns' [UDT: 355/189]. Adorno's alignment of the *ars inveniendi* with the imagination thus presents a deliberate adjustment of Benjamin's thought, by drawing it into a more Kantian understanding of genius as the product of the imagination (as is shown towards the end of his 1963 essay, 'Parataxis'). This adjustment corresponds to his use of the term 'model', which plays a similar role in Schoenberg's approach to composition.

29 The association with Surrealism is hardly arbitrary, especially when it is recalled how Breton attempted to link Surrealist thought and practice to the ideas of Marx and Freud in order to ground and extend its intended disruptions of the structures of bourgeois life. Six months after his inaugural lecture Adorno published some short sketches that he had written with Carl Dreyfus under the pseudonym of Castor Zwieback entitled 'Surrealistische Lesestücke'. These pieces are inconsequential observations of urban life whose inconsequentiality grants them a kind of anticlimactic jolt, a failure to convey the concreteness of everyday life, which is itself revealing of the gap between what exists and its representation in thought and language, alongside the banality of life as that which remains without consequence. However, they are not very effective, and republishing them thirty years later Adorno stated that their importance lay in their suggestion of a path not taken, a possibility that was not realized in his later development. See, 'Lesestücke', in *Vermischte Schriften II*, ed. Rolf Tiedemann (Frankfurt am Main: Suhrkamp, 1986), 587-97; tr. Susan H. Gillespie as 'Surrealist Readings', in *The Challenge of Surrealism: The Correspondence of Theodor W. Adorno and Elisabeth Lenk* (Minneapolis: University of Minnesota Press, 2015), 227-37.

30 This essay was published in 1961. It should be noted that Adorno does not title this essay 'Balzac lesen' (Reading Balzac) but uses the nominal form, 'Balzac-Lektüre', so that the translation should perhaps be 'A Balzac Reading', as if this was a course requirement, or even as if 'Balzac' was an adjective.

31 Lukács, *Die Theorie des Romans* (Darmstadt: Luchterhand, 1971), 95; tr. Anna Bostock as *The Theory of the Novel* (London: Merlin Press, 1971), 108-9. Although, even in this text, Lukács makes his position clear: 'Every form is the resolution of a basic dissonance of existence, a world in which the absurd has been put in its right place, as a bearer, as a necessary condition of meaning' [52/62].

32 Antonio Gramsci, *Quaderni del carcere*, ed. Valentino Gerratana (Torino: Einaudi, 1975), I: 311; *Selections from the Prison Notebooks*, ed. Quintin Hoare, tr. Geoffrey Nowell Smith (London: Lawrence & Wishart, 1971), 276.

33 This essay was first published as a preface to the Russian translation of Balzac's *Illusions perdues* in 1937, and was included in Lukács's 1939 collection, *К истории реализма* (Towards a History of Realism), before appearing in Hungarian in his *Balzac, Stendhal, Zola* in 1946, from which it was translated into English. The German version appeared in 1952 in *Balzac und der französische Realismus*.

34 Michael Löwy has suggested in *Georg Lukács: From Romanticism to Bolshevism*, tr. Patrick Camiller (London: New Left Books, 1979), 183, that the analysis of reification in *Geschichte und Klassenbewußtsein* is itself partly indebted to the descriptions found in Balzac's novels, especially *Illusions perdues*.

35 See especially on this point the account by Fredric Jameson in *Marxism and Form* (Princeton: Princeton University Press, 1971), 194-95, which goes beyond Lukács's own position by reading his later literary criticism on the basis of the earlier work in *Die Theorie des Romans* to suggest that 'realism is dependent on the possibility of access to the forces of change in a given moment of history' [204].

36 In an essay from 1955, Adorno uses the image of an intermittent dialectics to describe the structure of the Trauerspiel study (recalling Benjamin's own model in the foreword), which 'despite the most careful architecture of the whole, is built in such a way that each of the tightly woven and intrinsically uninterrupted sections draws breath, as it were, and starts anew [*von neuem anhebt*], instead of flowing into the next according to the schema of the continuous train of thought' [NL2: 571/223; UDT: 208/3].

Chapter Two: Dialectics of the Avant-Garde in Music

1 This undated manuscript, 'Über den Gebrauch von Fremdwörtern', was not published in Adorno's lifetime, but seems to date from the late 1920s or early 1930s.

2 Adorno was ambivalent about the Schubert essay: although it was his first long essay on music, he later regretted its excessive and ungrounded poetic evocations and, when he reprinted it in *Moments musicaux* in 1964, he removed references to

ontology that the original article had carried. Paddison has given a very helpful reading in 'Reading History in the Ruins of Nature: Images of Truth, Mortality, and Reconciliation in Adorno's Schubert Interpretation', in *Expression, Truth, and Authenticity: On Adorno's Theory of Music and Musical Performance*, ed. Mário Vieira de Carvalho (Lisboa: Colibri, 2009), 41-58. As Hans-Joachim Hinrichsen explains in 'Produktive Konstellation. Beethoven und Schubert in Adornos früher Musikästhetik', in *Musikalische Analyse und Kritische Theorie. Zu Adornos Philosophie der Musik*, ed. Adolf Nowak and Markus Fahlbusch (Tutzing: Hans Schneider, 2007), 157-75, the Schubert essay was also constitutive for the development of Adorno's thinking about Beethoven's late style.

3 This characterization of Beethoven's late period is not in itself novel, but how Adorno develops the notion is unique. It is accepted that Beethoven's last works are innovative and challenging, in particular the late string quartets and piano sonatas, along with the Diabelli Variations and the bagatelles for piano, but not the Ninth Symphony or the Missa Solemnis. The Ninth Symphony is seen to be more like the works of the middle period, while the mass is singular and unlike anything else Beethoven produced, which is one of the reasons why Adorno tried but failed to bring his analysis of it to any kind of completion. While there are some disagreements over the exact delineation of the middle and late periods, the general form of Adorno's analysis remains valid, see Jeffrey Swinkin, 'The Middle Style/Late Style Dialectic: Problematising Adorno's Theory of Beethoven', *Journal of Musicology* 30.3 (2013): 287-329.

4 See especially, Rose Rosengard Subotnik, 'Adorno's Diagnosis of Beethoven's Late Style: Early Symptom of a Fatal Condition', *Journal of the American Musicological Society* 29.2 (1976): 242-75. I am not competent to say whether Adorno's account of Beethoven is successful, although the consensus seems to be that it is largely accurate and insightful. However, my interest is not in the validity of Adorno's reading but in how he works through music to develop philosophical methods and concepts. For more musicological studies of Adorno's readings of Beethoven, see Carl Dahlhaus, 'Zu Adornos Beethoven-Kritik', in *Adorno und die Musik*, ed. Otto Kolleritsch (Graz: Universal Edition, 1979), 170-79; Colin Sample, 'Adorno on the Musical Language of Beethoven', *Musical Quarterly* 78.2 (1994): 378-93; Spitzer, *Music as Philosophy*; and, Daniel Chua, *Beethoven and Freedom* (Oxford: Oxford University Press, 2017).

5 In English, two terms are used for this movement of repetition, reprise and recapitulation, whereas in German there is only the term *Reprise*. Recapitulation refers more strictly to the concluding movement of the sonata form, while reprise refers to any repetition of a theme or motif. Considering that Adorno's concern with Beethoven is largely centred around the transformations in the sonata form, *Reprise* generally means recapitulation, but it should be recognized that it also occasionally means repetition more broadly. Robert Adlington provides an interesting analysis of

Adorno's thoughts on music and time by way of Paul de Man's discussion of allegory in 'Musical Temporality: Perspectives from Adorno and de Man', *Repercussions* 6.1 (1997): 5-60, and for a very helpful musical overview see, David B. Greene, *Temporal Processes in Beethoven's Music* (New York: Gordon and Breach, 1982).

6 Perhaps the best place to start with an analysis of Beethoven's late works is Mann's *Doktor Faustus*, since Adorno's article on late style is paraphrased in the words of the composer and organist Wendell Kretzschmar, see *Doktor Faustus*, in *Gesammelte Werke VI* (Frankfurt am Main: S. Fischer, 1974), 72ff; tr. John E. Woods as *Doctor Faustus* (New York: Vintage, 1999), 56ff. As Mann recalled in his account of the novel's genesis, this passage was directly informed by an impromptu performance by Adorno of Beethoven's Piano Sonata no. 32 in C minor (op. 111) in September 1943, which he delivered to elucidate his article on late style that Mann had just been reading. See, Mann, *The Story of a Novel: The Genesis of 'Doctor Faustus'*, tr. Richard and Clara Winston (New York: Alfred Knopf, 1961), 48.

7 Hegel lectured four times on aesthetics between 1820 and 1829 and these lectures were gathered up in the first edition of the *Ästhetik* in 1835. As has often been noted, the discussion of music is perhaps Hegel's weakest point; it is the shortest chapter of those dedicated to the individual arts and is regularly punctuated by Hegel's qualifications about his lack of detailed expertise in this area and given this lack, it seems as if this section was also subject to the most interventions by Hotho in his editing of the manuscripts. Useful overviews can be found in Julian Johnson, 'Music in Hegel's *Aesthetics*: A Re-Evaluation', *British Journal of Aesthetics* 31.2 (1991): 152-62; Alain Olivier, *Hegel et la musique* (Paris: Honoré Champion, 2003), 137-200; Richard Eldridge, 'Hegel on Music', in *Hegel and the Arts*, ed. Stephen Houlgate (Evanston: Northwestern University Press, 2007), 119-45; John Sallis, *Transfigurements: On the True Sense of Art* (Chicago: University of Chicago Press, 2008), chapter six; and, Lydia Moland, *Hegel's Aesthetics: The Art of Idealism* (Oxford: Oxford University Press, 2019), chapter nine.

8 In Hegel's words: 'The negation of the (separate) existence of material parts is itself negated as the restoration of their separation [*Außereinanderseins*] and their cohesion; it is *a single* ideality as an alternation of the determinations that sublate each other, the inner trembling [*Erzittern*] of the body in itself – *sound*' [NP: §299, 171/136]. The fact that sound occurs in the transition from materiality to ideality indicates its relation to the notion of *aufheben*, as the following notes show, and thus to its ambivalent combination of the sensuous and the abstract. It is of considerable significance that this account of the origin of sound remains true even in terms of digital synthesizers.

9 As Hegel writes: 'The birth of sound is difficult to pin down. The specific inner being [*Insichsein*], separated from gravity, is, in emerging, sound; it is the lament of the ideal in this force [*Gewalt*] of the other, but also its triumph over it, in that it is preserved in

it'. Hence the sublation of the material in the ideal is not simple or peaceful, as is demonstrated by reference to a cracked bell in which 'we not only hear the vibration [*Schwingen*], but also other material resistances, brittle and irregular, and so we have an impure sound that is noise'. Sound is characterized as a 'flight from materiality', and a transition to soulful ideality. Insofar as touch is the sense in which the determination of materiality takes place, sound is that sphere in which bodies are displaced in their spatial relations to each other (as they come to vibrate or rub against each other), which means that the sense of materiality is preserved as it is overcome and so there remains a sense of tangibility, or sensuousness, to sound as sublated touch in that it both feels and is felt in its vibrations [NP: §300 Z, 174-75/139-40]. Thus, while sound is determined by materiality, in being such it also becomes a way of tracking the determinations of materiality, a duplicity that is key to its development as a form of dialectical cognition. The place of violence in this sublation should not be overlooked, firstly in that vibration is a form of degradation, and secondly in that sound emerges against the restraining force of matter: 'The inner being in manifesting itself in sound is itself materialized, it dominates matter and thus maintains a sensuous existence by doing violence to matter' [NP: §302 Z, 184/147]. See especially on this point, Peter Hanly, 'Hegel's Voice: Vibration and Violence', *Research in Phenomenology* 39 (2009): 359-73.

10 Jeong-Im Kwon, 'Eine Untersuchung zu Hegels Auffassung der modernen Musik', *Journal of the Faculty of Letters* 37 (2012): 7-25, has examined the discussions of instrumental and vocal music in Hegel's lectures and finds that the former is never categorically rejected in favour of the latter. While the term 'absolute music' only arose later as a retrospective and somewhat disputed name for the music that later nineteenth-century composers wanted to differentiate themselves from, it remains highly useful because of the affinity it raises with the equivalent discovery of the absolute in literature and philosophy. The best study of the ways in which music emerged as formally independent remains Lydia Goehr's *The Imaginary Museum of Musical Works* (Oxford: Oxford University Press, 2007).

11 As Hegel is reputed to have said in relation to the revival of Bach's *St Matthew Passion*: 'this is not proper music; we have gone further now, although we are still a long way from being right' (*das sey keine rechte Musik; man sey jetzt weitergekommen, wiewohl noch lange nicht aufs Rechte*), as reported in a letter by Carl Friedrich Zelter to Goethe, 22 March 1829, *Briefwechsel zwischen Goethe und Zelter in den Jahren 1796 bis 1832. Fünfter Theil*, ed. Friedrich Wilhelm Riemer (Berlin: Duncker und Humblot, 1834), 190 (letter 643); *Goethe's Letters to Zelter with Extracts from those of Zelter to Goethe*, tr. and ed. A. D. Coleridge (London: George Bell, 1887), 352-53 (letter 265). Zelter was Felix Mendelssohn's tutor and was instrumental in the latter's revival of Bach's *Passion* in 1829, the first and second performances of which were attended by Hegel. It was at the second performance that he is said to have made this remark, as Zelter wrote in

his letter the following day. Mendelssohn also attended Hegel's lectures on aesthetics at this time, and was particularly critical of Hegel's ideas about the end of art. It should be noted that the performance was not a straightforward revival but modernized the work by making it shorter and more dramatic. As Dahlhaus suggests in 'Hegel und die Musik seiner Zeit', in *Kunsterfahrung und Kulturpolitik im Berlin Hegels*, ed. Otto Pöggeler and Annemarie Gethmann-Siefert (Bonn: Bouvier, 1983), 333-50, Hegel's response may have been stimulated by E. T. A. Hoffmann's article on church music from 1814. As is made clear in this article, religious music no longer has the resonance it once had, neither socially nor musically, and instrumental music has taken its place, see 'Old and New Church Music', tr. Martyn Clarke in *E.T.A. Hoffmann's Musical Writings*, ed. David Charlton (Cambridge: Cambridge University Press, 1989), 372. Hegel's scepticism is remarkable given the almost unanimous enthusiasm the revival received, both popular and critical, and the upsurge of religious and nationalist feeling it inspired, which on the surface seems to be an exact manifestation of the realization of the essence of music.

12 As is written in the *Naturphilosophie*: 'The specific *simplicity* of the determinacy that the body has in its density and the principle of its cohesion, this first *inner form*, passing through its immersion in the material separation, becomes *free* in the *negation* of the existence of this its separation. This is the transition from material *spatiality* to material *temporality*. What is in this form *as trembling* – i.e., through the momentary negation of the parts as well as the negation of their negation, which is bound to one another and awakened by each other, and so, as an oscillation of the existence and the negation of specific gravity and cohesion – is in the material as its *ideality*, the simple form *existing for itself* that appears as this mechanical animation' [NP: §300, 171/136-37].

13 An important contrast arises here, as Adorno writes in relation to Wagner that 'his music is conceived in the gesture of striking [*Schlagens*] and is dominated by the idea of striking' [VW: 28/30].

14 In reference to Marx, Adorno actually refers to this, deleted, passage from the Feuerbach chapter of *Die deutsche Ideologie*: 'We only know one science, the science of history. History can be viewed from two sides and divided into the history of nature and the history of mankind. These two sides, however, cannot be separated; as long as human beings exist, the history of nature and human history are mutually dependent', *The German Ideology*, tr. Salomea W. Ryazanskaya (London: Lawrence & Wishart, 1965), 34. In doing so, he reinstates his own version of the dialectic as one of natural-history, but one that has now become ramified with a much greater nuance of temporal and logical possibilities by way of his ideas about listening to music.

15 Adorno, 'The Radio Symphony: An Experiment in Theory', in *Current of Music, Elements of a Radio Theory*, ed. Robert Hullot-Kentor (Frankfurt am Main:

Suhrkamp, 2006), 226-28. Rosengard Subotnik provides a substantial critique of this notion in chapter three of her *Deconstructive Variations: Music and Reason in Western Society* (Minneapolis: University of Minnesota Press, 1996); while a more positive reconstruction has been attempted by Jeremy J. Shapiro, 'Adorno's Praxis of Individuation through Music Listening', *Música em Perspectiva* 3.2 (2010): 7-33.

16 Adorno, 'Form in der neuen Musik', in *Musikalische Schriften I-III*, 626; tr. Rodney Livingstone as 'Form in the New Music', *Music Analysis* 27.2-3 (2008): 215. The internal citation is from Arnold Schoenberg, *Theory of Harmony*, tr. Roy E. Carter (Berkeley: University of California Press, 2010), 417. Adorno abbreviates Schoenberg's statement: 'In composing I make decisions only according to feeling, according to the feeling for form. This tells me what I must write; everything else is excluded.' The other references to a speculative ear are as follows, 'Die Funktion des Kontrapunkts in der neuen Musik' (1956-57), *Klangfiguren*, in *Musikalische Schriften I-III*, 145; 'Über einige Arbeiten von Anton von Webern' (1958), in *Musikalische Schriften V*, 677; 'Schöne Stellen' (1965), in *Musikalische Schriften V*, 718. There is also a reference in Adorno's 1965 essay on Bloch, 'Henkel, Krug, und frühe Erfahrung' [NL2: 561/215]. Kierkegaard's use of the notion is found in his description of Mozart's *Don Giovanni* in *Either/Or*, tr. Howard and Edna Hong (Princeton: Princeton University Press, 1987), 122.

17 Adorno, 'Anweisungen zum Hören neuer Musik', *Der getreue Korrepetitor*, in *Gesammelte Schriften* 15, ed. Rolf Tiedemann (Frankfurt am Main: Suhrkamp, 1976), 189-90, and further along in this article: 'If the speculative ear has to hear simultaneous events together and apart in one, it has an analogous task to cope with them successively, one after the other, in the temporal course of the music. It must be prepared to build something like themes out of them, which are sharply opposed to motifs that are subterraneously connected, but that are hardly manifest as immediately sounding and yet relate to one another' [220]. Then, a few years later, in 'Schwierigkeiten II. In der Auffassung neuer Musik': 'The effort that the conception of new music requires is not one of abstract knowledge, not one of the knowledge of any systems, or theorems, let alone mathematical procedures. It is essentially imagination, what Kierkegaard called the speculative ear. The prototype of genuine experience of new music is the capacity to listen to divergent things together, to found in truly diverse areas a co-produced [*mitvollziehend*] unity. It is not for nothing that modernism emerged from the emancipation of the multiplicity of independent voices, from unleashed polyphony' [MS4: 290/674].

18 The notion of a productive imagination refers to the distinction Kant makes in the *Anthropologie* between derivative and original forms of presentation, in which the original presentation of the object 'precedes experience', and so conveys its own unfolding of temporality, see *Anthropology from a Pragmatic Point of View*, ed. and tr. Robert B. Louden (Cambridge: Cambridge University Press, 2006), 60.

19 Adorno finished the Schoenberg essay in May 1941, and it was then entitled 'Zur Philosophie der neuen Musik'. He had been writing on Schoenberg since 1925, but the larger project was stimulated by an invitation in October 1937 to write a book on Schoenberg (see the letter to Horkheimer, *Gesammelte Schriften* 16, 249-50). This invitation led to a sketch, 'Exposé zur Monographie über Arnold Schönberg', in *Musikalische Schriften VI*, 609-13, which although more ambitious didactically anticipates the themes and concerns of the later work. These points indicate the perspective Adorno has on Schoenberg's works, which focus mostly on the compositions made prior to Schoenberg's emigration in 1933. Of Schoenberg's American works, Adorno only studies the Fourth String Quartet, op. 37, from 1936, although there are significant footnotes on the Second Chamber Symphony, op. 38, and the String Trio, op. 45. While the Exposé was written shortly before Adorno sailed to New York, the later essay was already permeated by the beginnings of his discussions with Horkheimer on the history of the concept of reason, and it is thus that it is not only an 'excursus' to *Dialektik der Aufklärung*, as he remarks, but also a precursor.

20 On this point, Adorno refers to jazz as an example comparable to Schoenberg's late compositions, see his contemporary review of Wilder Hobson's *American Jazz Music* and Winthrop Sargeant's *Jazz: Hot and Hybrid*, in *Studies in Philosophy and Social Science* 9 (1941) in *Musikalische Schriften VI*, ed. Rolf Tiedemann (Frankfurt am Main: Suhrkamp, 1984), 392: 'Strangely, both authors missed the essential element of the jazz form: namely, that conventional design tends to suspend formal consciousness altogether and – also a parody of impressionism – to spatialize the music. In jazz there is simultaneity in the sense that the chronological sequence says nothing about the meaning of the individual phenomena: in principle, all events are interchangeable, and Sargeant occasionally correctly observes that a jazz piece can stop at any moment. Jazz is undialectical: the technique, which is praised as rhythmic, is basically neutral to musical time. That is why virtuoso jazz musicians like Ellington and Basie avoid caesuras as much as possible, which could also give the appearance of a temporal articulation of the form. In jazz one flees from time to the standstill of always the same movement'. Whether or not this diagnosis is true of later developments in jazz, it is of note that it could apply to some contemporary noise or drone works.

21 See my *Aesthetics of Negativity*, 94-99, for a discussion of Paulhan and the role his ideas played in the development of Blanchot's critical response to literature, which parallels Adorno's response to music.

22 The image of reading through overflowing eyes is mentioned in Adorno's early essays on Schubert and Kierkegaard, and it is evident that the later image of crying in relation to music alleviates some of his earlier Benjaminian melancholy by way of Schoenberg's critique of Romanticism [MMU: 33/31; K: 179/126]. The relation of

crying and music as a mimetic opening up of the face is also taken up in the 1949 draft of his theory of musical interpretation, see *Zu einer Theorie der musikalischen Reproduktion*, ed. Henri Lonitz (Frankfurt am Main: Suhrkamp, 2001), 237; tr. Wieland Hoban as *Towards a Theory of Musical Reproduction* (Cambridge: Polity, 2006), 179.

23 In September 1936 Adorno mentioned in a letter to Benjamin that he had recently been immersing himself in reading Hegel with much success, as is evident from his dissertation on Husserl and also from his response to Benjamin's 1935 sketch of the *Passagenwerk* a year earlier. In a letter to Horkheimer in July 1938, he again referred to his pleasure in reading Hegel and how this helped illuminate the work of Husserl. Adorno's more serious interest in Hegel would seem to derive from at least three sources at this time: from his work on Husserl and Sohn-Rethel in relation to the grounds of idealism, in response to Benjamin's ongoing historical and cultural work, which Adorno found unsatisfactory in dialectical terms, and because of his analysis of Beethoven that began in 1938. It should be added that his growing proximity to Horkheimer would also have stimulated Adorno to focus more carefully on Hegel's thought (as is found in the transcripts of their extended discussions in 1939 in Horkheimer, *Gesammelte Schriften* 12, 436-541), as would Marcuse's major essay *Reason and Revolution*, which Adorno read in 1940.

24 These points come from an article entitled 'Dissonanz in der neuen Musik' that Adorno wrote (along with eighteen other pieces) for an encyclopaedia in 1942, see *Musikalische Schriften V*, 73-75; *Night Music*, 199-201. The role of dissonance is discussed in the 1938 essay, *Versuch über Wagner* [VW: 61-64/64-68]. Wagner's role in the development of musical dissonance is exemplified by *Tristan und Isolde*, which provides the basis for Nietzsche's characterization of the Dionysian in the conclusion to *Die Geburt der Tragödie*, where he asks if we could imagine the incarnation (*Menschwerdung*) of dissonance, its becoming human, which would need to cover itself with the illusion of a veil of beauty in order to live, see *The Birth of Tragedy*, tr. Ronald Spiers, ed. Raymond Guess (Cambridge: Cambridge University Press, 1999), 113-15. This viewpoint is latent in the transformation of dissonance in Schoenberg.

25 Hegel, *Vorlesungen über die Philosophie der Kunst* (GW 28.3), ed. Walter Jaeschke and Niklas Hebing (Hamburg: Felix Meiner, 2020), 936: 'The time comes for a people when art flourishes, but it survives itself (it drives itself out)' (*Es tritt bei einem Volk die Zeit ein, wo die Kunst blüht, aber sie überlebt sich [sie treibt sich heraus]*), the last phrase appears in the transcript by Karol Libelt. The context of this remark is the changing status of art in relation to religion and philosophy, in which images of truth or divinity are sometimes acceptable and sometimes not. Art therefore outlives itself to the extent that it reformulates its relation to the idea, to the conceptual or non-representational.

26 See especially on this account, Roberts, *Revolutionary Time and the Avant-Garde*. As with other Adornian readings of contemporary art (e.g. Osborne's *Anywhere or Not at All*), the excellence of Robert's book is only marred by the absence of any discussion of Adorno's writings on music, an omission that if rectified would have provided much to counter the notion that Adorno is overly focused on the conceptual autonomy of the work of art.

27 Raoul Vaneigem, *Traité de savoir-vivre à l'usage des jeunes générations* (Paris: Gallimard, 1967), 191-92; tr. Donald Nicholson-Smith as *The Revolution of Everyday Life* (Oakland: PM Press, 2012), 162-63. Despite the note, this story does not appear to be from Brecht's *Geschichten vom Herrn Keuner*. A recent reformulation of this model can be found in Leslie Kaplan's *Désordre* (Paris: P.O.L. Éditeur, 2019); tr. Jennifer Pap as *Disorder: A Political Fable* (Chico, CA: AK Press, 2020), which becomes more compelling in its thought of reversal by instating the recoil of the punchline across the whole of its narrative.

28 The same aporia occurs in relation to the artwork, which bears a 'constitutive impossibility' that makes the artist's efforts futile in advance. As a result, the virtuosity that is necessarily involved in rendering the work is not 'limited to the rendering [*Wiedergabe*], but also has to be lived out in the structure [*in der Faktur sich ausleben*]; its sublimation urges it to do so. It relates [*verhält*] the paradoxical essence of art, the impossible as possible, to appearance' [AT: 415/279]. The artwork is thus itself an additional factor, in that it is a short circuit between theory and practice, and impossibility and possibility, which does not dissolve their contradiction but proceeds by way of it.

29 Adorno, *Probleme der Moralphilosophie*, ed. Thomas Schröder (Frankfurt am Main: Suhrkamp, 1996), 13-21; tr. Rodney Livingstone as *Problems of Moral Philosophy* (Cambridge: Polity, 2000), 4-9. The role of the additional factor has been taken up by Alexander Kluge and Oskar Negt in their understanding of the displacements of what they call bodily intelligence, where actions of the body subvert those of deliberate intentions, see for instance the account in *History and Obstinacy*, ed. Devin Fore, tr. Richard Langston et al. (New York: Zone Books, 2014), 204. One of the most useful studies of the additional factor can be found in Aaron Jaffe, 'Adorno's "Addendum"', *Philosophy and Social Criticism* 43.8 (2017): 855-76. Adorno returns to this account two years later by way of a reading of *Hamlet*, but this reading is less successful partly because he finds the additional factor in the final scenes of the play [LGF: 320-30/231-37]. It is unclear why Adorno should focus on this moment when the Mousetrap would appear to be a better candidate, insofar as it is the introduction of an extraneous element that causes Claudius to reveal his guilt, thereby triggering the resulting denouement. However, in line with its persistent doubling, *Hamlet* is marked by two climaxes, as the first one only leads to displacement and deferral, thus leading to the necessity for its recapitulation in the final act with the (doubly)

misplaced poison. I have attempted to develop an alternative account of the additional factor in Chapter Six, below.

30 Horkheimer, 'Traditionelle und kritische Theorie', in *Gesammelte Schriften* 4, ed. Alfred Schmidt (Frankfurt am Main: S. Fischer, 1988), 201; tr. Matthew J. O'Connell as 'Traditional and Critical Theory', in *Critical Theory*, 227. This account of the differing ways in which what 'is' appears converge in Alexander García Düttmann's reading in *So ist es. Ein philosophischer Kommentar zu Adornos 'Minima Moralia'* (Frankfurt am Main: Suhrkamp, 2004), where he shows that through the writing and reading of the aphorisms in *Minima Moralia* what 'is' can be shown to transform itself by way of its revision in the text. García Düttmann calls this revision the pure gesture of the 'so it is', which marks the distance that is taken from damaged life in a minimal moral philosophy. In perceiving what is, as it is, this gesture marks the transition from a false life to a true one, without determining or guaranteeing it, as the act of stating 'so it is' oscillates between its different elements and thereby finds scope for reflection. However, whether it makes sense to refer to this statement as a pure gesture (or indeed whether it encapsulates what is occurring in these aphorisms) seems doubtful. Moral philosophy, as Adorno will point out, is concerned with the production of consciousness, which here occurs through the change of perspective that each aphorism brings about and, as Hegel showed in his account of experience, this change not only affects the subject but also the object. Later remarks in *Ästhetische Theorie* confirm this view, for Adorno writes of the way that certain movements in Schubert and Beethoven bring about an incomplete change in experience by their demonstration of sheer facticity; the reprise in Beethoven's Ninth Symphony, for example, which resonates as an overwhelming 'So ist es', reveals the truth of the untruth of existence but does not yet formulate its dialectical reversal [AT: 363/245, cf. 171/112].

Chapter Three: Horkheimer, Sade, and Erotic Reason

1 It is in a letter from Adorno to Horkheimer, from 10 November 1941, that this phrase first occurs and, significantly, it does so in relation to Sade: 'I have just been reading Gorer's book on Sade, and a lot of things occurred to me that I think we will be able to use. Essentially, they concern the dialectic of enlightenment or the dialectic of culture and barbarism. By the way, have you ever investigated the deep relationship between Sade and Saint-Simon? I think there is much hidden there. I'm more and more inclined to see Sade as an industrial utopian. By the way, shouldn't the complex of Sade and anti-Semitism be an initial point of crystallisation for us?'

see, Horkheimer, *Gesammelte Schriften* 17, ed. Gunzelin Schmid Noerr (Frankfurt am Main: S. Fischer, 1996), 211. A couple of months earlier Horkheimer had remarked to Adorno, after reading his 1941 essay on Schoenberg and in anticipation of their work on *Dialektik der Aufklärung*, that 'de Sade's doctrine is in a peculiar way the counter-blow against the compulsion of the existing [*der Gegenschlag gegen den Zwang des Bestehenden*]. This is precisely what your essay proves of music. I see our task in the future as no longer being satisfied with critically demonstrating this function in cultural phenomena but as undertaking it ourselves. In your essay I see not merely a preliminary work, as you originally wanted it, but already the transition' [152]. Horkheimer's essay on Sade would be written a year later, but the connection to neither Saint-Simon nor anti-Semitism would be pursued. However, the notion of an industrial utopia in all its paradoxes is certainly apparent, as is the way in which this formulation would enable a transition of thought in contrast to the reality principle, as the drive towards what merely exists.

2 The most influential misreading of *Dialektik der Aufklärung* is by Jürgen Habermas, 'The Entwinement of Myth and Enlightenment: Re-reading *Dialectic of Enlightenment*', tr. Thomas Y. Levin *New German Critique* 26 (1982): 13–30, who construes the work as a pessimistic and self-contradictory polemic. While Robert Hullot-Kentor, 'Back to Adorno', *Telos* 81 (1989): 5–29; and, Amy Allen, 'Reason, Power, and History: Re-reading the *Dialectic of Enlightenment*', *Thesis Eleven* 120.1 (2014): 10–25, offer strong rebuttals of Habermas's criticisms, the work of Horkheimer in this excursus remains overlooked, which is indicative of a failure to recognize, let alone grasp, the thought he is attempting to develop. Some discussion of the excursus on Sade can be found in Marcel Hénaff, *Violence dans la raison? Conflit et cruauté* (Paris: L'Herne, 2014), 43–53; Gunzelin Schmid Noerr, 'Wie die "dunklen Schriftsteller des Bürgertums" die *Dialektik der Aufklärung* erhellen', *Zeitschrift für kritische Theorie* 44/45 (2017): 10–32.

3 Adorno, letter to Horkheimer, 29 June 1936, in Horkheimer, *Gesammelte Schriften* 15, 577–78.

4 The place of Freud in Horkheimer's essay may have been influenced by the work of Erich Fromm, whose essay on the sadomasochistic complex that derives from a repression of the libido – in which this denial is internalized as masochism and externalized as sadism and is instrumental to the formation of fascist ideology – was published in a volume edited by Horkheimer, *Studien über Autorität und Familie* (Paris: Felix Alcan, 1936), see esp. 110–35. Fromm had also reviewed Geoffrey Gorer's 1934 study of Sade, *The Revolutionary Ideas of the Marquis de Sade*, in *Zeitschrift für Sozialforschung* 3 (1934): 426–27.

5 The continuity of this thought with Horkheimer's underlying materialism is ably demonstrated by a line from his 1933 essay, 'Materialismus und Moral', where he states: 'Binding moral commands do not exist. Materialism does not find any

authority that transcends people and distinguishes between goodwill and lust for profit, kindness and cruelty, avarice and self-sacrifice. Logic also remains mute, it does not give priority to moral convictions.' See, 'Materialismus und Moral', in *Gesammelte Schriften* 3, 133; tr. Frederick Hunter as 'Materialism and Morality', in *Between Philosophy and Social Science*, 33.

6 This idea is taken up by Marcuse in his 1938 article 'Zur Kritik des Hedonismus', in explicit response to Horkheimer's essay: 'It is repressed cruelty that leads to sadistic terror and repressed self-surrender that leads to masochistic subjection. Left in their authentic intention, as modes of the sexual drive, they can end up in the increased pleasure not only of the subject but also of the object. They are no longer linked to annihilation', *Zeitschrift für Sozialforschung* 7 (1938): 78–79; tr. Jeremy J. Shapiro as 'On Hedonism' in *Negations: Essays in Critical Theory* (London: Penguin, 1968), 189. In saying as much he would seem to be ameliorating Horkheimer's thought by bringing it closer to Fourier's ideas.

7 The internal quotation comes from Kant's 1784 essay, 'Beantwortung der Frage: Was ist Aufklärung?' see, *Practical Philosophy*, tr. and ed. Mary J. Gregor (Cambridge: Cambridge University Press, 1996), 17, where enlightenment is described as the emergence from self-incurred immaturity (*Unmündigkeit*), in which the latter is defined as the 'inability to make use of one's own understanding without direction from another'. Horkheimer's interest in eighteenth-century materialism was not new, as he had taught a course in 1927 on modern philosophy in which he studied the Lumières, particularly La Mettrie, Helvétius, d'Holbach, Diderot, Voltaire, and Rousseau, but not Sade, see *Gesammelte Schriften* 9, ed. Alfred Schmidt (Frankfurt am Main: S. Fischer, 1987), 346–92.

8 Kant, *Critique of Practical Reason*, tr. and ed. Mary Gregor (Cambridge: Cambridge University Press, 1997), 27. These examples are not incidental to Kant's argument but attempt to be decisive, that is, they are not merely the application of a principle but a demonstration of its concrete justification. As a result, it is of major importance for the actualization of the law when these examples prove not to be decisive. This particular example is central to Jacques Lacan's readings of Sade, as Dany Nobus spells out in *The Law of Desire: On Lacan's 'Kant with Sade'* (London: Palgrave, 2017), 94–110.

9 Kant discusses apathy as the strength that is presupposed by virtue in the second part of *Die Metaphysik der Sitten*, from 1797, see *Practical Philosophy*, 536–37. Sade's possible response to this Kantian problem goes further, for in the distance taken from remorse there is also a distance from egoism as such, which reveals the greatest scope for ethicality, as Alenka Zupančič writes, 'if, as Kant claims, no other thing but the moral law can induce us to put aside all our pathological interests and accept our death, then the case of someone who spends a night with a lady even though he knows that he will pay for it with his life, *is the case of the moral law*', see 'The Subject

of the Law', in *Cogito and the Unconscious*, ed. Slavoj Žižek (Durham, NC: Duke University Press, 1998), 58–59.

While this reading supports the ambition of Horkheimer's account, it is necessary to pursue the question of what arises in place of egoism for Sade. For Zupančič, following Lacan, there is an alignment between jouissance and the death drive, where the formalism of Kantian ethics converges with that of Sadean sexuality. For Horkheimer, it is important to note that there is a distinction between instrumental reason, in which means are subordinated to ends, and a purely formal reason, in which reason has no ends other than the pursuit of its own systematicity. Although his account finds evidence of both in Sade's works, which to some extent blurs the relation to Kant, it is nevertheless his concern to show that reason in both its practical and theoretical aspects is divorced from morality. However, Sade goes even further by showing that the ascesis of the libertine requires a transformation from instrumental reason to a purely formal reason, and from this to an autonomous and erotic reason.

David James discusses the relation of formal and instrumental reason in 'From Kant to Sade: A Fragment of the History of Philosophy in the *Dialectic of Enlightenment*', *British Journal for the History of Philosophy* 26.3 (2018): 557–77, but does so without reference to the sensual, material distortion of reason in Sade's thought. This absence also mars Bernstein's reading in *Adorno*, 91–99, for whom 'the *dependence* of critique on the objects it seeks to desecrate' is the basis for the fact that 'reason must not simply avow but must *contain* these dependent moments as elements of itself'. The subsumption of these moments provokes an insistent critical negativity through which reason becomes self-defeating, as it becomes nothing more than the will willing its own assertion over things and thus 'a form of *irrationality*', which leads to the Nietzschean emphasis found in Horkheimer's reading of Sade. The dilemma of the model developed in *Dialektik der Aufklärung*, as it is explicated in Bernstein's Kantian reading, is found in the division between a sceptical and a dogmatic relation to objects, which becomes aporetic through the dialectic of enlightenment. But the Sadean reading is one where reason does not just contain these objective moments but is mimetically, sensuously transformed through them, which thereby overcomes the aporia of dogmatism or scepticism.

10 Horkheimer returns to Sade in the 1939 article 'Die Juden und Europa' to show how the contempt of the ruling classes for the people operates. He refers to the speech by the Bishop of Grenoble, which takes place towards the end of *La Nouvelle Justine*, who details the means by which governments can crush the freedoms of the people, see D. A. F. de Sade, *La Nouvelle Justine*, in *Œuvres II*, ed. Michel Delon (Paris: Gallimard, 1995), 1064–65, cited in 'Die Juden und Europa', in *Gesammelte Schriften* 4, 317–18.

11 The quotation, 'gardez vos frontières . . .', comes from the end of the republican pamphlet included in *La Philosophie dans le Boudoir*, in *Œuvres III*, ed. Michel Delon (Paris: Gallimard, 1998), 153; tr. Joachim Neugroschel as *Philosophy in the Boudoir* (London: Penguin, 2006), 148. The story of Zamé's utopia appears in *Aline and Valcour*, in *Œuvres complètes IV* (Paris: Cercle du Livre Précieux, 1966), 251–353; *Aline and Valcour*, Volume II, tr. Jocelyne Geneviève Barque and John Galbraith Simmons (New York: Contra Mundum, 2019), 262–360. As has been widely noted, this proto-socialist vision radically alters the perception of Sade's thinking as one that is only obsessed with cruelty.

12 The question arises here of whether Horkheimer's reading of Sade is closer to Benjamin or Hegel in its understanding of history. While it seems that the historical verdict of unending catastrophe is closer to Benjamin's thinking on this point, it is also the case that Horkheimer seems to approach this problem as one to be rationally endured, not in the hope of reconciliation but simply in terms of its recognition, which is closer to a Hegelian position. Most pointedly, as he had stated in 1933, materialism implies the following perspective: 'Past injustice will never be made up. The suffering of past generations receives no compensation.' See, 'Materialismus und Metaphysik', 86; 'Materialism and Metaphysics', 26.

13 Moishe Postone and Barbara Brick, 'Critical Pessimism and the Limits of Traditional Marxism', *Theory and Society* 11.5 (1982): 617–58. This article (revised and included in Postone's *Time, Labour, and Social Domination* (Cambridge: Cambridge University Press, 1993), 105–20) provides a Marxist analysis of the change in Horkheimer's thought by showing the shortcomings of Pollock's theory of state capitalism, which Horkheimer adopted. While this reading is mostly accurate, and political pessimism is undeniably present in Horkheimer's late work, this diagnosis should not lead us to jettison his early thinking as well, as evidence from his essay on egoism has hopefully shown. John Abromeit offers a detailed response to Postone's criticisms in his *Max Horkheimer and the Foundations of the Frankfurt School* (Cambridge: Cambridge University Press, 2011), 420–24.

14 During the composition of *Dialektik der Aufklärung* Horkheimer and Adorno were also involved in discussing Huxley's *Brave New World* with a group including Marcuse, Brecht, and others. In the article that arose from these discussions Adorno criticized Huxley for his failure to understand the implications of Sadean sexuality: 'In the foreword to the American edition added after the war, Huxley discovered the affinity between this principle [of the complete fungibility of bodily rights] and Sade's statement that human rights include the absolute sexual disposal [*Verfügung*] of all over all. In this he sees the perfection of the folly of consistent reason. But he fails to recognize the incompatibility of this heretical maxim with his future world-state [. . .] Domination could almost be defined as the disposal of one over others, not as the total disposal of all over all. The latter would not be thinkable

alongside any totalitarian order. The former relates far more to work relations than to the state of sexual anarchy'. See, Adorno, *Prismen*, ed. Rolf Tiedemann (Frankfurt am Main: Suhrkamp, 1977), 106–7; tr. Samuel and Shierry Weber as *Prisms* (London: Neville Spearman, 1967), 105. I have discussed Adorno's other, very fragmentary readings of Sade in *Without End: Sade's Critique of Reason* (New York: Bloomsbury, 2018), chapter one.

15 See, especially, García Düttmann, 'Thinking as Gesture: A Note on *Dialectic of Enlightenment*', *New German Critique* 81 (2000): 143–52; and, Pierre-François Noppen, 'Reflective Rationality and the Claim of *Dialectic of Enlightenment*', *European Journal of Philosophy* 23.2 (2015): 293–320.

16 Adorno goes on to make the link between orgasm and shudder evident when he speaks of the status of sexual experience: 'the aesthetic experience resembles the sexual one, and indeed its culmination. How the beloved image changes in it, how rigidification is united with the most lively, is, as it were, the bodily archetype [*Urbild*] of aesthetic experience' [AT: 263/176]. Note that Hullot-Kentor translates both *Schauer* and *Erschütterung* as shudder although the German terms are not identical; speaking rather broadly, the former is more uncanny, while the latter is more sublime, as such, *Schauer* is perhaps more subjective in that it is a sensation of unfamiliarity, while *Erschütterung* is more objective in that it is an actual occurrence of the disturbing. Sade's sense of ecstasy, it could be argued, is both subjective and objective, as I will go on to show. I have discussed the role of mimesis in Adorno's aesthetics and its relation to this sense of the unknown in *Aesthetics of Negativity*, chapter six

17 In a powerful analysis of Cindy Sherman's Disasters and Sex pictures, Bernstein makes much of the effect of encountering images that are extremely disgusting and notes how their repulsiveness is a marker of what can only be registered. However, this rebarbative effect is only seen to be a challenge to representation (insofar as Sherman's images are photographs) or epistemology (insofar as the image of indeterminate abjection marks the point at which thought can affirm itself in its distinction from the other, in its affirmation of distinction as such), see *Against Voluptuous Bodies*, 294–306. While these are important observations, the sensual affect and fascination of these images is sublimated, and the effects on reason avoided, by ignoring the objective significance of their bodily recapitulation. The nauseous effect of these pictures, much like that of Sade's writings, is not incidental but demonstrates how they exist in a form that is not purely visual or cognitive, and that marks the proximity that is conveyed in the mimetic response of disgust. As Kant writes, the singular nature of disgust is such that because 'the object is represented as if it were imposing the enjoyment that we are nevertheless forcibly resisting, the artistic representation of the object is no longer distinguished in our sensation from the nature of the object itself', *Critique of the Power of Judgment*, ed.

and tr. Paul Guyer (Cambridge: Cambridge University Press, 2000), 190. Although Bernstein cites this definition, he reads it in terms of a sublime contemplation rather than one in which the object imposes itself as a perpetual violation of aesthetic formulation, which is what is ongoing in Sade's excesses. There is a continual imposition of what cannot be assimilated and thereby rendered meaningful, and there is no scope to stand back from this encounter but rather the perverse attempt to enjoy it even as it insistently removes itself from enjoyment.

18 Sade, *Histoire de Juliette*, in *Œuvres III*, 752–53; tr. Austryn Wainhouse as *Juliette* (New York: Grove Press, 1968), 640–41.

19 Hénaff, *Sade: The Invention of the Libertine Body*, tr. Xavier Callahan (Minneapolis: University of Minnesota Press, 1999), 89–97; Josué Harari, 'Sade's Discourse on Method: Rudiments for a Theory of Fantasy', *MLN* 99.5 (1984): 1057–71; and, Michel Foucault, *Language, Madness, and Desire*, ed. Philippe Artières et al., tr. Robert Bononno (Minneapolis: University of Minnesota Press, 2015), 103–14. Harari's essay follows Foucault's 1970 lecture closely by focusing on the absolute solitude of the fantasy and its rational and repetitive operation but misses the explicitly material and pedagogical aspects that make this discourse an instance of contamination.

Chapter Four: Klossowski, Perversity, Criminality

1 Whitebook's major study, *Perversion and Utopia*, discusses perversity only in reference to Marcuse and Freud, a point that Tyrus Miller seeks to rectify in 'Perversion and Utopia: Sade, Fourier, and Critical Theory', *College Literature* 45.2 (2018): 330–59, but largely through a reading of Benjamin and Bataille. Both are useful accounts, but my aim here is to draw out the manner in which perversity takes up the dialectical argument about the basis of rationality in order to show its sensuous dissembling, which places it at a distance from both psychoanalysis and the broader readings of Marcuse and Benjamin. As will be seen, Klossowski's understanding of perversion is primarily in regard to its logic, a more psychoanalytic reading of Sade's perversity can be found in Lucienne Frappier-Mazur, *Writing the Orgy: Power and Parody in Sade*, tr. Gillian C. Gill (Philadelphia: University of Pennsylvania Press, 1996).

2 As this term is of key importance in Klossowski's reading it is worth considering its meaning more closely: *Scélérat* is a slightly archaic word that derives from the Latin verb, *scelero*, meaning to pollute or defile. As such, the translation offered by Lingis, 'villain', although generally adequate, does not reflect the etymological or rhetorical strength of the term. A *scélérat* is a criminal who violates or corrupts and is thus

engaged in major crimes, for example, Robert Damiens, who tried to kill Louis XV in 1757, was a *scélérat* because in seeking to kill the king he was not just guilty of attempted murder but of violating the very principle of the law. So, while it connotes a crime that is wicked or immoral, this is because it involves a perversion of the law itself. As a result, it is found in constructions like rogue agency (agence scélérate) and rogue wave (vague scélérate) and, following a series of anti-press laws passed by the French government in 1893–94, it has come to describe laws that are themselves harsh and repressive. Very helpful readings of Klossowski's essay can be found in Ian James, *Pierre Klossowski: The Persistence of a Name* (Oxford: Legenda, 2000), 56–65; and, Hervé Castanet, *Pierre Klossowski: The Pantomime of Spirits*, tr. Adrian Price and Pamela King (Bern: Peter Lang, 2014), 49–69.

3 Friedrich Nietzsche, *The Anti-Christ, Ecce Homo, Twilight of the Idols, and Other Writings*, ed. Aaron Ridley and Judith Norman (Cambridge: Cambridge University Press, 2005), 170. This passage from *Götzen-Dämmerung* comes directly before the account of how the 'true world' became a fable, which is of major importance for Klossowski's reading of Nietzsche.

4 This account forms the centrepiece of Klossowski's reading in 'Nietzsche, le polythéisme et la parodie', *Revue de métaphysique et de morale* 63.2-3 (1958): 328ff.; 'Nietzsche, Polytheism, and Parody', in *Such a Deathly Desire*, tr. Russell Ford (Albany: SUNY Press, 2007), 102ff. As is evident, Klossowski's reading of Nietzsche converges with that of Gilles Deleuze in *Nietzsche et la philosophie* in regard to the role and significance of impulses (*pulsions*) in Nietzsche's rethinking of the body.

5 Pierre Klossowski, *Les Lois de l'hospitalité* (Paris: Gallimard, 1995), 335–36, 346. This postface was first published as 'Du nom de 'Roberte' en tant que signe unique', *Les Lettres nouvelles* 19 (1961): 78–101. The contemporary notebooks collected in *Du Signe unique, feuillets inédits*, ed. Guillaume Perrier (Paris: Les Petits Matins, 2018), contain extensive elaborations of its thought. See also Klossowski's comments in the afterword to *The Baphomet*, tr. Sophie Hawkes and Stephen Sartarelli (Hygiene, CO: Eridanos Press, 1988), 163–64, and the interview with Jean-Maurice Monnoyer, 'Aux limites de l'indiscrétion', *La Nouvelle Revue française* 325 (1980): 70–86.

6 See my *Without End*, 124–27.

7 As Jeffrey Mehlman points out in 'Literature and Hospitality: Klossowski's Hamann', *Studies in Romanticism* 22.2 (1983): 329–47, the gesture of the open hand forms a critical point in Hegel's 1828 essay on Hamann, which Klossowski translated. Here the sense of language, in the contradiction between its meaning and its writing, constitutes a knot or, in Hamann's words, a clenched fist, which it is up to the reader to open, a point that Hegel criticizes for Hamann's failure to follow through on this suggestion, see *Hegel on Hamann*, ed. and tr. Lisa Marie Anderson (Evanston: Northwestern University Press, 2008), 39; J. G. Hamann, *Writings on Philosophy and Language*, ed. and tr. Kenneth Haynes (Cambridge: Cambridge University Press,

2007), 217–18. The contradiction in sense is what Klossowski will call a solecism, or, as he does in the introduction to the book on Hamann, a dialectical solecism of god, *dei dialectus solecismus*, see Klossowski, *Les Méditations bibliques de Hamann* (Paris: Minuit, 1948), 18–19.

8   It might be thought that, in reference to Klossowski's interest in secret societies, his 1966 preface to the French re-edition of Chesterton's *The Man Who Was Thursday* would be of relevance here. However, this preface does not expand on the points he makes in relation to Sade and Nietzsche but instead concerns the quasi-analogy that Chesterton pursues between the story of the seven days of creation and the seven members (or 'days') of the anarchist society depicted in his novel, which leads to an account of the nightmarish confusion that arises in relation to the possibility of a creation *ex nihilo*. As such, the possibility of examining the secret society as a self-unravelling series of bluffs and counterbluffs, as Chesterton also demonstrates, is passed over. See, Klossowski, 'Préface', in Gilbert Keith Chesterton, *Le nommé Jeudi*, tr. Jean Florence (Paris: Gallimard, 2002), 9–16.

9   Georg Simmel, *Sociology: Inquiries into the Construction of Social Forms*, tr. and ed. Anthony J. Blasi et al. (Leiden: Brill, 2009), 337–62. There is much more to this article, I have only drawn out its most relevant points. Klossowski's thoughts on conspiracy can be found in, *Nietzsche et le cercle vicieux* (Paris: Mercure, 1978), 242–49; tr. Daniel W. Smith as *Nietzsche and the Vicious Circle* (Chicago: University of Chicago Press, 1997), 165–71, and, 'Circulus Vitiosus', in *Nietzsche aujourd'hui? 1: Intensités*, ed. Maurice de Gandillac and Bernard Pautrat (Paris: Union Générale d'Éditions, 1973), 99–102; tr. Joseph D. Kuzma as 'Circulus Vitiosus', *The Agonist* 2.1 (2009): 37–39.

10 Plato, *Politeia* 351c-352c; Cicero, *De officiis* II, 11: 39–40. It is evidence of its fragility that the idiomatic form of this thought – that of the honour among thieves – always tacitly bears its own negation.

11 Hegel, *Grundlinien der Philosophie des Rechts*, ed. Klaus Grotsch and Elisabeth Weisser-Lohmann (Hamburg: Felix Meiner, 2009), §95, 89; *Elements of the Philosophy of Right*, ed. Allen W. Wood, tr. H. B. Nisbet (Cambridge: Cambridge University Press, 1991), 121–22. My reading here slightly pushes at the possibilities of Hegel's text, but a very helpful account of the more conventional interpretation can be found in Shannon Hoff, *The Laws of the Spirit* (Albany: SUNY Press, 2014), 136–37.

12 Conversely, in terms of the positive infinite judgement, as Blanchot writes in response to Gertrude Stein's description of a rose, its reiteration says both that nothing more can be said of the rose than that it is a rose, and also, that saying of the rose that it is nothing but a rose is to indicate that its very name is empty. While its identity is seemingly established and undercut in the same movement, more significantly, the thought of the rose becomes one of sheer resistance as it cannot be

developed into any kind of judgement, and so we move from 'rose is a rose is a rose' to 'rose [is] [a rose]', as both the copula and the nominalization fall away from the form of the predication, leaving a simple aporia, see Maurice Blanchot, *L'Entretien infini* (Paris: Gallimard, 1969), 503–4; tr. Susan Hanson as *The Infinite Conversation* (Minneapolis: University of Minnesota Press, 1993), 343. In both its positive and negative forms, infinite judgement, which as Klossowski shows is implicit in all forms of identity, presents a limit for thought.

13 Hegel, *Wissenschaft der Logik (1812/1813)*, ed. Friedrich Hogemann and Walter Jaeschke (Hamburg: Felix Meiner, 1978), 70; *Science of Logic*, tr. A. V. Miller (London: Allen & Unwin, 1969), 642.

14 Hegel, *Enzyklopädie der philosophischen Wissenschaften im Grundrisse 1830, Bd. I*, ed. Eva Moldenhauer and Karl Markus Michel (Frankfurt am Main: Suhrkamp, 1970), §173 Z, 325; *Encyclopedia Logic*, tr. T. F. Geraets et al. (Indianapolis: Hackett, 1991), 251.

15 Evgeny Pashukanis, 'The General Theory of Law and Marxism', tr. Peter B. Maggs in *Selected Writings on Marxism and Law*, ed. Piers Beirne and Robert Sharlet (London: Academic Press, 1980), 40–131; Georg Rusche, 'Labour Market and Penal Sanction', tr. Gerda Dinwiddie *Crime and Social Justice* 10 (1978): 2–8. Pashukanis's essay first appeared in Russian in 1924, Rusche's essay first appeared in the *Zeitschrift für Sozialforschung* in 1933 and would form the basis for the book completed by Otto Kirchheimer and published as *Punishment and Social Structure* in 1939. The work of critical theorists on criminology has developed widely since the 1960s and useful overviews can be found in Michael J. Lynch and Raymond J. Michalowski, *Primer in Radical Criminology* (Monsey, NY: Criminal Justice Press, 2006); Margaret Malloch and Bill Munro, eds, *Crime, Critique, and Utopia* (London: Palgrave, 2013); Vincenzo Ruggiero, *Power and Crime* (London: Routledge, 2015); and, Steve Hall and Simon Winlow, *Revitalising Criminological Theory* (London: Routledge, 2015).

16 Hegel, *Vorlesungen über die Philosophie des Rechts* (GW 26.1), ed. Dirk Felgenhauer (Hamburg: Felix Meiner, 2013), 499–500. This passage arises directly out of an argument that poverty can give rise to an inner anger or revolt (*Empörung*), in which the current circumstances of the individual are so distorted that right is in them, rather than the state, which has asserted its infinite criminal judgement over them. Such a point, although unique in its formulation is aligned with remarks at paragraphs 127 and 281 of the *Grundlinien der Philosophie des Rechts* that the relation between the individual and the state are contractual, so the individual is not duty bound to observe the law if the state has already broken its contract with the individual, or if no contractual relation exists (as in the case of an occupying force), hence there can be a right to revolt, as it were, in situations of distress where one's existence is at risk, as is found in Adorno's account of the additional factor. See Mark

Tunick, *Hegel's Political Philosophy* (Princeton: Princeton University Press, 1992), 115–19.

17 Marx, *Capital*, 896. See also the appendix to part one of *Theories of Surplus-Value* entitled, 'Apologist Conception of the Productivity of all Professions', tr. Emile Burns (London: Lawrence & Wishart, 1963), 387, in which the criminal is satirically acclaimed for producing 'not only crimes but also criminal law', and thus the entire social, political, and economic structure that depends on these laws. Less satirically, Marx also notes the importance of the role of criminality in relation to the problem of surplus labour.

Chapter Five: Beside Herself with Desire

1 The phrase 'freedom to the object' is used by Adorno quite often, and it appears to be a combination of the following lines from the Preface to Hegel's *Phänomenologie*: 'scientific cognition demands that it give itself over to the life of the object', and, 'argumentation [*Räsonieren*] is freedom from content and vanity over it; it is expected to make the effort to give up this freedom, and instead of being the arbitrarily moving principle of content, to sink this freedom into it, to let it move itself by its own nature, that is, through the self as its own self and to observe this movement' [PG: 39/32, 41–42/35–36].

2 The notion of the other state is central to the later parts of *Der Mann ohne Eigenschaften*, but Musil's understanding of it was first developed in two pieces from 1923 and 1925, see, 'Der deutsche Mensch als Symptom', in *Gesammelte Werke II. Prosa und Stücke*, ed. Adolf Frisé (Reinbek bei Hamburg: Rowohlt, 1978), 1392ff; tr. David S. Luft as 'The German as Symptom', in *Precision and Soul: Essays and Addresses*, ed. Burton Pike (Chicago: University of Chicago Press, 1990), 185ff, and, 'Ansätze zu neuer Ästhetik', in *Gesammelte Werke II*, 1143ff; tr. David S. Luft as 'Toward a New Aesthetic', in *Precision and Soul*, 198ff. The other state is not formulated as such in 'Die Vollendung der Liebe', and so I will not pursue the connection any further, but it is worth noting that its nascent appearance in this story is more sensual than mystical, which is largely how it will be developed in Musil's later thinking.

3 This story has attracted a considerable degree of commentary in German, and Birgit Nübel provides an overview in her 'Vereinigungen', in *Robert Musil Handbuch*, ed. Birgit Nübel and Norbert Christian Wolf (Berlin: De Gruyter, 2016), 120–56; but see especially, Wolfgang Riedel, 'Reise ans Ende des Ich. Das Subjekt und sein Grund bei Robert Musil', in *Geschichte und Vorgeschichte der modernen Subjektivität*, ed. Peter Schulz et al. (Berlin: De Gruyter, 1998), 1151–73. General guides to the background of Musil's story can be found in, Silvia Bonacchi and Philip Payne, 'Musil's 'Die

Vollendung der Liebe': Experience Analysed and Reconstituted', in *A Companion to the Works of Robert Musil*, ed. Philip Payne et al. (Rochester, NY: Camden House, 2007), 175–97; and, Armen Avanessian, 'Cubist Unions: Robert Musil's Novella "The Perfecting of a Love"', *The Germanic Review* 88.1 (2013): 5–27.

4 Aside from a couple of passing references in *Noten zur Literatur*, Adorno does not mention Musil, but in November 1933 he wrote to Berg to say: 'At your instigation I read Der Mann ohne Eigenschaften and in spite of a certain resistance found very beautiful and significant things in it; the head teacher is great, and so are the masks of Klages and Rathenau; Agathe is less well-grounded and it is a shame that there is an inadequate, amateurish philosophical theory running through it, worth about as much as the poetic effusions of some philosophers. Although, on the other hand, the dissatisfaction with blind forms and the urge towards the epistemological character of the novel have their rightful place. But this cannot be improvised simply from private considerations, any more than an amateur can construct counterpoint just from musical moods.' Adorno and Berg, *Briefwechsel 1925–1935*, ed. Henri Lonitz (Frankfurt am Main: Suhrkamp, 1997), 288; tr. Wieland Hoban as *Correspondence 1925–1935* (Cambridge: Polity, 2005), 202. Berg wrote back a week later to say '"D. Mann ohne Eigenschaften": Imagine: I certainly remember the title – but not the novel. Who is it by? What happens?' Adorno's comments are interesting for what they imply about the possibility and status of the philosophical novel, since he commends the aims of Musil's work while criticizing his technique. In a sense, what is flawed in Musil's approach for Adorno is the philosophical nature of his reflections, which appear only to be inserted into the novel rather than to have arisen from the material through its working through. Whether or not this is true of Musil's later work, it is not the case for 'Die Vollendung der Liebe', as I will show.

Discussion of Adorno and Musil is uncommon, and it would seem that readers of Adorno have perhaps unconsciously shared his response to Musil, but see Roger Foster, *Adorno and Philosophical Modernism* (Lanham, MD: Lexington, 2016), chapter six, who looks at the ethical implications of Musil's essayism.

5 Jürgen Schröder, 'Am Grenzwert der Sprache. Zu Robert Musils *Vereinigungen*', *Euphorion* 60 (1966): 311–34, gives a detailed analysis of Musil's language and the effects of its persistent allusions and approximations. See also, Fred Lönker, *Poetische Anthropologie: Robert Musils Erzählungen 'Vereinigungen'* (München: Wilhelm Fink, 2002), 21–69, although whether it is an 'anthropology' that emerges from this transformation of language is doubtful.

6 Musil, letter to Franz Blei, 15 July 1911, *Briefe 1901–1942*, ed. Adolf Frisé (Reinbek bei Hamburg: Rowohlt, 1981), 87. Although he felt he had come closer to achieving this aim here than in any of his other writings, Musil was never satisfied with the result. As he noted at a critical moment during the composition of 'Die Vollendung der Liebe', the desire for precision and rigour seemed to lead to no more than a form

of intellectual paraphrase, see *Tagebücher*, ed. Adolf Frisé (Reinbek bei Hamburg: Rowohlt, 1976), 213; *Diaries 1899–1941*, ed. Mark Mirsky, tr. Philip Payne (New York: Basic Books, 1998), 116–17.

As Adorno wrote in relation to the Expressionism of Schoenberg's *Erwartung*, its stance ultimately sublates both object and subject by the rigour of its attention to the material:

> If one calls the compulsion to coherent construction objectivity [*Sachlichkeit*], then objectivity is not a mere countermovement to Expressionism. It is Expressionism in its otherness. Expressionist music took the principle of expression out of traditional Romanticism so precisely that it assumed the character of a transcript [*Protokollcharakter*]. But that turns it around. Music as a transcript of expression is no longer "expressive". What is expressed no longer hovers over it in an indeterminate distance and lends it the lustre of the infinite. As soon as the music sharply and unambiguously fixes what is expressed, its subjective content freezes under its gaze to that very objective [*Objektiven*] whose existence denies its purely expressive character. In the transcript-based stance to its object [*Gegenstand*], it itself becomes "objective" ["*sachlich*"]. With its outbursts, the dream of subjectivity explodes no less than do the conventions. The transcript-like chords burst the subjective semblance. In doing so, however, they ultimately sublate [*aufheben*] their own expressive function. Whatever they depict as an object [*Objekt*], however precisely, becomes indifferent: it is the same subjectivity whose magic fades before the exactness of the gaze that the work directs on it.
>
> PNM: 53/42–43

7   Although it is not clear exactly what this term would have meant in Berlin in 1910, it refers to a rank of senior civil servant that is perhaps of the same level as an assistant director. That is, he is clearly senior, but not so much that he avoids the crass arrogance of an ambitious figure from the lower ranks. Musil's intention is thus to make him anonymous but also specific to a certain order of masculinity.

8   As Adorno remarks in one of the unpublished appendices to *Minima Moralia*, entitled 'Post festum': 'it is unavoidable for passion to reflect on that very moment in the experience of the indispensable boundary between two people and thus to see the nothingness of being overwhelmed at the same moment that one is overwhelmed by it' [MM: 291]. These appendices have appeared as 'Messages in a Bottle', tr. Edmund Jephcott *New Left Review* 200 (1993): 5–14 [9].

9   Musil, *Gesammelte Werke II*, 972. The 'path of the smallest steps' is a phrase that is central to Adorno's analyses of the music of Alban Berg, and would seem to derive from the notion of organic evolution.

10 These and many other important details about the historical and cultural background of this change in thinking can be found in Harry Oosterhuis, *Stepchildren of Nature: Krafft-Ebing, Psychiatry, and the Making of Sexual Identity* (Chicago: University of Chicago Press, 2000), and, Benjamin Kahan, *Book of Minor Perverts: Sexology, Etiology, and the Emergences of Sexuality* (Chicago: University of Chicago Press, 2019).

11 The question of masochism is handled very well by Stephanie Bird, 'Masochism and its Limits in Robert Musil's "Die Vollendung der Liebe"', *Modern Language Review* 100.3 (2005): 709–22.

12 Adorno, 'Sexualtabus und Recht heute', in *Kulturkritik und Gesellschaft II*, ed. Rolf Tiedemann (Frankfurt am Main: Suhrkamp, 1977), 538; tr. Henry W. Pickford as 'Sexual Taboos and Law Today', in *Critical Models: Interventions and Catchwords* (New York: Columbia University Press, 1998), 75. This thought pursues an idea posed twenty years earlier: 'Only those who are able to determine utopia in blind somatic pleasure, which is without intention and stills the end [*die letzte stillt*], would be capable of an idea of truth that would endure' [MM: 66/61]. The emphasis, as Adorno makes clear, is equally on the blind somatic pleasure and its determination since it is only as such that it can endure its lack of end.

Chapter Six: Modernity and Utopia

1 The problem of the status of Adorno's aesthetic theory was first raised by Rüdiger Bubner in a widely cited article, 'Kann Theorie ästhetisch werden? Zum Hauptmotiv der Philosophie Adornos', in *Materialien zur ästhetischen Theorie Theodor W. Adornos*, ed. Burkhardt Lindner and W. Martin Lüdke (Frankfurt am Main: Suhrkamp, 1979), 108–37; tr. Nicholas Walker as 'Can Theory Become Aesthetic? On a Principal Theme of Adorno's Philosophy', in *Theodor W. Adorno: Critical Evaluations in Cultural Theory*, ed. Simon Jarvis (London: Routledge, 2007), Volume I, 14–39. In this article Bubner glosses aesthetic theory as 'the convergence of knowledge/cognition [*Erkenntnis*] and art' [109/15]. Such an idea would, he wrote, bring about a disservice to both aspects and a failure to grasp the significance of each, thereby preventing an understanding of the challenge of modern art. This gloss is then repeated as 'the convergence of [philosophy and art] at the point of cognition', and 'the convergence of artistic and philosophical cognitive intentions' [120/24, 131/34]. These glosses are authorized by Bubner's claims that they present Adorno's basic proposition (*unableitbaren Satz*) that he stressed everywhere (*allenthalben betont*), although Bubner does not provide evidence of these claims, or explicate them and, when he reprinted this essay in his 1989 collection *Ästhetische Erfahrung*,

he did so without changing it. However, when Adorno does speak of convergence it is between art and philosophy and in relation to truth-content, not knowledge, as he makes clear when he writes that critique 'recognises in the spirit of the works their truth-content or separates it from it. In this act alone, not through any philosophy of art that dictated to it what its spirit should be, do art and philosophy converge' [AT: 137/88, cf. 197/130–31, 422/284, 507/341]. So, in terms of aesthetic theory, convergence is exactly what does not take place, for the reflective aspect of aesthetics and the aesthetic aspect of theory oscillate in a mutually determining and disrupting, and thereby unresolved, dialectic that is its unravelling of the truth-content of the work, which thus cannot be understood simply in terms of cognitive content.

Although Bubner's paper is often cited it is rarely discussed, and so it is worth highlighting the way that he frames his argument, since this is critical to his negative perception of Adorno's intentions. Bubner's argument is that Adorno's thinking of aesthetics is limited by its circularity, for while aesthetics is said to be the other of philosophical thought, which art attempts to broach, this alterity is itself conceived and determined by philosophy. Hence the apparent aestheticization of theory that Adorno seems to propose only indicates the prior determination of aesthetics by theory, and thus the lack of a genuine aesthetic encounter [133/35]. This charge of circularity and narrowness is widely made and derives from the suspicion that the socially and historically determined nature of Adorno's thinking leads him to find only that which he had sought in the various phenomena that he discusses, and indeed, that what he finds is in all cases merely evidence of reification or its resistance. There is a certain validity to this complaint, although it often arises in response to historical materialist accounts, but the problem with it is that it is precisely the complaint of philosophy, that is, it views Adorno's thought solely in terms of its position as theory, and hence only finds theory or its failings. However, it is in Adorno's extensive discussions of music or literature that we find more than just a confirmation of a prior theory; in the detail and the way that this perspective is distorted and fragmented. Equally, while aesthetic experience is always related to theory, this is not the full extent of what is ongoing in the encounter with artworks. Here the speculative aspect of Adorno's thought presents its honesty, both in terms of the awareness of the prior determinations that mark its perspective and how these are transformed in the encounter with art. Bubner fails to grasp this aspect because his reading remains within a Kantian/Schillerian position of considering art and conceptual thought to be opposed and thus unavailable for mutual determination or disruption. In Bubner's view, art fosters the free play of reflection, which liberates consciousness from previous forms of perception and conceptual modes of thinking [130/33]. As such, artworks are mere vehicles of reflection that are unaffected by thinking and detached from their own contexts.

2   As Paulhan explains, the mutual use of and by language draws out its doubled relation to alienation: '*Flee from language, it will pursue you. Pursue language, it will*

flee from you', see Jean Paulhan, *Les Fleurs de Tarbes, ou La Terreur dans les lettres* (Paris: Gallimard, 1941), 153; *The Flowers of Tarbes: Or, Terror in Literature*, tr. Michael Syrotinski (Urbana: University of Illinois Press, 2006), 82.

3 Following the initial shudder in the encounter with the beautiful, the individual becomes hot as the soul feels its wings beginning to swell and throb and ache (*Phaedrus*, 251b-c). The language that Socrates uses in this description is obviously and deliberately euphemistic, as is often his way, but in this instance, it registers the impossibility of talking about the experience of the beautiful without referring to the physical arousal that it brings about. Stimulation and excitement can never be wholly intellectual, by their nature they refer to an actual bodily response, which is impossible to ignore.

4 Adorno makes the point very clearly: 'modern art is indeed different from the traditional, but it is also identical to traditional art, except that everything that was subcutaneous in the way of problems and difficulties, which was previously hidden by the closed surface of communication, now emerges actually and essentially' [AS: 239/150]. However, it would have to be added that 'now' is a receding horizon against which works of art are continually coming to expose previously subcutaneous tensions.

5 Adorno, 'Wozu noch Philosophie', in *Kulturkritik und Gesellschaft II*, 473; tr. Henry W. Pickford as 'Why Still Philosophy', in *Critical Models*, 17.

6 Kant, 'Towards Perpetual Peace', in *Practical Philosophy*, 317. Hegel, *Wissenschaft der Logik (1832)*, ed. Friedrich Hogemann and Walter Jaeschke (Hamburg: Felix Meiner, 1985), 56; *Science of Logic*, 69. It is also worth recalling the lines that Adorno wrote before his noted description of *musique informelle* and the form of artistic utopia: 'Informal music is a little like Kant's perpetual peace, which he conceived of as a real, concrete possibility that can be actualized, and yet again as an idea' [QF: 540/322]. See, *Kranichsteiner Vorlesungen*, 446; *The New Music: Kranichstein Lectures*, 272.

7 Guy de Maupassant, 'Out on the River', tr. David Coward in '*A Day in the Country' and Other Stories* (Oxford: Oxford University Press, 1990), 3–9; *Sur l'eau*, ed. Jacques Dupont (Paris: Gallimard, 1993); tr. Douglas Parmée as *Afloat* (New York: NYRB, 2008). See, Gerhard Schweppenhäuser, *Theodor W. Adorno: An Introduction*, tr. James Rolleston (Durham, NC: Duke University Press, 2009), chapter six; and, Damien Marwood, '*Sur l'Eau*, or How to Read Adorno: Guy de Maupassant and the Negative Dialectic of Utopia', *Modernism/Modernity* 23.4 (2016): 833–54. García Düttmann appears uncertain of how to read this aphorism in *So ist es*, 59–62, for while he states that the density of its last lines eliminates the nonsense of seeing it as simply edifying, or of breaking the taboo on images of utopia, he then suggests that the image that Adorno draws is such that it ironically suspends the dialectic with the result that it should be taken literally, as indicating a state without ambiguity or resonance, which is its utopian gesture. While this fits with his general reading in *So*

ist es, the image that Adorno draws is instead more like a dialectical image in its careful combination of dissonant elements.

It is worth looking at Maupassant's short story closely, as its dimensions indicate that it is not simply a tale of finitude. As is stated at the beginning of the narrative, rivers are in some way more mysterious and sinister than the ocean, at least for the narrator, because of their darkness and quiescence. They lack the wildness of the ocean but bring to the land a strange lack of finitude, as if the land had lost its borders and, as such, sailors on these inland waterways often find themselves in more treacherous and unknown waters. Although this is a typically gothic opening for the story, it bears an intriguing contrast in terms of the mundane quality of the waterways and their combination of danger and mystery, interiority and exteriority, as if the land touched upon its otherness in these places more powerfully than it would at the seashore, precisely because they are so far from the edge of land. This mundane quality is further reflected in the muddiness of the waters, which, like their interiority, is both literal and figurative. These rivers are, he says, like cemeteries without tombs, where you see and hear things that are not there.

The conclusion also follows a fairly typical gothic denouement, but its significance lies with the contrast it sets up with the wondrous vision the boatman had seen, an entirely commonplace vision in its parts, but one that becomes fantastic through the effects of the situation. The river is on the other side of the border that encloses the land, just as is the night, but it is an exteriority that is bound to this interiority even as it is itself boundless. It is the latter confusion that is felt in the disorientating movements and sounds that assail him, which is perhaps the source of his fear as they indicate a place without place, and thus without limit or direction. Only by way of the black mass of mortality, which he has come up against, does this other place become oriented and through it he becomes witness to a brilliant constellation of lights. Throughout this display the river remains 'absolutely free', merely a dark line between below and above, its darkness a reminder of the mud in which everything rots, in his words. The discovery of the body comes with morning, with the return to everyday reality, to those grey, rainy days that bring sadness and misfortune, as he says. The discovery is suggestive, but little can be made of it; the woman would appear to have killed herself, but why and when are of course unknown and this only adds to the grotesque banality of the revelation. There is nothing more here than an irreducible negativity, no honour or justice or truth in this discovery, no empowering knowledge or morality, simply a black mass on which the boatman had become stranded that is related and unrelated to the marvellous sights he had seen, and by way of which he had for a time become completely displaced.

The later travelogue draws out this tension in more extreme but also more quotidian terms, as nihilism and idleness, between whose poles the narrator oscillates, as in the following passage:

> Certainly, on some days, I have a horror of what is to the point of longing for death. I feel, to the extent of acute suffering, the invariable monotony of landscapes, figures, and thoughts. The mediocrity of the universe amazes and revolts me, the smallness of all things fills me with disgust, the poverty of human beings annihilates me.
> On some others, on the contrary, I enjoy everything like an animal. If my restless mind, tormented, hypertrophied by work, rushes to hopes that are not of our race, and then falls back into contempt for everything after having noticed its nothingness, my animal body becomes drunk with all the intoxications of life.
>
> 78/36

As the narrative develops these extremes are ameliorated into tragicomic anecdotes, which dissipates their tension but also suggests how the banality of life makes it almost impossible to maintain.

8 Adorno's thoughts on metaphysical experience as fallibility can be found in his 1965 lecture course, *Metaphysik. Begriff und Probleme*, ed. Rolf Tiedemann (Frankfurt am Main: Suhrkamp, 1998), 218ff; tr. Edmund Jephcott as *Metaphysics: Concept and Problems* (Cambridge: Polity, 2000), 140ff.

9 This meeting took place in August 1960. Kracauer included some of its points in his *History: The Last Things Before the Last* (Oxford: Oxford University Press, 1969), 201. Adorno's response can be found in his notes for his 1965–66 course on negative dialectics [VND: 188–91/144–47; cf. ND: 43/33].

10 The persistence of this popular image is itself remarkable, for as Osborne noted in 1989 ('Adorno and the Metaphysics of Modernism', in *The Problems of Modernity: Adorno and Benjamin*, ed. Andrew Benjamin (London: Routledge, 1989), 23–48), it was already a caricature then, but as a result it says much about the resistance to Adorno's ideas, and the need to confine or dismiss their challenge.

11 Honoré de Balzac, *Illusions perdues*, ed. Antoine Adam (Paris: Garnier Frères, 1956), 346–47; tr. Raymond N. MacKenzie as *Lost Illusions* (Minneapolis: University of Minnesota Press, 2020), 247. Interestingly, Adam notes that the style of Lucien's review resembles that of the critic Jules Janin – whose 1830 review of a play by Georges Ozaneaux pioneered this new style – even to the degree of borrowing its opening from Janin's review of Balzac's own novel, *La Peau de chagrin*. While this indicates Balzac's satirical approach, it also marks the odd position of the review as that which only partly exists within the novel.

Index

a prima vista 39, 40, 48
absolute music 92–107
abstraction 14, 24–5, 27, 119, 217 n. 23
   Beethoven, Ludwig van 90
   Kant, Immanuel 138
   Sade, Marquis de 138
activity regulation 97
actuality 203
additional factor, the 122–4, 125, 205
Adorno, Theodor W.
   academic career 56
   aesthetic theory 183
   aesthetics lectures (1958–59) 6–15, 165
   'Aktualität der Philosophie, Die' (inaugural lecture) 38, 51, 52, 60, 73–4
   art 184
   Ästhetische Theorie 6, 193, 194
   Balzac, Honoré de 67–72, 195–8, 206
   Beethoven, Ludwig van 81, 83, 86–91, 102, 104, 108, 113
   Benjamin, Walter 23, 50, 52, 55, 59, 61–2, 76, 82
   Berg, Alban 59
   career 107
   Darmstadt Summer School address (1961) 17–18
   Dialektik der Aufklärung (with Horkheimer, Max) 13, 107, 111, 116, 125–6, 131–2, 136, 141–2, 143, 144–5, 148
   dissertation 55
   Expressionism 240 n. 5
   'Form in der neuen Musik' 106
   Hegel, Georg Wilhelm Friedrich 104–5, 106–7, 117, 190
   Horkheimer, Max, 132–3, 135, 148
   'Idee der Naturgeschichte, Die' 50–3
   Kierkegaard 41, 43, 55–6, 57, 62, 76, 85–6
   Kierkegaard, Søren 56, 57
   Kracauer, Siegfried 38–40, 44, 45, 48, 73–4, 201

   Křenek, Ernst 44, 46, 51, 55
   marriage 148
   Minima Moralia. See *Minima Moralia*
   Moments musicaux 193
   as musician and composer 209 n. 6
   Musil, Robert 239 n. 4
   'Nachtmusik' 84–5
   Negative Dialektik 193
   Noten zur Literatur 193
   opera 199
   Parva Aesthetica 193
   Philosophie der neuen Musik 3, 107, 108, 111, 125, 193
   Plato 184–7
   Prismen 107, 193
   Schoenberg, Arnold 47–8, 55, 57, 58–9, 106, 108–9, 112–13, 114, 116–17, 198
   Schubert, Franz 83–4
   sociological work/writings 107
   'Spätstil Beethovens' 86
   Stichworte 193
   thinking, status of 50
   Versuch über Wagner 107
   'Zur gesellschaftlichen Lage der Musik' 55
   Zur Metakritik der Erkenntnistheorie 107
aesthetic material 183–4
aesthetic theory 183
aesthetics lectures (1958–59) 6–15, 165
'Aktualität der Philosophie, Die' (inaugural lecture) (Adorno, Theodor W.) 38, 51, 52, 60, 73–4
alienation 30–1, 56, 68, 177, 184
   employment 35
   language 82
   Schoenberg, Arnold 58
allegory 82–3
   landscapes 82, 83, 84
Angerstein murder case 25–7

248

Angestellten 27–8, 32, 36–7, 40 *see also* employment
Angestellten, Die (Kracauer, Siegfried) 32–40, 42, 43
antinomies 122–3
apathy 138
aphorisms 77
aporia 19, 122
appearance 144–5
architecture 92
Aristotle 135
ars inveniendi 65–6
art 13, 119, 184
    appearance of 119
    avant-garde 109, 119
    end of 118–19
    history 84–5, 119
    philosophy 55
    spirit 92
    utopia 188–9
artworks 9–10, 13–15, 57, 203–4
    abstract 217 n. 23
    alienation 184
    aporia 227 n. 28
    approaching 195–206
    avant-garde 109
    conceptual approach 203–4
    disinterest 181
    dissonance 181
    essence of 84
    experience 192
    form 75
    fragmentary 115–16
    history 84–5, 119
    knowledge 115
    language 184
    modern 187–8
    natural-history 11, 46–7, 55
    ornament 112
    Schoenberg, Arnold 59
    sensuality 179, 181, 189, 192
    shudder 145
    thought 204–5
    utopia 188–9
Ästhetische Theorie (Adorno, Theodor W.) 6, 193, 194
atheism 151–2
audience response 46–7
automation 34–5
'Autoritärer Staat' (Horkheimer, Max) 141
avant-garde, the 109, 119, 120

Bach, Johann Sebastian
    St Matthew Passion 222 n. 11
Balzac, Honoré de 67–72
    Comédie humaine, La 69, 198
    Illusions perdues 71, 195–200, 205–6
beauty 185–7
    standards of 119
Beethoven, Ludwig van 81, 83, 86–91, 100, 102, 103, 104, 113
Benjamin, Walter 51, 52–3, 73, 215 n. 14
    Adorno, Theodor W. 23, 50, 52, 55, 59
    allegory 82–3
    constellation notion 186
    history 141
    Passagenwerk, Das 61
    Ursprung des deutschen Trauerspiels 38, 44, 52, 61–2, 74, 82
    Wahlverwandtschaften (Goethe) 59, 83
Bentham, Jeremy 135
Berg, Alban 59, 114–15
Berlin 27–8
Bernstein, Jay 208 n. 4
Bubner, Rüdiger 241 n. 1
burglary metaphor 64–6
businesses *see also* employment
    automation 34–5
    organization 35
    recruitment 33–4, 35, 36

capitalism 30, 70, 134, 141, 163 *see also* employment
Cent Vingt Journées de Sodome, Les (Sade, Marquis de) 127
change 45, 46
Chesterton, G. K., 236 n. 8
chiasmus 122–3, 124
Cicero 160
clichés 113
Comédie humaine, La (Balzac, Honoré de) 69, 198
commodity-exchange 163 *see also* capitalism
communication 58
completion 170

concept, the 43–4
concreteness 24–5, 27, 119, 193, 194–5
  negative 201–2
consonance 117–18, 119
constellation notion 186
contradictions 36, 115, 118, 122
conventions 87–8, 89
creative expression 113
crime 25–7, 42–4, 162–4 *see also* detective fiction
  criminal acts 161, 162
  Hegel, Georg Wilhelm Friedrich 162–3
  scélérat 234 n. 2
  secret societies 160
  sexuality 126
  trust among criminals 160
criminal philosophy 150–8
critical theory 2, 55, 73, 125–7, 141, 143
cruelty 134, 136, 138, 140
  association with happiness 135–6
crying 116

death 84, 87, 177
death drive 134
decadence 69–70
decay 80, 82, 83
Denke, Karl 212 n. 2
desire 10–11, 126–7, 138,
  insatiability 142–3
  Musil, Robert 174, 175, 177–8
detective novels 40–4
Detektiv-Roman, Der (Kracauer, Siegfried) 41
diaballo 45
dialectic, the 88
Dialektik der Aufklärung (Adorno, Theodor W. and Horkheimer, Max) 13, 107, 111, 116, 125–6, 131–2, 136, 141–2, 143, 144–5, 148
disgust 233 n. 17
disintegration 79–91
disinterest 181
dissonance 2, 5, 10, 117–18, 181
  music 45, 111, 113–14, 115, 117–18
  sensuality 13
  sublime 193
Doktor Faustus (Mann, Thomas) 45, 69, 221 n. 6

ecstasy 145, 146–8
egoism 133, 134–5, 230 n. 9
'Egoismus und Freiheitsbewegung' (Horkheimer, Max) 132–6, 139, 141–2
emancipation 133–4
employment 28–9, 32–5 *see also* capitalism *and* labour market
enjoyment 138 *see also* pleasure
enlightenment, the 4, 7, 112, 114
  Dialektik der Aufklärung 131–2
  Horkheimer, Max 138, 139
Enlightenment, the 126, 132
  pure insight 116–17
  revolution 133–4
enthusiasm 185
eros 194
Erwartung (Schoenberg, Arnold) 175, 240 n. 6
essays 66, 73–5, 196, 197
excess 10
experience 144, 145, 194
  intellectual experience 203
expression 52, 56, 58, 59, 112
  formal and dissonant 107–18
  historico-material 112
  music 94, 99–101, 107–18
Expressionism 240 n. 5
expressionless 59
extravagance 146, 147, 148

fairy tales 31, 33
feeling 93–4, 95–8, 100–1, 102
  Musil, Robert 166, 168, 171, 175–7
fidelity 171, 172, 173, 174
Fleurs de Tarbes, Les (Paulhan, Jean) 113, 114
foreign words 81–2
form 40, 45–8, 57, 73–5, 88
  conventions 87
  Hegel, Georg Wilhelm Friedrich 9
  Kierkegaard, Søren 55, 57
  music 19, 46
  Schoenberg, Arnold 56, 57
'Form in der neuen Musik' (Adorno, Theodor W.) 106
Frankfurt discussions 55

freedom 9, 10, 133–4, 160–1, 189–90
   loss of 161
   melody 102
   music 45, 103
'freedom to the object' 9, 165, 182, 201, 202, 238 n. 1
Freud, Sigmund 134, 143
Fromm, Erich 229 n. 4

García Düttmann, Alexander 228 n. 30, 243 n. 7
gesture 155–8, 161
Goethe, Johann Wolfgang von
   Wahlverwandtschaften 59, 83, 196
Gramsci, Antonio 70

Haarmann, Fritz 212 n. 2
habit 24, 27
Hammer, Espen 209 n. 8
happiness 133, 134, 140 *see also* pleasure
   association with cruelty 135–6
harmony 98, 99, 102, 118
hearing 93
   speculative ear 104–6
   structural listening 104–5, 108
Hegel, Georg Wilhelm Friedrich 7, 9, 67, 104–5, 106–7, 214 n. 11
   aphorisms 77
   art, obsolescence of 118–19
   crime 162–3
   gesture 157
   history 198
   Milder-Hauptmann, Anna 199
   modernity 69
   music 90, 92–107
   Naturphilosophie, Die 93, 96
   Phänomenologie des Geistes 105
   pure insight 116–17
   Rechtsphilosophie 69, 100, 162
   universal history 50
   Vorlesungen über die Ästhetik 101
   Wissenschaft der Logik 24, 190
Heidegger, Martin 51
   Frankfurt discussions 55
   philosophers 64–5
   sociologists 64–5
Herbertz, Richard 25, 212 n. 2
hiatus 121

historical images 63, 64–5, 66, 70
historico-material expression 112
history 9, 46, 50–1, 63, 223 n. 14 *see also* natural-history
   art/artworks 84–5, 119
   Balzac, Honoré de 72
   Benjamin, Walter 52–3, 141
   disintegration 83, 84, 85
   Hegel, Georg Wilhelm Friedrich 198
   judgement 125
   language 57–8
   literature 67
   Lukács, Georg 52
   music 108, 115
   state 198
   truth-content 57–8
   universal 50
Hoffmann. E. T. A 223 n. 11
homeostasis 198
hope 110
Horkheimer, Max 2, 4, 47, 62, 131, 207 n. 3
   'Autoritärer Staat' 141
   Adorno, Theodor W., 132–3, 135, 148
   Dialektik der Aufklärung (with Adorno, Theodor W.) 13, 107, 111, 116, 125–6, 131–2, 136, 141–2, 143, 144–5, 148
   'Egoismus und Freiheitsbewegung' 132–6, 139, 141–2
   judgements 125
   Sade, Marquis de 126–7, 132–3, 135–44
   science 60
   'Vernunft und Selbstbehauptung' 141
Huxley, Aldous 232 n. 14

ideas 53–4
'Idee der Naturgeschichte, Die' (Adorno, Theodor W.) 50–3
idée fixe 155
idleness 190–1
Illusions perdues (Balzac, Honoré de) 71, 195–200, 205–6
imagination 65–6, 146–8
imperative, the 188

individuality 34–5, 77, 134 *see also* self-interest
dialectic, the 88
infidelity 171, 172, 173, 174
infinite judgements 162
intellectual experience 203
intelligibility 5–6
interiority 92, 95–6
intermittent dialectics 75–7
interpretation 39, 52, 53, 60–6, 84

jazz 225 n. 20
judgements 125
Juliette (Sade, Marquis de) 131, 136, 136, 139, 144, 148, 155, 157

Kant, Immanuel 6, 7,
  beauty and the sublime 8, 9–10
  elemental power 9–10
  experience 145
  Kritik der Urteilskraft 7
  morality 136–8
  peace 190
  self-interest 136–7
Karplus, Gretel 148
Kierkegaard, Søren 55, 56, 57
Kierkegaard (Adorno, Theodor W.) 41, 43, 55–6, 57, 62, 76, 85–6
Klossowski, Pierre 4
  gesture 156, 157–8
  perversion 4, 149–50, 158, 161
  'Philosophe scélérat, Le' 149
  Roberte ce soir 154
  Sade mon prochain 149
  Sade, Marquis de 149, 150–6, 161
  secret societies 159
  thought 154–5
knowledge 115
Kracauer, Siegfried 3, 29, 36, 40, 44, 48, 55
  a prima vista 39, 40, 48
  Adorno, Theodor W. 38–40, 44, 45, 48, 73–4, 201
  alienation 35
  Angerstein murder case 25–7
  Angestellten, Die 32–40, 42, 43
  concept, the 43–4
  detective novels 40–4
  Detektiv-Roman, Der 41

fairy tales 31, 33
form 73–5
ornament, the 29
'Ornament der Masse, Das' 29–32
totality 40, 41
urban culture 23–4
Kraus, Karl 5, 121
Křenek, Ernst 44, 46, 51, 55
Kritik der Urteilskraft (Kant, Immanuel) 7

labour market 163 *see also* employment
  negative labour 160, 163–4
labourers 28, 29
landscapes, barren 82, 83, 84
language 53, 57–8, 76
  alienation 184
  artworks 184
  foreign words 81–2
  gesture 155–8
  hiatus 121
  Klossowski, Pierre 153–4
  music 59, 98, 114, 124–5
  Musil, Robert 172, 175
  perversion 151–3, 155, 156–7
  punctuation 124–5
  purism 81–2
  Sade, Marquis de 151–7
  sensations 172–3
  sensuality 173
  subjectivity 151–2
liberation 94–5
libertinism 160–1, 189
listening 93
  speculative ear 104–6
  structural listening 104–5, 108
literature 67–72
  poetry 95, 101
  realism 200
loneliness 109–10
love 173, 177, 178, 182
Lukács, Georg 24, 26, 51
  Balzac, Honoré de 69, 70–1
  Studies in European Realism 69
  Theorie des Romans, Die 52, 69

Malte Laurids Brigge (Rilke, Rainer Maria) 175
Mann, Thomas

Doktor Faustus 45, 69, 221 n. 6
Tod in Venedig 175
Mann ohne Eigenschaften, Der (Musil, Robert) 169
Marcuse, Herbert 2, 50, 211 n. 1, 230 n. 6
Marx, Karl 63, 64, 163, 211 n. 1
mass ornaments 30, 31–3
material/temporal antagonism 113
materialism 1, 47, 73–4, 229 n. 5
  interpretation 63–4
  philosophy 89
materiality 44, 46, 183–4
Maupassant, Guy de 190
  'Sur l'eau' 190–1, 193
mediation 24–5
melancholy 57, 62
melody 98–9, 102
Mendelssohn, Felix 222 n. 11
metaphysical questions 60
metaphysics 72
Milder-Hauptmann, Anna 199
Minima Moralia (Adorno, Theodor W.) 40, 54, 73, 75, 77, 125, 196
  tact 79, 80
  thought 193
  utopia 189–90, 191
modern, the 187–8
modernism 187–8
modernity 69–70, 126, 184
  Musil, Robert 171
  tact 79–80
Moments musicaux (Adorno, Theodor W.) 193
monstrosity 151–2, 156
morality 135, 136–8, 139–40, 180
music 3, 15–20, 89–91, 124
  absolute 92–107
  as accompaniment 99
  activity regulation 97
  ahistoricity 112
  as art of feeling 93–4, 95–8, 100–1, 102
  aufheben 101–2
  Bach, Johann Sebastian 222 n. 11
  Beethoven, Ludwig van 81, 83, 86–91, 100, 102, 103, 104, 113
  Berg, Alban 59, 114–15
  clichés 113
  composing 111, 114

  conventions 87–8, 89
  crying 116
  dissonance 45, 111, 113–14, 115
  expression 94, 99–101, 107–18
  Expressionism 240 n. 5
  form 88–9, 99–100, 111–12
  freedom 102, 103
  harmony 98, 99, 102, 118
  Hegel, Georg Wilhelm Friedrich 92–107
  history 108, 115
  Hoffmann, E. T. A 223 n. 11
  improvisation 39–4
  as independent 99
  informal 17–18
  instrumental 94, 99, 100, 102–3
  interiority 92, 95–6
  jazz 225 n. 20
  language 59, 98, 114, 124–5
  late style 86–8, 90–1, 92, 103–4
  liberation 94–5
  material/temporal antagonism 113
  meaning 111
  melody 98–9, 102
  Mendelssohn, Felix 222 n. 11
  New Music 105, 106, 108
  objectivity 17–18, 19, 93–4, 106, 240 n. 6
  ornament 112
  philosophy 89–90, 106–7, 108
  recapitulation 90
  religious 223 n. 11
  repetition 17–18
  reproduction 98, 100
  resonance 93–4
  rhythm 98, 102
  Schoenberg, Arnold. *See* Schoenberg, Arnold
  Schubert, Franz 83–4
  sound 93, 95
  spatiality 92, 93, 101
  speculative ear 104–6
  spirit 101, 108
  structural listening 104–5, 108
  subjectivity 17–18, 19, 93–4, 97–8, 103–4, 240 n. 6
  temporality 86, 90, 91, 97, 98, 101, 102, 104, 111, 124

themes 94, 114
twelve-tone technique 47, 109, 110–15
variation 114
Webern, Anton 114–15
Zelter, Carl Friedrich 222 n. 11
musical material 24, 44–9, 84–91, 108, 124
Musil, Robert 3, 4
   Adorno, Theodor W. 239 n. 4
   Mann ohne Eigenschaften, Der 169
   Vereinigungen 175, 178
   'Vollendung der Liebe, Die' 165–78, 179–80, 181–2
myth 53

'Nachtmusik' (Adorno, Theodor W.) 84–5
natural-history 2, 3, 7, 23, 50–3, 86
   artworks 11, 46–7, 55
   Benjamin, Walter 52–3
   Lukács, Georg 52
   musical material 44–9
   of ornamentation 27–44
   theatre 54
nature 50–1, 52–3, 180 *see also* natural-history
Naturphilosophie, Die (Hegel, Georg Wilhelm Friedrich) 93, 96
negative dialectics 3, 13, 17, 44, 59, 118
Negative Dialektik (Adorno, Theodor W.) 193
negative infinite judgements 162
negative labour 160, 163–4
negativity 192, 201–1
New Music 105, 106, 108
Nietzsche, Friedrich 135, 139–40
Noten zur Literatur (Adorno, Theodor W.) 193

object/objectivity 9, 11, 12, 165
   absence 88–9
   abstract/concrete 24
   artworks 13–14
   conventions 87
   experience 194
   freedom to the 9, 165, 182, 201, 202
   interpretation 60–1
   music 17–18, 19, 93–4, 106, 240 n. 6
opacity 48
orgasm 145, 146

'Ornament der Masse, Das' (Kracauer, Siegfried) 29–32
ornaments/ornamentation 29–33, 43, 44, 60
   music 112
other state, the (*anderen Zustand*) 3, 165

pain. *See* suffering
painting 92
Parva Aesthetica (Adorno, Theodor W.) 193
Passagenwerk, Das (Benjamin, Walter) 61
Paulhan, Jean
   Fleurs de Tarbes, Les 113, 114
perversion 1–2, 149–58, 161
   gesture 155–8, 161
   Klossowski, Pierre 4, 149–50, 158, 161
   loss of will 161
   Musil, Robert 171, 179–80
   Sade, Marquis de 146–58, 161
   secret societies 159
   sensuality 179
   sodomy 179–80
Phaedrus (Plato) 184–7, 199
Phänomenologie des Geistes (Hegel, Georg Wilhelm Friedrich) 105
'Philosophe scélérat, Le' (Klossowski, Pierre) 149
philosophers 64–5
Philosophie der neuen Musik (Adorno, Theodor W.) 3, 107, 108, 111, 125, 193
philosophy 57–8, 64, 202–3
   art 55
   avant-garde, the 120
   criminal 150–8
   imagination 65–6
   interpretation 60–6
   materialism 89
   metaphysical questions 60
   music 89–90, 106–7, 108
Plato 160
   Phaedrus 184–7, 199
   Symposium 185
pleasure 5, 126, 133, 134, 135, 138–9, 181
   see also happiness
   libertinism 160–1, 189

poetry 95, 101, 113
Pollock, Friedrich 141
positive infinite judgements 162
poverty 163
Prismen (Adorno, Theodor W.) 107, 193
psychology 12
　Angerstein murder case 25–6
punctuation 124–5, 175
pure insight 116–17

rationality/reason 12, 13, 27, 138, 140, 231 n. 9
　coerciveness 142
　crime 42–3
　detectives 41
　Horkheimer, Max 138, 140–2
　Kracauer, Siegfried 41
　perversion 151, 152, 153–4
　Sade, Marquis de 142, 144, 148
　sensuality 142
　violence 142
realism 69–72, 200
recapitulation 90 *see also* repetition
Rechtsphilosophie (Hegel, Georg Wilhelm Friedrich) 69, 100, 162
recruitment 33–4, 35, 36
reification 24, 25, 26–7
repetition 220 n. 5 *see also* recapitulaiton
　Schoenberg, Arnold 58
reprise 220 n. 5
reproduction 179, 180
resistance 10
resonance 93–4
reversal 56, 57
reversal of perspective 120–1
rhythm 98, 102
Rilke, Rainer Maria
　Malte Laurids Brigge 175
Rimbaud, Arthur 188
Roberte ce soir (Klossowski, Pierre) 154
Romanticism 8–9, 113

Sade, Marquis de 4, 125–7, 135–8, 150
　atheism 151–2
　Cent Vingt Journées de Sodome, Les 127
　ecstasy 145, 146

Horkheimer, Max 126–7, 132–3, 135–44
Juliette 131, 136, 137, 139, 144, 148, 155, 157
Klossowski, Pierre 149, 150–6, 161
perversion 146–58, 161
rationality/reason 142, 144, 148
sensuality 143, 145–7, 180–1
sexuality 232 n. 14
Sade mon prochain (Klossowski, Pierre) 149
scélérat 234 n. 2
Schiele, Egon 175
Schoenberg, Arnold 47–8, 56, 58–9, 108–9, 116–17
　composition 55, 56, 111, 115
　dissonance 113
　enlightenment 114
　Erwartung 175, 240 n. 6
　fractured style 57
　harmonic innovations 106
　homeostasis 198
　material/temporal antagonism 113
　twelve-tone technique 47, 112, 115
Schubert, Franz 83–4
science 60–1
sculpture 92
second nature 24, 27, 52, 53
secret societies 158–60
self-denial 133
self-interest 133, 134, 148
　Kant, Immanuel 136–7
semblance 200
semicolons 124
sensuality 1, 2, 12, 125, 142, 143, 179–82, 194
　artworks 179, 181, 189, 192
　beauty 186–7
　dissonance 13
　intelligibility 5–6
　language 173
　Musil, Robert 166, 168, 169, 170, 171
　perversion 179
　Sade, Marquis de 143, 145–7
sexual freedom 2, 126
sexuality 2, 4–5, 143, 232 n. 14 *see also* perversion

crime 126
female 182
shock 194
shudder 145, 186, 193-4
Simmel, Georg 158-9
social change 32, 45, 79
social class 28-9, 33, 36-7
  revolution 133-4
society 68, 77, 108
  Balzac, Honoré de 68, 70-1
  dialectic, the 88
  modernity 79
  secret societies 158-60
  social change 32, 45, 79
  tact 79-80
sociologists 64-5
sodomy 179-80
sound 93, 95, 193
  feeling 96-8
sovereignty 161
spatiality
  music 92, 93, 101
'Spätstil Beethovens' (Adorno, Theodor W.) 86
speculative ear 104-6
speech 96
spirit 67, 72, 92
  interiority of 92, 95-6
  music 101, 108
  poetry 101
St Matthew Passion (Bach, Johann Sebastian) 222 n. 11
state, the 198
Stichworte (Adorno, Theodor W.) 193
structural listening 104-5, 108
Studies in European Realism (Lukács, Georg) 69
Stumpf, Carl 175
subject/subjectivity 8-10, 11, 12, 56
  absence 88-9
  artworks 13-14
  conventions 87
  language 151-2
  music 17-18, 19, 93-4, 97-8, 103-4, 240 n. 6
sublimation 12-13
sublime, the 8, 9-10, 193

suffering 5, 11, 109, 135, 138, 140, 181, 185
  see also cruelty
coercion 142
rationality 142
'Sur l'eau' (Maupassant, Guy de) 190-1, 193
Surrealism 66
Symposium (Plato) 185

taboo 137, 138, 181
tact 79-80, 82, 102, 124
Takt 102
temporality 86, 90, 91, 97, 98, 101, 102, 104, 111, 124
  material/temporal antagonism 113
theatre 54
Theorie des Romans, Die (Lukács, Georg) 52, 69
thought 17, 18-20, 49-50, 193-4
  artworks 204-5
  avant-garde, the 120
  essays 196
  imagination 146-8
  Kant, Immanuel 138
  Klossowski, Pierre 154-5
  negativity 192
  perversion 151
  pure insight 116-17
  Sade, Marquis de 138, 146-7
  shudder of 193-4
Tod in Venedig (Mann, Thomas) 175
totality 40, 41
  Balzac, Honoré de 71
transcendence 145
transgression 137, 148, 149 see also crime and perversion
transience 52-3
truth 83, 85
  unintentional 63, 64
truth-content 57-8

uncertainty 193-4
unconscious, the 26
unintentional, the 62-3, 64
urban culture 23-4
Ursprung des deutschen Trauerspiels (Benjamin, Walter) 38, 44, 52, 61-2, 74, 82

utopia 2, 3, 10, 187, 188–93, 200
  beauty 185
  pain 185
  sexual freedom 126
  sexuality 143
  thought 19–20

Vereinigungen (Musil, Robert) 175, 178
'Vernunft und Selbstbehauptung'
  (Horkheimer, Max) 141
Versuch über Wagner (Adorno, Theodor
  W.) 107
vertigo 201
violence 126–7, 134, 136, 142
'Vollendung der Liebe, Die' (Musil, Robert) 165–78, 179–80, 181–2
Vorlesungen über die Ästhetik (Hegel,
  Georg Wilhelm Friedrich) 101

Wagner, Richard 117, 226 n. 24
Wahl, Jean 211 n. 1
Wahlverwandtschaften (Goethe,
  Johann Wolfgang von) 59, 83,
  196
Webern, Anton 114–15
whole, nature of the 49–50
will, the 4
Wissenschaft der Logik (Hegel,
  Georg Wilhelm Friedrich)
  24, 190
world-spirit 67, 72

Zelter, Carl Friedrich 222 n. 11
'Zur gesellschaftlichen Lage der Musik'
  (Adorno, Theodor W.) 55
Zur Metakritik der Erkenntnistheorie
  (Adorno, Theodor W.) 107

www.ingramcontent.com/pod-product-compliance
Lightning Source LLC
Chambersburg PA
CBHW062125300426
44115CB00012BA/1818